AF335040

EDITOR'S NOTE

WHEN WE LAUNCHED OUR BRIEFS SERIES in 2016, we knew the books would be a hit: briefer (of course) even than our already-concise standard titles, and therefore a deeper dive within a tighter scope, like a shot of espresso rather than a cup of coffee. And the twelve titles that emerged certainly delivered, offering readers quick learning on specific topics within web design, development, and content.

What we didn't expect was how much readers would request these titles in print. We intended for the Briefs series to be digital-only—and in 2016, that sounded like a solid bet. All around us, publishers were singing the praises of ebooks and claiming that paper was an artifact of the past. But even—or perhaps especially—within our audience of tech workers, readers asked for tangible reading experiences.

We closed the Briefs series after twelve amazing titles, but they continue to teach readers new skills, and deserve their own moment of ink. So we've brought them together in three new anthologies, available in a special edition printed hardcover format.

Volume 1, the Development Anthology, covers the how-tos of programming essentials like CSS Grid Layout, the command line, images, and pair programming. We hope this collection of Briefs continues to reach readers in a meaningful way.

1

SECOND EDITION

GET READY FOR CSS GRID LAYOUT

RACHEL ANDREW

FOREWORD BY
ERIC MEYER

Publisher: Jeffrey Zeldman
Designer: Jason Santa Maria
Executive Director: Katel LeDû
Managing Editor: Lisa Maria Martin
Editor: Caren Litherland
Copyeditor: Katel LeDû
Proofreader: Katel LeDû
Book Producer: Ron Bilodeau

Editor, first edition: Caren Litherland
Technical Editor, first edition: Paul Lloyd
Copyeditor, first edition: Lisa Maria Martin
Compositor, first edition: Rob Weychert
Ebook Producer, first edition: Ron Bilodeau

ISBN: 978-1-937557-91-1

A Book Apart
New York, New York
http://abookapart.com

TABLE OF CONTENTS: GET READY FOR CSS LAYOUT

FOREWORD

WHAT DOES IT LOOK LIKE, when a new web feature is tested for years, honed to a fine edge, and launched in multiple browsers almost simultaneously, catapulting its global support from nothing to well over eighty percent in the space of a few weeks?

It looks like CSS Grid.

For those of us who have watched web standards develop for lo these many years, what happened with Grid was almost incomprehensible. We're used to watching one browser pick up a new standard, and then wait years for the others to join the fun. We're used to seeing these slowly emerging implementations riddled with gaps, or having to change defined behaviors midstream because flaws in the specification were uncovered long after shipping. Flexbox suffered this.

But Grid—no, Grid arrived in a fusillade of browser updates, with robust consistency and a small rump of glitches and oddities that were quickly smoothed out. The ship that Internet Explorer (yes!) launched in 2012 set sail as an armada in the spring of 2017.

That was then. What about now?

Now we have two years of slowly growing experience with Grid. Sites have shipped using it for layout almost unheralded, because there was no need for clever hackery to make it work. It does what it claims to do, what it was *designed* to do, with efficiency and elegance.

And now, with that experience behind us, the specification is being updated to address some of the rare limitations that existed in the first version of Grid. That's why you're lucky to have this book in front of you. No one is better qualified than Rachel Andrew to explain the basics *and* the evolution of Grid. Whether this is your first foray into Grid or a refresher course on a technology you already rely on, you'll find what you need here. And, quite probably, you'll find nearly everything you might *want* in a layout language. Savor it. We may not see its like again.

—Eric Meyer

INTRODUCTION

WHEN I BEGAN WORKING ON THE WEB in 1996, the only real skill a front-end developer had to master was chopping up images into tiny bits and reassembling them into a table to create a layout.

Netscape 4 still held a huge market share when I started using CSS for layout. The browser's implementation of absolute positioning was so poor that when a user resized their screen, all of the positioned elements would stack up in the top left corner. I've watched CSS evolve from a simple single specification—concerned primarily with changing text colors and adding borders to things—to the increasingly complex language it is today. We live in a very different world from the one in which I learned my craft!

Along the way, I've witnessed browser wars, and, during my time as a Web Standards Project member, have encouraged browser and tool vendors alike to innovate through the standards process. We can now see that process playing out in many of the specifications currently wending their way through the W3C.

One such specification, CSS Grid Layout, is the subject of this little book. The specification debuted under this name as a proposal by Microsoft in April 2011. This early version of the specification appeared in Internet Explorers 10 and 11 and was adopted by the W3C. Updated versions of the specification ultimately shipped in Chrome, Firefox, and Safari within weeks of one another in March 2017. Microsoft Edge updated from the old Internet Explorer specification in October of that year.

I began experimenting with CSS Grid Layout as soon as I discovered the IE10 implementation. For several years, I've been frustrated that layout hasn't advanced much, despite our ability to round corners, create drop shadows, use a wider variety of fonts, and even animate things in CSS. We now have better ways to cope with floating and positioning elements, and our browsers are less buggy—yet the techniques we use for layout are not far removed from the ones we used in the early days of CSS. As soon as I started experimenting with Grid Layout,

I could see its potential. I really believe that Grid Layout is the layout method we've been waiting for.

The first edition of this book was written in 2015, before Level 1 of the specification shipped in browsers. As I write this update four years later, Level 2 of the specification is being implemented in Firefox, and Grid Layout support hovers around eighty-nine percent globally, according to CanIUse.com. The second edition, like the first, is an ode to the elegance and power of the specification. And now that Grid has shipped in browsers, I hope this book can also serve as your guide as you start using Grid Layout in your projects today.

WHAT IS CSS GRID LAYOUT?

THE CSS GRID LAYOUT MODULE defines a two-dimensional grid layout system. Once a grid has been established on a containing element, the children of that element can be placed into a flexible or fixed layout grid. The grid can be redefined using media queries. This makes CSS Grid Layout an incredibly powerful tool—one that the web has been waiting for ever since we began doing layout with CSS instead of tables.

Rather than talk about CSS Grid Layout (or just plain "Grid," as I will call it often throughout this text) in abstract terms, I'll demonstrate its functionality through a series of examples. The example code is linked so you can use it as a starting point for your own explorations. Everything described—with the exception of the final section on Grid Layout Level 2—is supported in Chrome, Firefox, Safari, and Edge, plus the myriad Chromium-based browsers available today.

GRID BASICS

In this first chapter, I want to use some simple examples to provide a rundown of the essential concepts of the CSS Grid Layout Module. Grid is a very flexible module, so there are a number of ways to use it. In the following chapters, we'll look at some more "real-world" examples, building on what I describe here.

Defining a grid

A grid is defined using a new value of the display property, `display: grid`.

In my HTML markup, I want to create a grid on the wrapper and position the child elements on that grid.

```
<div class="wrapper">
  <div class="box a">A</div>
  <div class="box b">B</div>
  <div class="box c">C</div>
```

```
  <div class="box d">D</div>
  <div class="box e">E</div>
  <div class="box f">F</div>
</div>
```

In my CSS, I start by declaring a grid on the element with a class of `.wrapper`, making this element our *grid container*.

```
.wrapper {
  display: grid;
}
```

Next, I need to describe what the grid looks like. Grids have rows and columns, which the CSS Grid Layout Module gives us new properties to describe:

```
grid-template-rows
grid-template-columns
```

```
.wrapper {
  display: grid;
  grid-template-columns: 100px 100px 100px;
  grid-template-rows: 100px 100px;
}
```

Code example: http://bkaprt.com/cgl-2/01-01/

You can find this, and all of the examples in this book, on GitHub. I'll reference the file below each example, like I've done above.

Here, I've created a grid with three 100-pixel-wide columns, and two 100-pixel-tall rows.

If we take a look at our page after we've declared a grid, we'll see that the child elements have placed themselves on the grid (**FIG 1.1**). They do this according to Grid's auto-placement rules, which simply fill each cell in turn with a direct child of the grid container.

FIG 1.1:
Grid automatically fills each consecutive cell with a direct child of the grid container.

FIG 1.2: The highlighted grid line is column line 2.

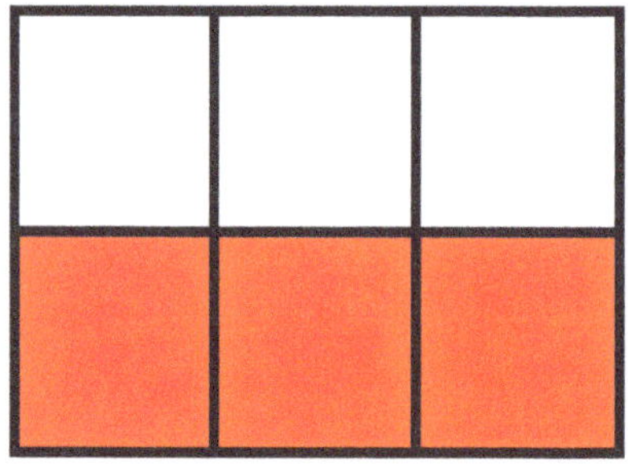

FIG 1.3: Here, I've highlighted the track between row lines 2 and 3.

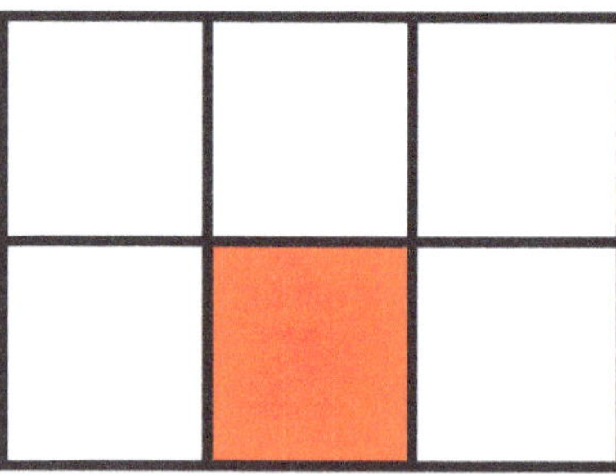

FIG 1.4: The highlighted grid cell in this image is between row lines 2 and 3 and column lines 2 and 3.

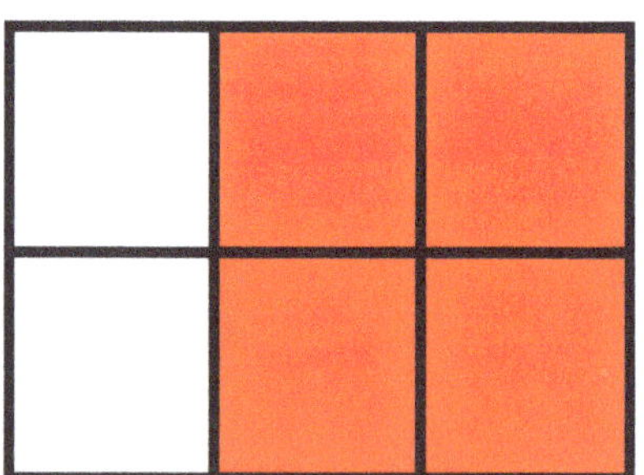

FIG 1.5: The highlighted grid area in this image falls between row lines 1 and 3 and column lines 2 and 4.

Grid terminology

Before going any further, let's take a few moments to understand some of the terminology used when talking about Grid Layout.

Grid lines

Grid lines make up the grid and can be horizontal or vertical. They can be referred to by number, but they can also be named (**FIG 1.2**).

Grid track

A *grid track* is the space between two grid lines. It can be either horizontal or vertical (**FIG 1.3**).

Grid cell

A *grid cell*—the space between four grid lines—is the smallest possible unit on the grid (**FIG 1.4**). Conceptually, it is exactly like a table cell.

Grid area

A *grid area* is any area of the grid bound by four grid lines (**FIG 1.5**). It can contain a number of grid cells.

To see a visual representation of your grid as you work on it, you can use the Grid Inspector included with Firefox Developer Tools. Select your Grid Container and then look at the Layout Panel, where you can turn on the grid lines, see line numbers, and highlight grid cells (**FIG 1.6**).

FIG 1.6: Inspecting our grid with the Firefox Grid Inspector highlights many of the parts of a grid layout.

The explicit and implicit grid

In our initial example, we created an *explicit* grid: we declared `grid-template-columns` and `grid-template-rows`, and the child elements of our grid container automatically slotted into the cells created by those grid tracks.

If we don't create enough cells, or place something outside of the explicit grid, Grid creates *implicit* grid tracks for us. This means that we can remove our `grid-template-rows` property, and our items will still place themselves on the grid. The rows are no longer 100 pixels tall; instead, they are auto-sized. It's safe to assume that an auto-sized track will be large enough to fit the content.

More ways to define your grid

When using Grid Layout, we do a lot of work on the grid container, setting up our grid so that it's ready for us to place items into it. But before we move on to placing items, let's have a look at some of the additional ways we can define our grid.

FIG 1.7: The `gap` property creates gaps between our tracks. It's shorthand for `column-gap` and `row-gap`.

Gaps between grid tracks

Sometimes we might want to create gaps between our items. We can do this by using the `gap` property, or individual properties of `column-gap` and `row-gap`.

```
.wrapper {
  display: grid;
  grid-template-columns: 100px 100px 100px;
  grid-template-rows: 200px 200px;
  gap: 10px;
}
```

Code example: http://bkaprt.com/cgl-2/01-03

Sizing implicit rows

When describing the implicit grid, I explained that the tracks created in it are auto-sized. This is the initial value of such tracks—but we can specify a size for them using the `grid-auto-rows` and `grid-auto-columns` properties.

In the following example, I've used `grid-auto-rows` with a value of `100px` to create rows in the implicit grid that are 100 pixels tall, rather than specifying explicit tracks.

```
.wrapper {
  display: grid;
  grid-template-columns: 100px 100px 100px;
  grid-auto-rows: 100px;
  gap: 10px;
}
```

Code example: http://bkaprt.com/cgl-2/01-04

The minmax() function

If we create rows that have a fixed height, as in the previous example, and then add more content to our items, we'll probably run into a situation where the content overflows the fixed-height track (**FIG 1.8**).

Designs that appear to have fixed-size rows but that can accommodate extra content are a nice feature of Grid Layout. We can achieve this flexibility by using the `minmax()` function for our track sizing.

The `minmax()` function allows us to pass in a minimum and a maximum value. In the following example, I've passed in a minimum of `100px` and a maximum of `auto`. This means that if there is less content in the track than would make it 100 pixels tall, it will nevertheless be at least 100 pixels tall. The maximum of `auto` means that the track can get as tall as necessary to fit the content. You can use `minmax()` anywhere you can add a fixed track size.

```
.wrapper {
  display: grid;
  grid-template-columns: 100px 100px 100px;
  grid-auto-rows:minmax(100px, auto);
  gap: 10px;
}
```

Code example: http://bkaprt.com/cgl-2/01-05

FIG 1.8: Content overflows if it exceeds the fixed-height track.

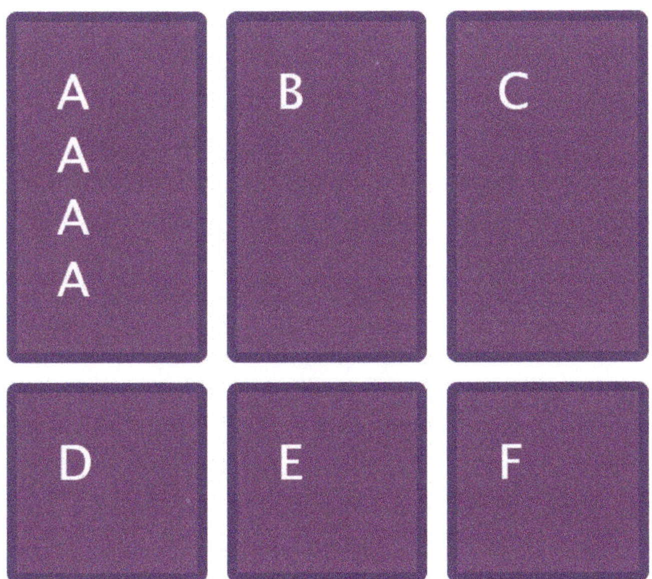

FIG 1.9: By using `minmax()`, we can make the track expand as necessary.

The fr unit

You can create your tracks with any valid CSS length unit, or with percentages. But you can also size tracks using the Grid-specific `fr` unit. This value represents a fraction of the available space in the grid container. If we change our example to use `fr` units, we can see how it works:

```
.wrapper {
    width: 600px;
  display: grid;
  grid-template-columns: 2fr 1fr 1fr;
    grid-auto-rows:minmax(100px, auto);
  gap: 10px;
}
```

I've made my first track `2fr`, and the second and third tracks `1fr` each. This means that the available space in the grid container is divided into four: two parts are assigned to the first track, and one part each to the second and third tracks (**FIG 1.10**).

Note that we're not distributing *all* of the available space in the grid container, only the space left over after laying out the content. A larger amount of content in the third track means less remaining space to assign to the others (**FIG 1.11**).

Now that you know about `minmax()`,it might be useful to understand that `1fr` is really `minmax(auto, 1fr)`. In other words, Grid assigns `auto` (enough space for the content) and then parcels out the leftover space. If we want to force even space distribution, we can use `minmax(0, 1fr)` explicitly. This treats each track as if it has a size of `0`, and shares out all of the space the items need to fit into.

```
.wrapper {
  display: grid;
  grid-template-columns: minmax(0,2fr) minmax(0,1fr)
  minmax(0,1fr);
    grid-auto-rows:minmax(100px, auto);
  gap: 10px;
}
```

Code example: http://bkaprt.com/cgl-2/01-06

FIG 1.10: Using the `fr` unit to create flexible tracks.

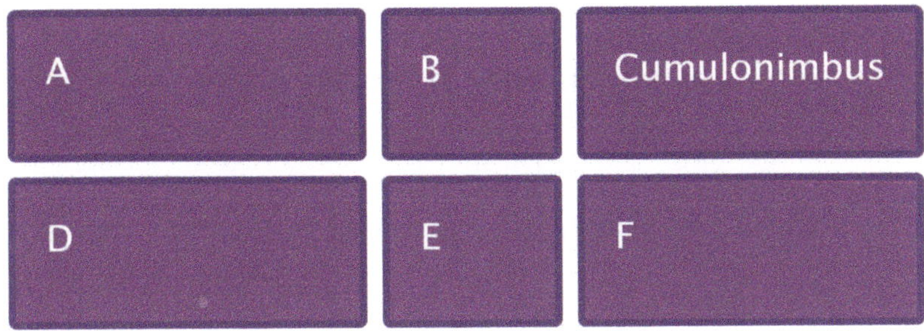

FIG 1.11: Something that takes up a lot of room in one track means less space is left over for other tracks.

FIG 1.12: We can use `minmax(0,1fr)` to force an even distribution of all space, not just leftover space.

Using repeat() notation

If we're creating a grid with a large number of tracks of equal size, we can repeat all, or a section of, our track listing. For example, say we want to create a twelve-column grid using `minmax(0,1fr)` to make every column the same size. To do this, we could use the following code:

```
.wrapper {
  display: grid;
  grid-template-columns: minmax(0,1fr) minmax(0,1fr)
  minmax(0,1fr) minmax(0,1fr) minmax(0,1fr)
  minmax(0,1fr) minmax(0,1fr) minmax(0,1fr)
  minmax(0,1fr) minmax(0,1fr) minmax(0,1fr)
  minmax(0,1fr);
}
```

Or, we could dramatically simplify our CSS with `repeat()`:

```
.wrapper {
  display: grid;
  grid-template-columns: repeat(12, minmax(0,1fr));
}
```

Code example: http://bkaprt.com/cgl-2/01-07

When we use `repeat()`, we place comma-separated values between parentheses. The value before the comma stands for the number of times a pattern should repeat; the value after the comma refers to the pattern. We can repeat a single track value or a track listing.

Using the auto-fill and auto-fit keywords

We can combine all of the things we've learned so far to create a very useful pattern. Let's say we want to have as many tracks as will fit into our grid container, and we want the tracks to have a minimum size. This enables a responsive number of column tracks without relying on media queries to add breakpoints.

The following example creates a repeating pattern of tracks that are exactly two hundred pixels wide. If we open the code example in a browser and resize the window, we'll see that additional grid tracks are created or removed depending on how much space is available, and the auto-placed items are reflowed. This is achieved by using the `auto-fill` keyword instead of a number before the comma in our repeat notation.

```
.wrapper {
  display: grid;
  grid-template-columns: repeat(auto-fill, 200px);
}
```

Code example: http://bkaprt.com/cgl-2/01-08

This isn't quite what we want, though—these automatically created tracks are always two hundred pixels wide. So unless our grid container can be neatly divided by two hundred, we'll have a gap at the end.

We can get the result we're after by combining `repeat`, `auto-fill`, and `minmax()`:

```
.wrapper {
  display: grid;
  grid-template-columns: repeat(auto-fill,
  minmax(200px, 1fr));
}
```

Code example: http://bkaprt.com/cgl-2/01-09

The `minmax()` function has a minimum value of `200px` (our desired minimum). It has a maximum value of `1fr`, which distributes any leftover space across the tracks that have been created. Thus we get as many flexible tracks as will fit into our container, with a minimum size of two hundred pixels.

Placing items by line number

All of the work we've done so far has been on the grid container. Our items have been auto-placed into cells created by our tracks. Now let's turn to the grid items themselves, and see how they can be placed on the grid.

The simplest method to use is line-based placement. We can use the following rules to place an element whose class is `.a` so that it spans two column tracks and two row tracks, from line 1 to line 3 for both columns and rows:

```
.a {
  grid-row-start: 1;
  grid-column-start: 1;
  grid-row-end: 3;
  grid-column-end: 3;
}
```

Code example: http://bkaprt.com/cgl-2/01-10

We can also express this in shorthand by using the `grid-column` and `grid-row` properties, in which the first value represents the column or row *start* and the second value represents the column or row *end*.

```
.a {
  grid-row: 1 / 3;
  grid-column: 1 / 3;
}
```

Code example: http://bkaprt.com/cgl-2/01-11

By drawing a box around the area we want our content to go into, line-based placement creates a *grid area*. An even shorter shorthand than the `grid-column` and `grid-row` properties is the `grid-area` property. Here is the order of values:

1. `grid-row-start`
2. `grid-column-start`
3. `grid-row-end`
4. `grid-column-end`

This gives us:

```
.a {
  grid-area: 1 / 1 / 3 / 3;
}
```

Code example: http://bkaprt.com/cgl-2/01-12

Personally, I find the shorter shorthand a little difficult to read. For clarity, I prefer the `grid-column` and `grid-row` shorthand.

A grid area can span as many individual grid cells as required. We just need to specify the line where the content will start and the line where it will end. In the code example, I've placed four items onto the grid using line-based positioning (FIG 1.13).

The Firefox Grid Inspector makes it easy to place items because it indicates the line numbers (FIG 1.14).

Note that the source order of these child elements doesn't affect where we can place each one. Having said that, though, it's not a good idea to make the visual display of items diverge from the order of items in the source. The source determines the order that screen readers read out the content, and the order in which a user navigating with a keyboard can tab around the document. It's possible to create a very confusing experience by disconnecting the visual display from the source order, so we should take great care not to do so.

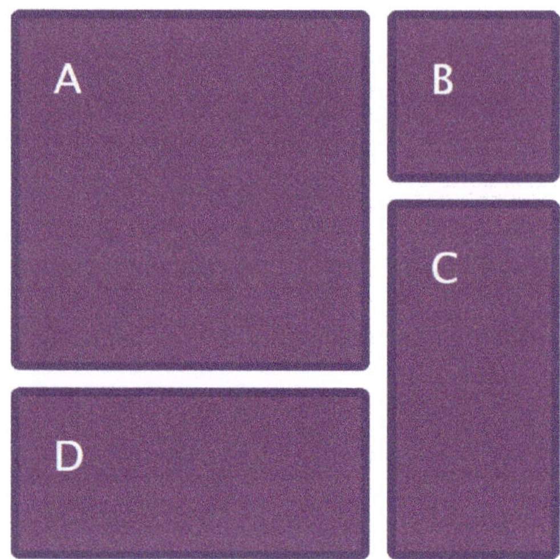

FIG 1.13: Our grid after we've used line-based placement to position the items.

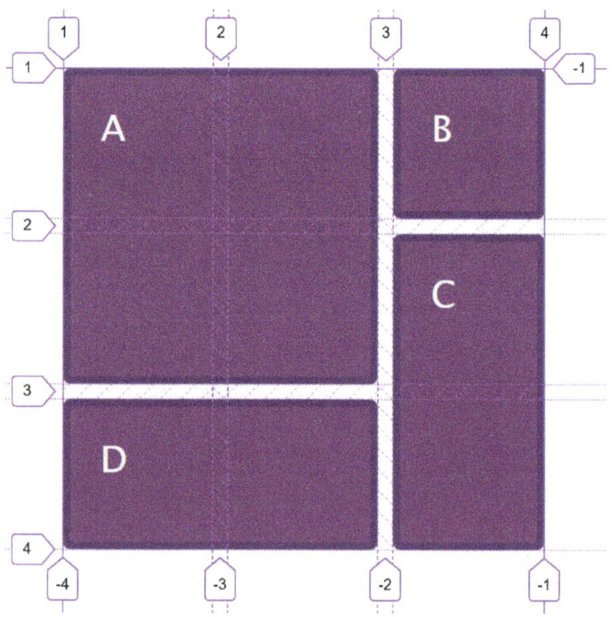

FIG 1.14: Lines highlighted using the Firefox Grid Inspector.

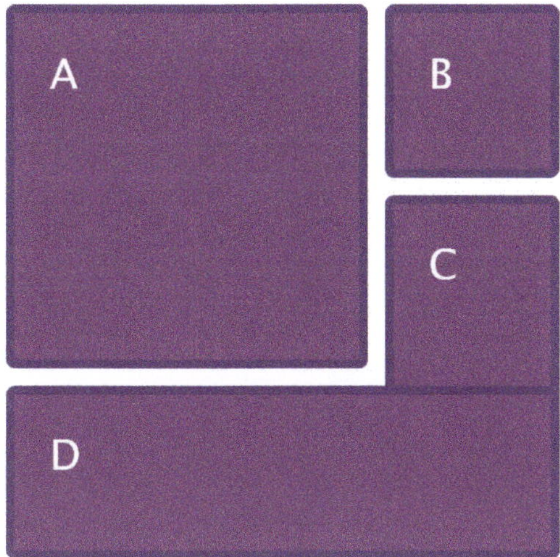

FIG 1.15: Overlapping items.

Overlapping items on the grid

When placing items using lines, we can place an item into the same cell as another item. My next example shows some elements that overlap. Items that are lower in the source display on top of items that come before them; however, we can use the `z-index` property (just as we would with absolute positioning) to change the stacking order of items (**FIG 1.15**).

Line-based placement and the `span` keyword

As I have demonstrated, we don't need to use any kind of spanning properties to create a grid area that spans multiple grid lines. But the Grid Layout Module does include a `span` keyword, which we can use instead of explicitly specifying the end line.

The layout shown in **FIG 1.13** could also be written like this:

```
.a {
        grid-row: 1 / span 2;
        grid-column: 1 / span 2;
```

```
}
.b {
    grid-row: 1;
    grid-column: 3;
}
.c {
    grid-row: 2 / span 2;
    grid-column: 3;
}
.d {
    grid-row: 3;
    grid-column: 1 / span 2;
}
```

Code example: http://bkaprt.com/cgl-2/01-13

Two new things show up here. The first is the span keyword. Instead of positioning the div with a class of .a by saying, "Start at column line 1 and end at column line 3," I say, "Start at column line 1 and span 2 column tracks." The result is the same.

I've also omitted the row- or column-end value where the content only spans to the next line because that is the default—no need to specify it.

LINE-BASED PLACEMENT WITH NAMED LINES

Keeping track of all of these line numbers soon gets old. Luckily, the Grid Layout Module provides a way to name lines, making it far easier to remember what goes where on the grid.

Let's continue with our example layout. When defining our grid, we can assign names to the lines, like so:

```
.wrapper {
  display: grid;
  grid-template-columns:
       [main-start col1-start] 100px
```

```
[col1-end col2-start] 100px
    [col2-end col3-start] 100px [col3-end main-
  end];}
```

Remember: *we are naming grid lines, not tracks*. In the value for `grid-template-columns` above, I've named our first line `main-start` and `col1-start`. After that comes the `100px` track size. I move across the columns, giving the lines names. Note that lines can have multiple names, which should be separated by a space.

We can then position our items using those names, instead of numbers.

```
.a {
    grid-row: 1 / 3;
    grid-column: main-start / col2-end;
  }
  .b {
    grid-row: 1 / 2;
    grid-column: col3-start / col3-end;
  }
  .c {
    grid-row: 2 / 4;
    grid-column: col3-start / col3-end;
  }
  .d {
    grid-row: 3 / 4;
    grid-column: main-start / main-end;
  }
```

Code example: http://bkaprt.com/cgl-2/01-14

The nice thing about naming lines this way is that once we've defined a grid, we can quickly arrange things without needing to think about their numerical position. For example, we can define `sidebar-start` and `sidebar-end` and feel confident that any element positioned there will sit in the sidebar area.

GRID TEMPLATE AREAS

The final method for creating and positioning items on the grid involves using *grid template areas*. It's usually when I show people this method that they start to get almost as excited about Grid as I am. Here we create named grid areas, and then use the new property `grid-template-areas` to describe where on the grid these named areas sit.

My HTML consists of a small layout with a header, a sidebar, a content area, and a footer:

```
<div class="wrapper">
  <div class="box header">Header</div>
  <div class="box sidebar">Sidebar</div>
  <div class="box content">Content</div>
  <div class="box footer">Footer</div>
</div>
```

In my CSS, I have rules set up for each of the areas. I use the `grid-area` property to give these areas a name to refer to when defining the layout on the grid.

```
.sidebar { grid-area: sidebar; }
.content { grid-area: content; }
.header { grid-area: header; }
.footer { grid-area: footer; }
```

Now I just need to declare my grid on the wrapper like I did before. This time, though, I also use `grid-template-areas` to define the layout using a kind of ASCII-art syntax.

```
.wrapper {
  display: grid;
  grid-template-columns: 1fr 1fr 1fr;
  grid-template-areas:
  "header  header header"
  "sidebar content content"
  "footer  footer  footer";
}
```

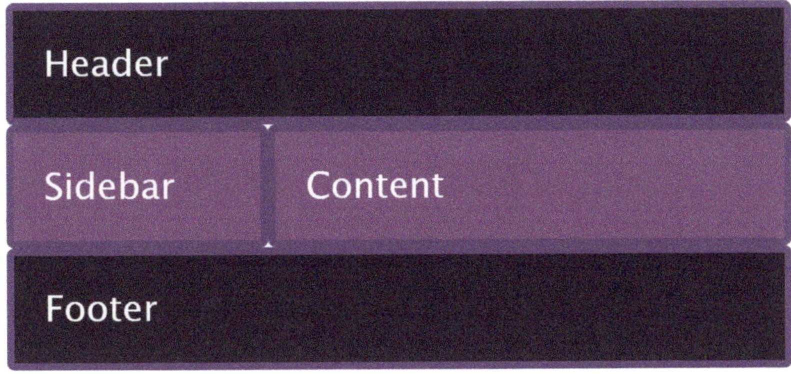

FIG 1.16: A simple layout using `grid-template-areas`.

Code example: http://bkaprt.com/cgl-2/01-15

Repeating the name of an area causes the content to span those cells. That's all we need to do to lay out a page using the CSS Grid Layout Module.

There are a few ground rules to remember when using this method. For starters, every cell on the grid must be filled. If we want to leave a cell empty, we need to use a period (`.`) For example, if we only want the footer to sit under the content, leaving an empty cell below the sidebar, our code should look like this:

```
.wrapper {
  display: grid;
  grid-template-columns: 1fr 1fr 1fr;
  grid-template-areas:
  "header  header header"
  "sidebar content content"
  ".   footer  footer";
}
```

If we want to line up the names of the cells more neatly, we can use multiple periods. We can use additional spaces between the names for the same purpose.

```
.wrapper {
  display: grid;
  grid-template-columns: 1fr 1fr 1fr;
  grid-template-areas:
  "header  header header"
  "sidebar content content"
  "........  footer  footer";
}
```

Also, the areas we create must be a complete rectangle—no Tetris-style pieces. And the rectangle must be connected; we can't use this as a way to duplicate content. If we make an incorrect grid, then the whole value will be invalid, and we won't get a layout. If you find your layout isn't working, make sure every cell is filled.

No clearing is required. We can add as much or as little content as we want into either the sidebar or the content area; the footer will always stay below both columns. The columns will also be the same height. No need for any weird hacks!

Finally, we don't have to add any additional class names to our document to describe the number of columns or rows an element spans. We can simply position the elements using the classes already applied to describe the content.

All of this explains why I love the CSS Grid Layout Module so much. Read on to see more examples and discover what else is possible with Grid.

LAYING THINGS OUT ON THE GRID

NOW THAT WE'VE COVERED some of the basics of Grid, let's take a look at a few common layouts and see how we might achieve them using this new method.

A THREE-COLUMN LAYOUT USING grid-template-areas

To start, let's create a simple three-column layout (**FIG 2.1**).

Our HTML has the layout nested inside a wrapper div and includes a header; an article containing a heading, a div, and an aside; an aside; and finally a footer.

```
<div class="wrapper">
<header class="mainheader">
  <h1>Excerpts from the book <cite>The Bristol
Royal Mail</cite></h1>
</header>
<article class="content">
  <h1>Post letter boxes: position, violation,
peculiar uses</h1>
  <div class="primary">
    <p>[code omitted for brevity]</p>
  </div>
  <aside>
    <p>[code omitted for brevity]</p>
  </aside>
</article>

<aside class="sidebar">

</aside>

<footer class="mainfooter">
  <p>[code omitted for brevity]</p>
</footer>
</div>
```

Excerpts from the book *The Bristol Royal Mail*

Post letter boxes: position, violation, peculiar uses

A remarkable case was that of a servant who was a somnambulist, and who for some time wrote letters in her sleep, night after night, and took them to adjacent letter boxes to post. Sometimes she was fully attired, and at other times only partially so. As a rule, the letters were properly addressed, but the girl did not always place postage stamps upon them.

Occasionally the postmen have to encounter the difficulties arising from a frost-bound letter box. Such a case occurred with a box situated on the summit of the Mendip Hills. The letter box and the wall in which the box is built were found by the postman to be covered with ice, caused by rain and snow having frozen on them. The door resisted all his efforts to open it, and he had to leave it for the night. On making another effort when morning came, it taxed his ingenuity and that of other interested and willing helpers to get the box open. Hot water was tried, paraffin was poured into the lock, and it was only after a hammer had been used and a fire in a movable grate had been applied for a time that the lid could be opened.

A letter box erected in a brick pillar in a secluded spot on the East Harptree road, about a mile distant from any habitation, was, late one night, damaged to the extent of having its iron door completely smashed off, apparently either by means of a large stone which lay at its base when the violation was discovered, or by means of a hammer and jemmy. Although the adjacent ground, ditches, and hedges were searched, no trace of the iron door could be found. As three roysterers were known to have passed the box on the night in question, it was assumed that the damage was done by them out of pure mischief and not from any desire to rob Her Majesty's mails. Whether such were the case or not, they had the unpleasant experience of being locked up over the Sunday on suspicion.

The three hundred and fifty pillar and wall letter boxes are placed at convenient points, regard being had to the wants of the immediate neighbourhood that each has to serve—to approach by paved crossings, to contiguity to a public lamp, to being out of the way of pedestrians and as far removed from mud-splashing as possible. At the same time, the inspectors endeavour to place the boxes so that they may be an attraction, rather than an eyesore, to the spot where erected.

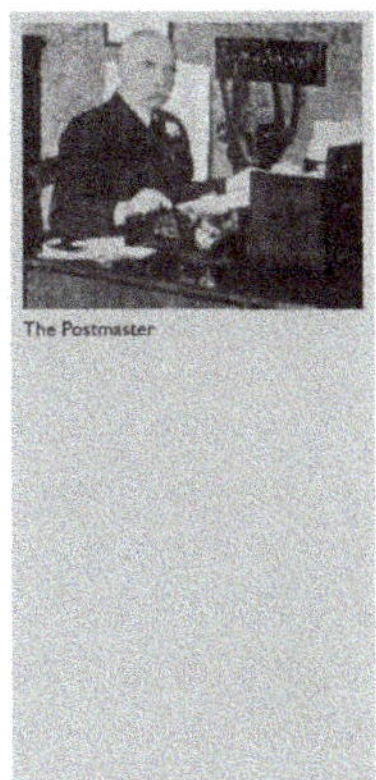

The Postmaster

Excerpts from The Project Gutenberg EBook of The Bristol Royal Mail, by R. C. Tombs.

FIG 2.1: A simple three-column layout.

If we take a look at this in the browser, we'll see the content displayed in the document source order, since no positioning has yet been applied (**FIG 2.2**).

I want to use `grid-template-areas` to position my content in this example, so the first step is to define the main areas using the selectors that identify them.

```
.mainheader { grid-area: header; }
.content { grid-area: content; }
.sidebar { grid-area: sidebar; }
.mainfooter { grid-area: footer; }
```

I then create a grid on the `div` with a class of `.wrapper`. My grid has two columns: a `3fr`-unit column and a `1fr`-unit column. I have not added a value for `grid-template-rows`, since I simply want as many auto-sized rows as we need to accommodate our content.

Excerpts from the book *The Bristol Royal Mail*

Post letter boxes: position, violation, peculiar uses

A remarkable case was that of a servant who was a somnambulist, and who for some time wrote letters in her sleep, night after night, and took them to adjacent letter boxes to post. Sometimes she was fully attired, and at other times only partially so. As a rule, the letters were properly addressed, but the girl did not always place postage stamps upon them.

Occasionally the postmen have to encounter the difficulties arising from a frost-bound letter box. Such a case occurred with a box situated on the summit of the Mendip Hills. The letter box and the wall in which the box is built were found by the postman to be covered with ice, caused by rain and snow having frozen on them. The door resisted all his efforts to open it, and he had to leave it for the night. On making another effort when morning came, it taxed his ingenuity and that of other interested and willing helpers to get the box open. Hot water was tried, paraffin was poured into the lock, and it was only after a hammer had been used and a fire in a movable grate had been applied for a time that the lid could be opened.

A letter box erected in a brick pillar in a secluded spot on the East Harptree road, about a mile distant from any habitation, was, late one night, damaged to the extent of having its iron door completely smashed off, apparently either by means of a large stone which lay at its base when the violation was discovered, or by means of a hammer and jemmy. Although the adjacent ground, ditches, and hedges were searched, no trace of the iron door could be found. As three roysterers were known to have passed the box on the night in question, it was assumed that the damage was done by them out of pure mischief and not from any desire to rob Her Majesty's mails. Whether such were the case or not, they had the unpleasant experience of being locked up over the Sunday on suspicion.

The three hundred and fifty pillar and wall letter boxes are placed at convenient points, regard being had to the wants of the immediate neighbourhood that each has to serve—to approach by paved crossings, to contiguity to a public lamp, to being out of the way of pedestrians and as far removed from mud-splashing as possible. At the same time, the inspectors endeavour to place the boxes so that they may be an attraction, rather than an eyesore, to the spot where erected.

The Postmaster

Excerpts from The Project Gutenberg EBook of The Bristol Royal Mail, by R. C. Tombs.

FIG 2.2: The layout before any positioning is added.

Finally, I define the layout as the value of the `grid-template-areas` property. I repeat the `header` across both columns of the first row. In the second row, I put the content in the left column and the sidebar on the right. The `footer` makes up the final row.

```
.wrapper {
  display: grid;
  width: 90%;
  margin: 0 auto 0 auto;
  grid-template-columns: 3fr 1fr;
  gap: 40px;
  grid-template-areas:
    "header header"
    "content sidebar"
    "footer footer";
```

Excerpts from the book *The Bristol Royal Mail*

Post letter boxes: position, violation, peculiar uses

A remarkable case was that of a servant who was a somnambulist, and who for some time wrote letters in her sleep, night after night, and took them to adjacent letter boxes to post. Sometimes she was fully attired, and at other times only partially so. As a rule, the letters were properly addressed, but the girl did not always place postage stamps upon them.

Occasionally the postmen have to encounter the difficulties arising from a frost-bound letter box. Such a case occurred with a box situated on the summit of the Mendip Hills. The letter box and the wall in which the box is built were found by the postman to be covered with ice, caused by rain and snow having frozen on them. The door resisted all his efforts to open it, and he had to leave it for the night. On making another effort when morning came, it taxed his ingenuity and that of other interested and willing helpers to get the box open. Hot water was tried, paraffin was poured into the lock, and it was only after a hammer had been used and a fire in a movable grate had been applied for a time that the lid could be opened.

A letter box erected in a brick pillar in a secluded spot on the East Harptree road, about a mile distant from any habitation, was, late one night, damaged to the extent of having its iron door completely smashed off, apparently either by means of a large stone which lay at its base when the violation was discovered, or by means of a hammer and jemmy. Although the adjacent ground, ditches, and hedges were searched, no trace of the iron door could be found. As three roysterers were known to have passed the box on the night in question, it was assumed that the damage was done by them out of pure mischief and not from any desire to rob Her Majesty's mails. Whether such were the case or not, they had the unpleasant experience of being locked up over the Sunday on suspicion.

The three hundred and fifty pillar and wall letter boxes are placed at convenient points, regard being had to the wants of the immediate neighbourhood that each has to serve—to approach by paved crossings, to contiguity to a public lamp, to being out of the way of pedestrians and as far removed from mud-splashing as possible. At the same time, the inspectors endeavour to place the boxes so that they may be an attraction, rather than an eyesore, to the spot where erected.

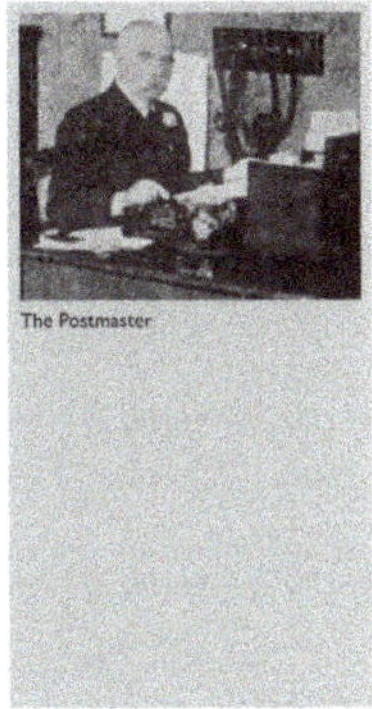

The Postmaster

Excerpts from The Project Gutenberg EBook of The Bristol Royal Mail, by R. C. Tombs.

FIG 2.3: Our layout after positioning the main content areas.

```
}
```

We now have a layout taking shape, all with just a few lines of CSS (**FIG 2.3**). That footer will stay put no matter which column is the longest. The background color on the sidebar extends right down to the footer.

Inside our `article` we have a heading, a `div` containing the primary content, and an `aside`. I'm also going to use Grid to position these, since it lets us create nested grids. I'll set up the grid areas of the nested items the same way I did with the main items.

```
.content .primary { grid-area: article-primary; }
.content aside { grid-area: article-secondary; }
.content > h1 { grid-area: chapterhead; }
```

I then create a new grid on `.content` and lay out our elements with the heading in the top left column, the primary content below it, and the `aside` to the right.

```
.content {
  display: grid;
  grid-template-columns: 3fr 1fr;
  gap: 40px;
  grid-template-areas:
    "chapterhead ."
    "article-primary article-secondary";
  }
```

Code example: http://bkaprt.com/cgl-2/02-01

That's all there is to it. We now have the layout shown at the beginning of this chapter (**FIG 2.1**).

Nested grids and subgrids

Our nested grid in this example is completely independent of the main grid. The container `.content` is positioned by the main grid, but the child elements are not—they acquire their grid from the way we set up `.content`.

This means we can't inherit column widths from the parent, which is a problem if we want to use flexible-length units: it's tricky to get the elements in the nested grid to line up with those in the outer grid.

At the end of this book, I'll explain something that will solve this problem: the subgrid feature, which is part of Grid Level 2. For now, though, let's continue with features that have good browser support and that we can safely use in our work today.

A BOXY LAYOUT

Placement using template areas is straightforward and makes it very easy to position items into known page containers. If we want to achieve more complex layouts, however—for example, if we want to work with multiple-column grid systems—then line-based placement is the tool to use. My next example is an

FIG 2.4: The completed boxy layout.

image layout, which could just as easily be a set of containers holding any type of content (**FIG 2.4**).

The HTML for this example is very simple: a `div` with a class of `.wrapper` containing a `header` and our images.

```
<div class="wrapper">
  <header>
    <h1>Little boxes layout</h1>
  </header>

  <img src="images/balloon1.jpg" alt="Hot-air
  balloons being inflated" class="box1">
  <img src="images/balloon2.jpg" alt="Hot-air
  balloons lit up at night" class="box2">
  <img src="images/balloon3.jpg" alt="Hot-air
  balloons launching" class="box3">
  <img src="images/balloon4.jpg" alt="Mass launch of
  hot-air balloons" class="box4">
  <img src="images/balloon5.jpg" alt="A bunch of
  hot-air balloons in the sky" class="box5">
```

```
  <img src="images/balloon6.jpg" alt="Inflated hot-
  air balloons in a field" class="box6">
  <img src="images/balloon7.jpg" alt="A hot-air
  balloon with a cartoon face on it" class="box7">
  <img src="images/balloon8.jpg" alt="Hot-air
  balloons waiting to leave the field" class="box8">
</div>
```

I declare a grid of twelve `1fr` columns on the .`wrapper` element. This means I'm creating a grid containing thirteen column lines in total. For the rows, I start with a row whose height value is `auto` for my heading. I then create fixed-size tracks, each `100px`. Since I'm only displaying images here, the fixed height isn't a problem. My images all use the `object-fit` property with a value of `cover`, so any excess image will be cropped.

```
.wrapper {
  display: grid;
  grid-template-columns: repeat(12, 1fr) ;
  grid-template-rows: auto;
  grid-auto-rows: 100px;
  gap: 10px;
}
```

Positioning the boxes

With a grid defined, I can start to position the boxes. The `header` is going into the first row and will stretch across the layout.

```
header {
  grid-column: 1 / -1;
  grid-row: 1;
}
```

I'm using `-1` as the value for `grid-row-end`. This means that the header will end at the end column line of the explicit grid.

If we look at this layout in a browser, we can see that the images have been automatically slotted into available cells on

Little boxes layout

FIG 2.5: Images automatically placed one by one into each consecutive cell of the grid, before we start to lay them out.

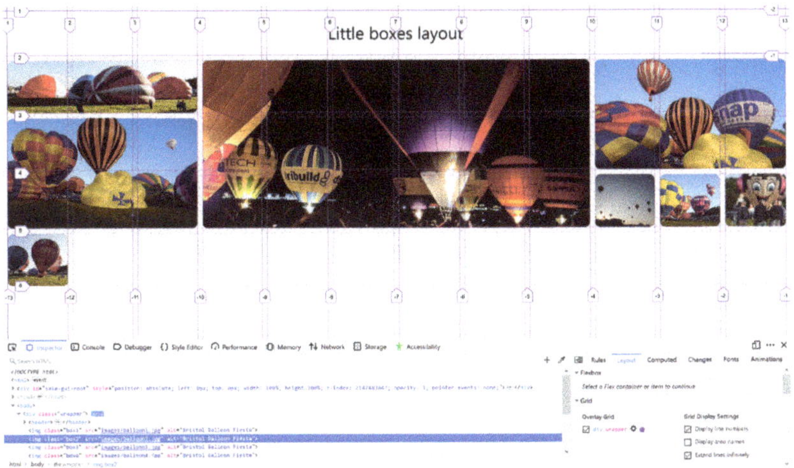

FIG 2.6: Our layout in progress, using the Grid Inspector to position items.

the grid, making them tiny (**FIG 2.5**). We can now start to place those images using line-based placement.

Using Firefox Developer Tools to highlight the lines of the grid makes creating our layout straightforward; it shows us a visual representation, with line numbers. We can even use the Grid Inspector to try out different placements of images before copying the values into our CSS (**FIG 2.6**).

Notice, as we add a rule at a time, how the remaining images continue to automatically place themselves, never overlapping. Grid is trying to give us a reasonable layout of the items as we work.

My completed set of rules looks like this:

```
.box1 {
        grid-row: 2 ;
        grid-column: 1 / 4;
    }

    .box2 {
        grid-column: 4 / 10;
        grid-row: 2 / 5;
    }

    .box3 {
        grid-row: 2 / 4;
        grid-column: 10 / -1;
    }

    .box4 {
        grid-row: 3 / 5;
        grid-column: 1 / 4;
    }

    .box5 {
        grid-row: 5 / 7;
        grid-column: 1 / 10;
    }

    .box6 {
        grid-row: 4 / 6;
        grid-column: 10 / -1;
    }

    .box7 {
        grid-row: 6 ;
        grid-column: 10 / -1;

    }

    .box8 {
        grid-column: 1 / -1;
        grid-row: 7 / 9;
    }
```

Code example: http://bkaprt.com/cgl-2/02-02

We now have the boxy grid layout. Since this is a collection of images, we don't need to worry so much about source order. If this were a set of items that a user needed to tab between, though, we'd want to take care not to disconnect the visual view from the logical source order of our content when positioning elements.

LAYERING ITEMS ON THE GRID

If you're as old as I am, you may remember the days of using tables for layout. Conceptually, using Grid is a lot like using a table, but with a key difference: the table is not defined semantically, but in CSS. This means it can be *redefined*, as we will see when we look at using Grid in responsive layouts.

Another important difference when using Grid Layout over table layout is that elements on the grid can overlap, as we learned in Chapter 1. I'm going to use this to create a detail view for an image.

First, I'll use the `box-shadow` property on `img.overlay` to make sure the selected image has a shadow. Adding a class of `overlay` to an image adds a shadow to it.

```
img.overlay {
  box-shadow: 10px 10px 20px 0px rgba(0,0,0,0.75);
}
```

Next, I'll redefine the grid for an image with a class of `overlay` to place the image on top of the other images. Because this `overlay` class comes last in the CSS, it will override any previous positioning. However, I also need to add a `z-index` value to make this element display on the top of the stack. Otherwise, images arriving later in the source will display on top.

```
      img.overlay {
        z-index: 10;
        box-shadow: 10px 10px 20px 0px
  rgba(0,0,0,0.75);
```

```
        grid-column: 2 / -2;
        grid-row: 3 / 8;
}
```

The image now displays on top of the other images (**FIG 2.7**).

Code example: http://bkaprt.com/cgl-2/02-03

As a finishing touch, I've added a class of `.active` to the grid container so I can easily lower the opacity of images that don't have a class of `.overlay` (**FIG 2.8**).

```
.active img:not(.overlay) {
  opacity: .4;
}
```

This is essentially a very simple grid—and yet we're able to create some interesting layout patterns with it using very few lines of code. Experimenting with what is now easily possible is one of the most fun things about starting to learn Grid Layout, and I encourage you to play around and create interesting designs of your own.

So far, we've gone over the two main ways of using the CSS Grid Layout Module, and have talked about some of the finer points of the specification. Next, we'll see how the Module makes it easier for us to control our layouts at multiple breakpoints.

FIG 2.7: Now that we've defined a `box-shadow` and a `z-index` value on `img.overlay`, the active image sits on top of the other images.

FIG 2.8: Fading out the inactive images.

CSS GRID LAYOUT AND RESPONSIVE DESIGN

IF YOU'VE MADE IT THIS FAR, you probably already have an inkling of how useful CSS Grid Layout is when working with responsive layouts. With float-based layouts, we were constrained by the need to give everything a width, and to painstakingly make sure our boxes didn't add up to more than a hundred percent across a row. With a responsive design, this often meant adding many breakpoints using media queries so we could adjust our layout.

GRID AND MEDIA QUERIES

Grid and Flexbox have flexibility built into them, which often translates into needing fewer media queries and breakpoints. That doesn't mean Grid doesn't play well with media queries, though. In this chapter, we'll put their compatibility to the test by creating responsive versions of the layouts we've worked on so far.

Let's start with the three-column layout using `grid-template-areas` from Chapter 2 (**FIG 2.1**).

Redefining `grid-template-areas` with media queries

Once again, I start by setting up all of my grid areas, for both the main grid and the nested grid on the `article`, with a class called `.content`.

```
.mainheader { grid-area: header; }
.content { grid-area: content; }
.sidebar { grid-area: sidebar; }
.mainfooter { grid-area: footer; }
.content .primary { grid-area: article-primary; }
.content aside { grid-area: article-secondary; }
.content > h1 { grid-area: chapterhead; }
```

At a breakpoint of 460 pixels, I start laying this out as a grid. For the main grid, I place the sidebar—which contains an image and is positioned last in the source—between the header and content.

I also declare a grid on `.content`, pulling the `aside` (defined as `article-secondary`) between the `chapterhead` and `article-primary` content (**FIG 3.1**).

```
@media only screen and (min-width: 460px) {
  .wrapper {
    display: grid;
    width: 90%;
    margin: 0 auto 0 auto;
    grid-template-areas:
      "header"
      "sidebar"
      "content"
      "footer";
  }

  .content {
    display: grid;
    grid-template-areas:
      "chapterhead"
      "article-secondary"
      "article-primary";
   }
   article aside { font-size: .75rem;}
}
```

Once we hit the 700-pixel breakpoint, we can go to two columns by redefining the grid on `.wrapper` (**FIG 3.2**). At this breakpoint, I'm going to leave the inner grid alone; three columns would feel a little cramped.

```
@media only screen and (min-width: 700px) {
  .wrapper {
    grid-template-columns: 3fr 1fr;
    gap: 40px;
    grid-template-areas:
      "header header"
      "content sidebar"
      "footer footer";
```

FIG 3.1: Our layout at 460 pixels.

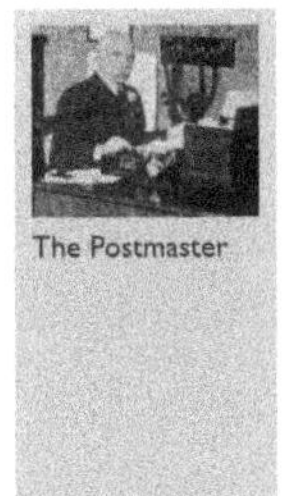

FIG 3.2: Our layout goes to two columns as we reach the 700-pixel breakpoint.

```
  }
}
```

Finally, I redefine the inner grid at 980 pixels, returning to the three-column layout I created in the last chapter.

```
@media only screen and (min-width: 980px) {
  .content {
    grid-template-columns: 3fr 1fr;
    grid-template-areas:
      "chapterhead ."
      "article-primary article-secondary";
  }
  article aside { font-size: 100%;}
}
```

Code example: http://bkaprt.com/cgl-2/03-01

Redefining the grid when using `grid-template-areas` is incredibly straightforward. It makes it much easier to tweak the layout at multiple breakpoints, allowing the content to determine what works best.

Redefining line-based placement

The second example we created in Chapter 2 was an image layout. A fair amount of screen real estate is necessary to view the layout in that format. We can add some media queries to adjust the layout to suit the viewport.

The layout is built on a twelve-column grid. I'm going to keep that grid, which means that at narrow widths, the column tracks will be very narrow, and items will need to span more tracks (**FIG 3.3**).

Outside of any media queries, I add this CSS:

```
.wrapper > img {
  grid-column: 2 / -2;
}
```

Little boxes layout

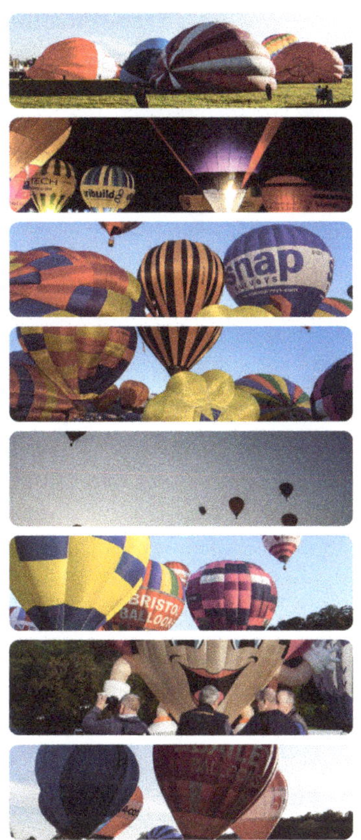

FIG 3.3: Narrow-width display on a twelve-column grid.

All this does is make every direct image child of the grid container span from the second line to the second-to-last line. Note that you can count backward from the end line of the explicit grid, which is -1.

At 600 pixels, I continue taking advantage of auto-placement, and set the column and row start to `auto`—which places it wherever it naturally goes when automatically placed. However, I span the end column line six tracks, and the row line two.

FIG 3.4: Mid-width display.

```
@media only screen and (min-width: 600px) {
  .wrapper > img {
    grid-column: auto / span 6;
    grid-row: auto / span 2;
  }
}
```

After that, we're back to the layout we created in the last chapter, wrapped in media queries with a 1000-pixel minimum. A tiny amount of code makes this layout responsive.

Of course, we can also redefine our grid for different breakpoints, or use any combination of these methods in one layout. Grid Layout and Flexbox give us the flexible-grids part of responsive design; media queries give us the ability to change the layout at different breakpoints. Grid makes it easier to do that second part, too.

GRID, ANOTHER TOOL IN OUR KIT

THE CSS GRID LAYOUT MODULE works alongside other layout methods to bring CSS layout up to date. Together with the Flexible Box Layout Module (Flexbox) and media queries, Grid can help us achieve the kind of sites and layouts we need to build today.

People new to Grid Layout commonly wonder how Grid works with Flexbox. When should we choose to use one over the other (in an ideal world where both have support)? On the www-style mailing list, Tab Atkins offered an excellent answer to this question:

> *Flexbox is for one-dimensional layouts—anything that needs to be laid out in a straight line (or in a broken line, which would be a single straight line if they were joined back together).*
>
> *Grid is for two-dimensional layouts. It can be used as a low-powered flexbox substitute (we're trying to make sure that a single-column/row grid acts very similar to a flexbox), but that's not using its full power.*
>
> *Flexbox is appropriate for many layouts, and a lot of "page component" elements, as most of them are fundamentally linear. Grid is appropriate for overall page layout, and for complicated page components which aren't linear in their design.*
>
> *The two can be composed arbitrarily, so once they're both widely supported, I believe most pages will be composed of an outer grid for the overall layout, a mix of nested flexboxes and grid for the components of the page, and finally block/inline/table layout at the "leaves" of the page, where the text and content live.*

We can better grasp this concept of one versus two dimensions through a very simple demo. In the first example below, I use Flexbox to lay out a set of five items. I've set `flex-wrap` to `wrap`, and the items display in two flex lines. The first line contains three items; the second line contains two. On the second line, the items grow to fill the space (**FIG 4.1**).

```
.wrapper {
  display: flex;
  flex-wrap: wrap;
```

FIG 4.1: Boxes laid out with Flexbox—a one-dimensional layout.

```
}

.box {
   flex: 1 1 200px;
}
```

Code example: http://bkaprt.com/cgl-2/04-02

In Flexbox, we control one line at a time; space distribution happens per line. In other words, items don't line up in columns and rows. This is one-dimensional layout.

If we look at a similar example in Grid (again with five items), our second line contains two items, but they're lined up in columns as well as in rows. This is two-dimensional layout (**FIG 4.2**).

```
.wrapper {
   display: grid;
   grid-template-columns: repeat(auto-fill,
  minmax(200px, 1fr));
}
```

Code example: http://bkaprt.com/cgl-2/04-03

We can better understand the choices in play by creating a layout that combines Grid with other methods. Let's make a fairly standard layout: navigation, followed by a large feature image and a main `article`, then a set of boxes featuring content of different heights, and, finally, a `footer` (**FIG 4.3**).

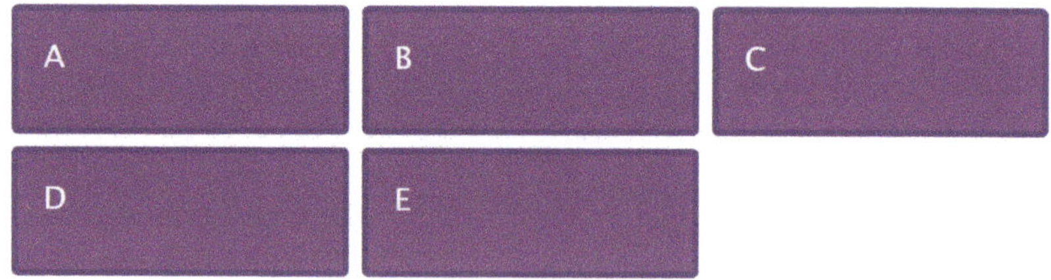

FIG 4.2: Boxes laid out with Grid—a two-dimensional layout.

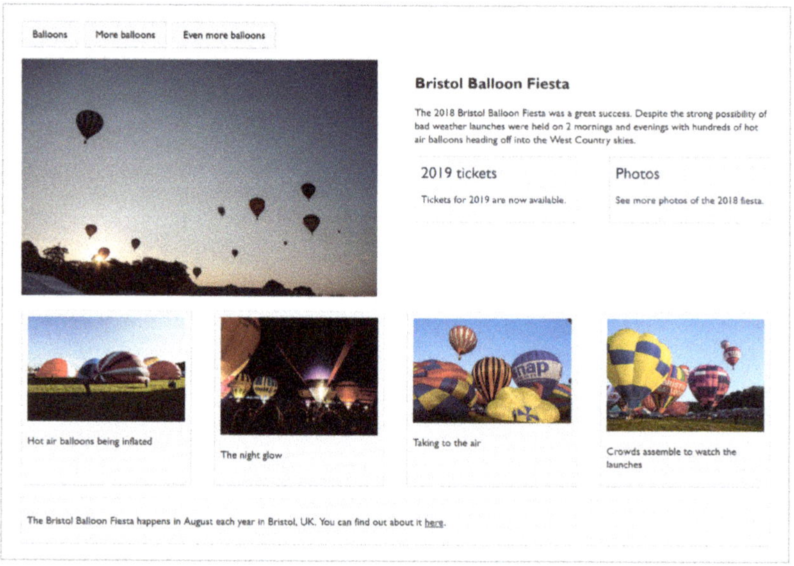

FIG 4.3: A layout combining Grid with other methods.

The HTML for the body of our page looks like this:

```
<div class=”wrapper”>
  <header class=”mainheader”>
    <nav>
      <ul>
    <li><a href=””>Balloons</a></li>
    <li><a href=””>More balloons</a></li>
```

```
      <li><a href="">Even more balloons</a></li>
    </ul>
      </nav>
    </header>

    <aside class="feature-pull"><img src="images/
    balloon5.jpg" alt="Bristol Balloon Fiesta"></
    aside>

    <article class="feature">
      <h1>Bristol Balloon Fiesta</h1>
      <p>[code omitted for brevity]</p>

      <ul class="cta-list">
        <li class="box"><li>
     <li class="box"><li>
      </ul>
    </article>

    <ul class="gallery">
      <li class="box"><img src="images/balloon1.jpg"
    alt="Inflating balloons">
      <p>Hot air balloons being inflated</p></li>
      <li class="box"></li>
      <li class="box"></li>
      <li class="box"></li>
    </ul>
    <footer class="mainfooter box"></footer>
  </div>
```

Here, I've added a class called `.box` to the elements to give them a basic box style so we can clearly see the layout. I've also written some CSS for basic styling. This gives us a linearized view (**FIG 4.4**).

At a 460-pixel breakpoint, I start using Grid Layout to position the main content areas on the page. Inside the media query, I set up those main areas and then create a linearized layout to arrange them in the order I want.

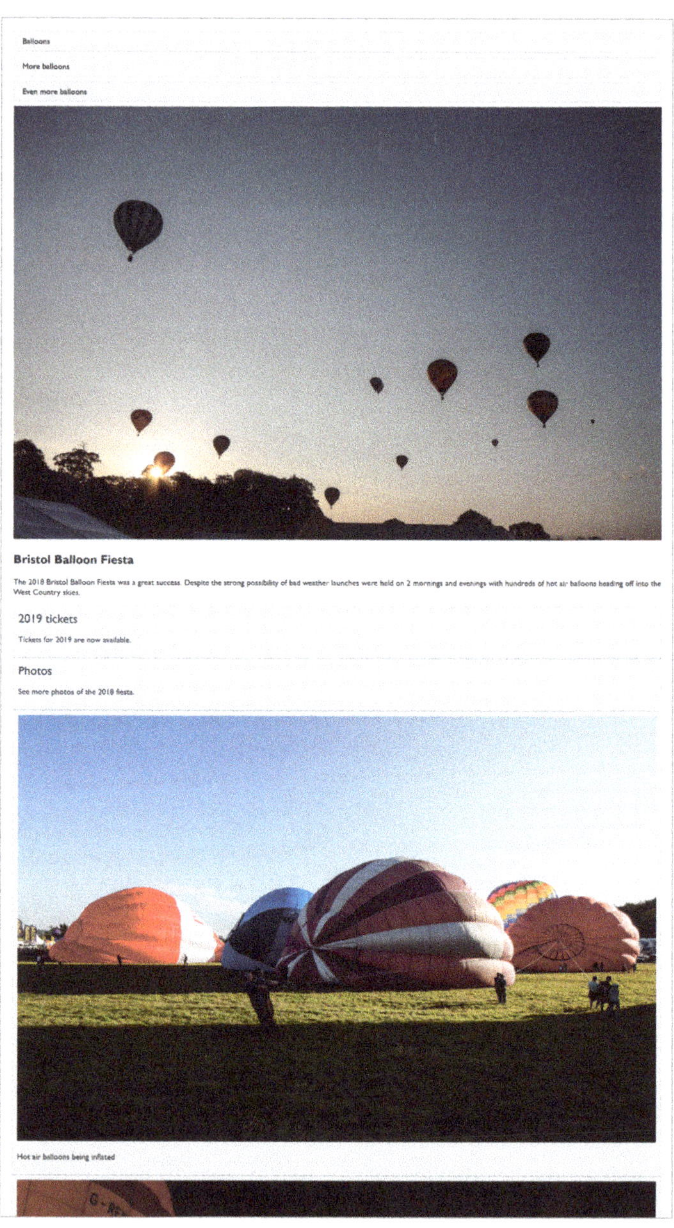

FIG 4.4: Our layout prior to adding CSS to position elements.

```
@media only screen and (min-width: 460px) {

  .mainheader { grid-area: header; margin: 0 0 20px
  0;}
  .feature-pull { grid-area: featurepull; }
  .feature { grid-area: feature; }
  .gallery { grid-area: secondary; }
  .mainfooter { grid-area: footer; }

  .wrapper {
    display: grid;
    width: 90%;
    margin: 0 auto 0 auto;
    grid-template-areas:
      "header"
      "feature"
      "featurepull"
      "secondary"
      "footer";
  }
}
```

At 760 pixels, I move to a two-column layout with a gutter. This allows me to place the feature image to the left of the `article` (**FIG 4.5**).

```
@media only screen and (min-width: 760px) {
  .wrapper {
    grid-template-columns: 1fr 1fr;
    column-gap: 5%;
    grid-template-areas:
      "header header"
      "featurepull feature"
      "secondary secondary"
      "footer footer";
}
```

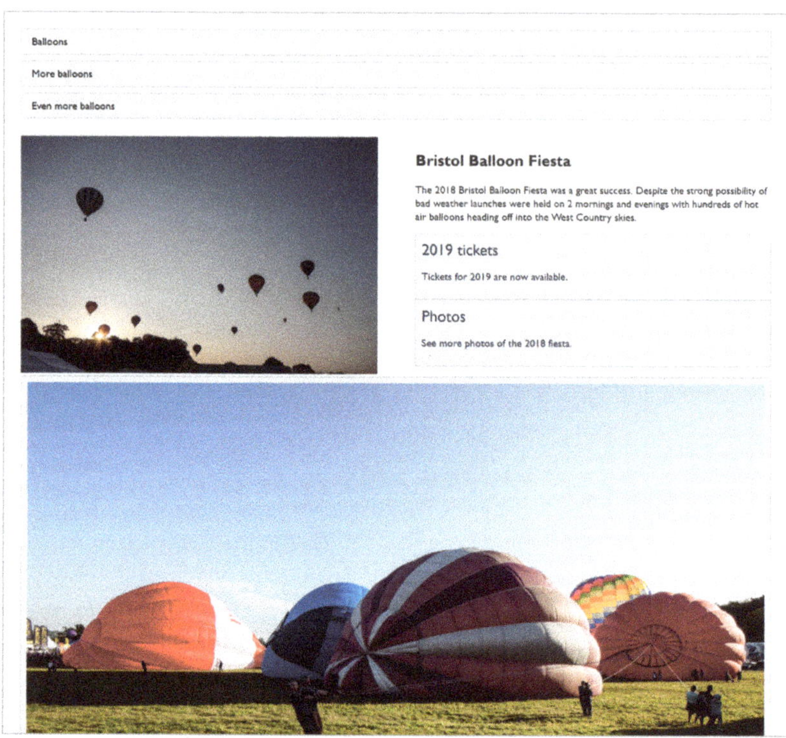

FIG 4.5: Our layout after positioning the main page areas.

At this point, we have a number of elements on the page that haven't yet been laid out to match the initial design (**FIG 4.3**). The navigation runs right across the page, the small images need to be formatted into a row of four, and two calls to action that should be side by side are stacked under the main content.

We could achieve the desired result with Grid, but Flexbox is probably a better fit for such small interface elements. Flexbox not only has the ability to wrap rows, but also has other useful features for dealing with the smaller parts of a user interface.

Inside the media query for the first breakpoint, I set the `.mainheader ul` and `.gallery` selectors to `display: flex`. I add to that at the second breakpoint by turning the wrapper for the two call-to-action boxes (`.cta-list`) into a Flex container.

Our simple layout is now complete and resembles the first design (**FIG 4.3**).

Code examples: http://bkaprt.com/cgl-2/04-04 and http://bkaprt.com/cgl-2/04-05

One thing I appreciate about using Grid and Flexbox like this is how infrequently we need to add wrapper divs purely to create the layout. Most of the existing layout methods currently require redundant markup. It's nice to know I'm not adding bulk to my pages merely for CSS purposes. Here's the deal: we can often use *either* Flexbox or Grid for any particular component. Don't worry about it too much. If you find yourself struggling to get the layout you want, try the other method!

WHAT'S NEXT FOR GRID?

MY GREATEST HOPE FOR THIS BOOK is that it will give you a good introduction to CSS Grid Layout and encourage you to explore further. In this final chapter, I'd like to take a look at a feature currently being designed and implemented for the next level of the specification.

GRID LEVEL 2 AND SUBGRID

CSS specifications are developed in *levels*. Think of a level as a bit like a feature release of a product. A new level contains everything in the previous level, plus some extra features or enhancements to features. Level 2 of the Grid specification was quickly embarked on to specify a feature that had been dropped from Level 1 due to complexity. That feature is *subgrid*, and I touched on why it would be useful in Chapter 2. Let's take a closer look.

Only the direct children of a grid container become grid items. The children of the grid items return to displaying in normal flow. In the following example, the grid container has three direct children: a `div`, a `ul`, and a third `div`. Let's start with a three-column layout and place those items on the grid (**FIG 5.1**).

```
.wrapper {
  display: grid;
  grid-template-columns: 2.5fr 1fr .5fr;
  gap: 20px;
}

.box1 {
  grid-column: 1;
  grid-row: 1;
}

.box2 {
  grid-column: 2 / 4;
  grid-row: 1;
}
```

```
.box3 {
  grid-column: 1 / -1;
  grid-row: 2;
}
```

Code example: http://bkaprt.com/cgl-2/05-01

If we want the list items to be displayed using Grid Layout, we need to create a completely new grid, with its own columns and rows. In the case of a flexible, content-based grid, this may mean that the items in the list do not line up neatly with the outer grid.

With subgrid, we can make the unordered list a grid, but specify the value of `grid-template-columns` to be `subgrid`. This opts the tracks into the parent grid. They will now line up with any items positioned as direct children of the parent grid (**FIG 5.2**).

```
.box3 {
  grid-column: 1 / -1;
  grid-row: 2;
  display: grid;
  grid-template-columns: subgrid;
}
```

Code example: http://bkaprt.com/cgl-2/05-02

This makes it possible to use correct semantic markup, even with multiple levels of nesting, and lets our layout use a grid defined on an overall parent element.

At the time of writing, one browser (Firefox) actively implements subgrid. I hope that in the very near future, subgrid will be usable in more browsers.

Offering feedback on the specification

When I wrote the first edition of *Get Ready for CSS Grid Layout*, one of my aims was to introduce the emerging specification so that more designers and developers would offer feedback on it.

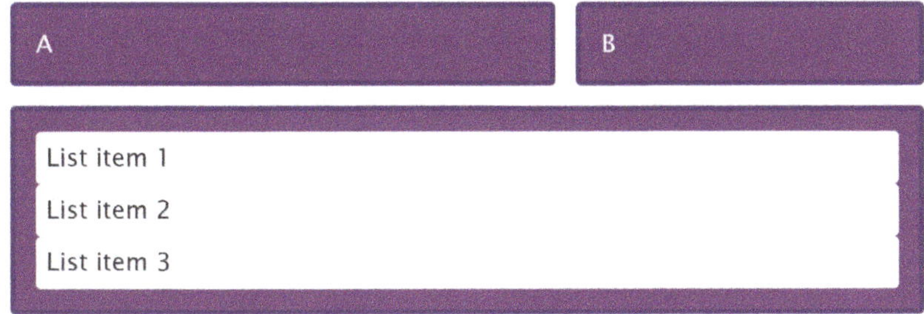

FIG 5.1: Indirect children are not part of the grid layout.

FIG 5.2: The `subgrid` value allows indirect children to participate in the grid layout.

And indeed, a comparison of the first and second versions of the spec reveals a feature that directly benefited from the web community's feedback.

The `gap` properties were added to the spec right before the first edition of this book came out. I had been pushing for the inclusion of a proper way to do gutters almost for as long as I had been using Grid Layout. Whenever I talked and wrote about Grid, I kept introducing this issue and getting enthusiastic responses from other developers who felt as strongly about it as I did. The feature was added to the spec in time for me to put a note into the first edition about it, but all of my examples still used small tracks as gutters. The result was that auto-placement was not useful—Grid would try to place an item into those tiny gaps. The examples in this edition have been updated to take advantage of the `gap` properties, and to show layouts that were impossible back when we needed to use tracks for our gutters.

Convinced of the power of community feedback, I'd like to conclude this second edition with the same call to action. I want to urge you to provide feedback for web-platform features that are still in the early stages of development. Although CSS Grid Level 1 has shipped in browsers, and Level 2 is currently being implemented, new features for CSS are continually being designed. You can—and should!—comment on them.

The CSS Working Group discussion has now moved to GitHub. You can view issues, comment on them, or raise your own questions about any specification. Many of the discussions are heavily technical, but sometimes feedback is requested on terminology, or on whether or not developers actually use a certain feature. This is crucial: developers sometimes complain that a specification does not meet their needs, so it's imperative that they get involved at a point when their concerns could be addressed. Specification writers are usually not practicing web developers, but the documents they work on are available as Editor's and Working Drafts. The process is open for our feedback if we are willing to give it.

Take a look at the resources I've listed here, experiment with the examples in this book, and start offering feedback on the specification or logging bugs against browser implementations. We're all busy, but contributing to the web platform can truly be seen as helping our collective future selves. Our contributions have the potential to make the platform better not only for us, but for everyone who uses the web.

RESOURCES

Read the specification to find out more about CSS Grid Layout and to stay current with browser support and developments.

Search for "css-grid" in the CSSWG GitHub repo issues to read and participate in current discussion on the Grid spec.

Grid by Example, my resource site on CSS Grid Layout, is a collection of step-by-step examples and experiments with Grid.

ACKNOWLEDGMENTS

I owe a debt to many people who have spent time discussing Grid with me, pointing out my mistakes, and being interested in my opinions. In particular, I'm grateful to Spec editors Tab Atkins Jr. and fantasai, the developers at Igalia, and Jen Simmons. Also, I appreciate every conference audience member who has come up and chatted with me after my Grid presentations. My ability to understand and teach Grid is informed by these conversations—revealing which things are confusing, and which are truly exciting for other developers and designers. Thank you.

REFERENCES: GET READY FOR CSS LAYOUT

Shortened URLs are numbered sequentially; the related long URLs are listed below for reference.

Introduction

00-01 http://www.w3.org/TR/2011/WD-css3-grid-layout-20110407/

00-02 https://caniuse.com/#feat=css-grid

Chapter 1

01-01 https://github.com/abookapart/css-grid-layout-code/blob/master/2e/ch1-basic.html

01-02 https://github.com/abookapart/css-grid-layout-code/

01-03 https://github.com/abookapart/css-grid-layout-code/blob/master/2e/ch1-gaps.html

01-04 https://github.com/abookapart/css-grid-layout-code/blob/master/2e/ch1-auto-rows.html

01-05 https://github.com/abookapart/css-grid-layout-code/blob/master/2e/ch1-minmax.html

01-06 https://github.com/abookapart/css-grid-layout-code/blob/master/2e/ch1-fr.html

01-07 https://github.com/abookapart/css-grid-layout-code/blob/master/2e/ch1-repeat.html

01-08 https://github.com/abookapart/css-grid-layout-code/blob/master/2e/ch1-auto-fill.html

01-09 https://github.com/abookapart/css-grid-layout-code/blob/master/2e/ch1-auto-fill-flexible.html

01-10 https://github.com/abookapart/css-grid-layout-code/blob/master/2e/ch1-line-based.html

01-11 https://github.com/abookapart/css-grid-layout-code/blob/master/2e/ch1-line-based-shorthand.html

01-12 https://github.com/abookapart/css-grid-layout-code/blob/master/2e/ch1-line-based-grid-area.html

01-13 https://github.com/abookapart/css-grid-layout-code/blob/master/2e/ch1-line-based-span.html

01-14 https://github.com/abookapart/css-grid-layout-code/blob/master/2e/ch1-line-based-named-lines.html

01-15 https://github.com/abookapart/css-grid-layout-code/blob/master/2e/ch1-grid-template-areas.html

Chapter 2

02-01 https://github.com/abookapart/css-grid-layout-code/blob/master/2e/ch2-layout.html

02-02 https://github.com/abookapart/css-grid-layout-code/blob/master/2e/ch2-boxy.html

02-03 https://github.com/abookapart/css-grid-layout-code/blob/master/2e/ch2-boxy-overlay.html

Chapter 3

03-01 https://github.com/abookapart/css-grid-layout-code/blob/master/2e/ch3-layout.html

Chapter 4

04-01 http://lists.w3.org/Archives/Public/www-style/2013May/0114.html

04-02 https://github.com/abookapart/css-grid-layout-code/blob/master/2e/ch4-layout.html

04-03 https://github.com/abookapart/css-grid-layout-code/blob/master/2e/ch4-layout-styles.css

04-04 https://github.com/abookapart/css-grid-layout-code/blob/master/2e/ch4-layout.html

04-05 https://github.com/abookapart/css-grid-layout-code/blob/master/2e/ch4-layout-styles.css

Chapter 5

05-01 https://github.com/abookapart/css-grid-layout-code/blob/master/2e/ch5-nosubgrid.html

05-02 https://github.com/abookapart/css-grid-layout-code/blob/master/2e/ch5-subgrid.html

05-03 https://github.com/w3c/csswg-drafts/issues

Resources

06-01 http://www.w3.org/TR/css-grid-1/

06-02 https://github.com/w3c/csswg-drafts/issues

06-03 http://igalia.github.io/css-grid-layout/index.html

INDEX: GET READY FOR CSS LAYOUT

ABOUT THE AUTHOR

Rachel Andrew is half of the web development firm edgeofmyseat.com and editor-in-chief of *Smashing Magazine*. She is a member of the CSS Working Group and a Google Developer Expert.

Rachel has been working on the web since 1996 and writing about the web for almost as long. She's written several books including *Get Ready for CSS Grid Layout*, the bestselling *CSS Anthology* from Sitepoint, and recent ventures into self-publishing have produced *The Profitable Side Project Handbook* and *CSS3 Layout Modules, Second Edition*. She is a regular columnist for *A List Apart* as well as other publications online and in print. When she's not writing, Rachel often works with other authors as a technical editor.

Rachel is a keen distance runner who encourages people to join her for a run when attending conferences, with varying degrees of success!

3

WORKING THE COMMAND LINE

REMY SHARP

FOREWORD BY
JEREMY KEITH

BRIEFS

Publisher: Jeffrey Zeldman
Designer: Jason Santa Maria
Executive Director: Katel LeDû
Editor: Caren Litherland
Technical Editor: Anna Debenham
Copyeditor: Lisa Maria Martin
Proofreader: Katel LeDû
Compositor: Rob Weychert
Ebook Producer: Ron Bilodeau

ISBN: 978-1-937557-49-2

A Book Apart
New York, New York
http://abookapart.com

10 9 8 7 6 5 4 3 2 1

TABLE OF CONTENTS: WORKING THE COMMAND LINE

FOREWORD

STOP ME if you've heard this one before.

You've just followed a link to a cool-sounding new resource that one of your friends has recommended. Now you're reading about how this could help you in your day-to-day work on the web. You excitedly click through to the documentation; the installation instructions are laid out before you. That's when your heart sinks. "This is moon language!" you cry.

You are not alone. I don't just mean that there are many of us who feel the same way. I mean that you are literally not alone. You have Remy with you.

As I navigate the intimidating dark depths of the Command Line Interface, I'll keep this book close to hand. But it isn't a reference book. It's more like a self-help book. It will help me—and you—become a more efficient developer, better equipped to battle moon language. "It's a Unix system," you'll whisper. "I know this!"

Having finished the book, I now have one question I ask myself before I confront an unavoidable task on the command line: *What Would Remy Do?*

When it comes to the command line, WWRD will serve you in good stead. (Warning: when it comes to just about any other aspect of your daily life, WWRD will almost certainly be disastrous.)

What Would Remy Do? The answer lies within these pages.

—Jeremy Keith

“JUST OPEN THE TERMINAL...”

AT SOME POINT IN YOUR LIFE, dear reader, you may have opened the terminal and found yourself staring into a black void—or, if you're of the Mac persuasion, a white void (**FIG 1.1**).

A flashing cursor and a dollar symbol invite you to enter a command. But *then* what? What does this void want from you?

In my first experiences with a terminal, I remember typing words like "Hello." "Run." "Open." I tried entire sentences. I'm not even kidding. And, no, none of it worked.

This book is for those of you who are new—or even not so new—to the terminal. Maybe you're a front-end developer or a designer who has read countless blog posts that start with this magical incantation: "Just open the terminal..." Or perhaps you have a few command-line skills, but have found yourself sucked into the void, stuck inside a command, unable to quit—ever.

By the end of this book, you'll feel quite comfortable firing up the terminal, and you'll be able to speak enough terminal black-void gobbledygook that you may very well start telling other people to "just" run `echo pling dollar`.

WHY USE THE TERMINAL?

Damn good question. Who in their right mind would punish themselves by using the terminal instead of a beautifully designed app with an interface that would make Jony Ive shed a tear?

The answer is that decades of development have gone into the tools available from the *terminal and the command line* (or the *command-line interface*, or CLI, as it's also known). Lots and lots and lots of tiny tools—programs that are built to do one simple thing well, but that often join forces to solve more complex problems. This practice of designing tiny tools is known as the *Unix philosophy*.

> *There is no single, standardized statement of the philosophy. But if it had to be described with only a single word, that word would be modularity, which refers to a system that is composed of components (i.e., modules) that can be fitted together or arranged in a variety of ways. —The Linux Information Project*

FIG 1.1: Faced with a dollar symbol and nothingness, you'd be forgiven for bailing out immediately.

Consider a tiny command-line utility called *cat*, which allows you to print the contents of a file to the screen. On its own, cat is fine, if somewhat limited—but it can be used as part of a larger system. Now, if I combine cat with *grep*, I can quickly find out on which line the words "black void" appear in my manuscript. I can even count how many times I've used the phrase "black void," simply by combining these two tools. Then I can plug that output into another program and manipulate the text, or do something else entirely. (We'll return to the grep tool in Chapter 3.)

One can't easily plug something like Adobe Photoshop into Sublime Text and then into another application. But in the terminal, such acrobatics are common practice.

TERMINAL APPLICATIONS

You really only need one terminal application to get to the command line. You can apply customization and personalization to any and all terminals—even remote machines. I personally look for a few key features that make working with the terminal application more productive:

- **Tabs**. We're used to tabbed browsers, and tabs have become a standard requirement for terminal applications these days, too.
- **Split screens**. Some of us are fortunate enough to work with large screens. Being able to split the terminal to view more than one task at a time is very powerful.
- **Select-to-copy**. If you've never had this feature, it might sound strange, but being able to quickly double-click (to select) any text in the terminal and then paste (so it goes straight into the prompt) is very powerful and quickly becomes muscle memory.

If you're a Linux desktop user and have Gnome Terminal, then you're pretty much set, since it includes all of these great features by default. Both Windows and Mac include terminal applications by default, but you'd be wise to upgrade away from them because of their inherent limitations. The default Mac terminal is pretty good, but it's not ideal; if you want to use a split screen, or a feature as simple (and powerful) as select-to-copy, consider using something else. The default Windows terminal is called Command Prompt; it has a number of restrictions, including not being able to resize the window.

Let's take a closer look at the Mac and Windows terminals.

Mac terminal

Out of the box, the Mac operating system comes with a terminal application called, aptly enough, "Terminal." It's a passable terminal, but being a Mac user myself, I highly recommend installing iTerm2, a free, open-source app that includes all sorts of great features. iTerm2 will be the terminal app I'll continue to use throughout this book (**FIG 1.2**).

Let me suggest a few tweaks that make working with iTerm2 extremely slick. Go to the app's preferences:

- In General, uncheck "Use Lion-style Fullscreen windows." This means that when you expand the terminal to fullscreen, you won't have to wait for the annoying full-screen animation to run before actually being able to use the terminal.

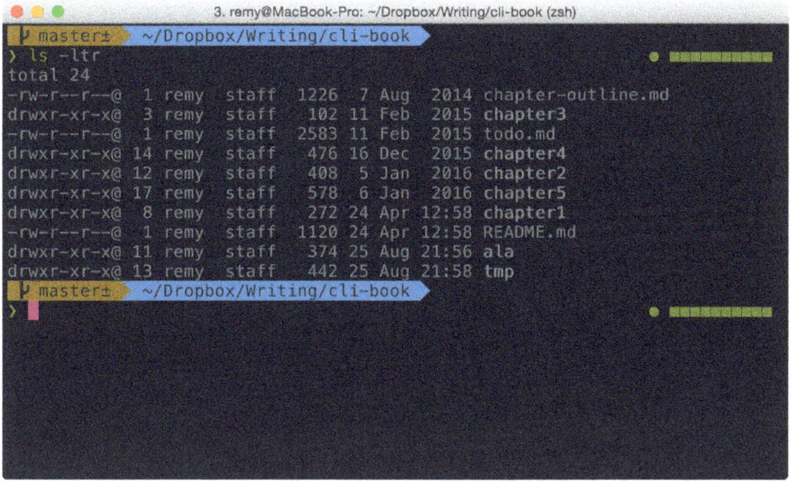

```
3. remy@MacBook-Pro: ~/Dropbox/Writing/cli-book (zsh)
 master±  ~/Dropbox/Writing/cli-book
› ls -ltr
total 24
-rw-r--r--@  1 remy  staff  1226  7 Aug  2014 chapter-outline.md
drwxr-xr-x@  3 remy  staff   102 11 Feb  2015 chapter3
-rw-r--r--@  1 remy  staff  2583 11 Feb  2015 todo.md
drwxr-xr-x@ 14 remy  staff   476 16 Dec  2015 chapter4
drwxr-xr-x@ 12 remy  staff   408  5 Jan  2016 chapter2
drwxr-xr-x@ 17 remy  staff   578  6 Jan  2016 chapter5
drwxr-xr-x@  8 remy  staff   272 24 Apr 12:58 chapter1
-rw-r--r--@  1 remy  staff  1120 24 Apr 12:58 README.md
drwxr-xr-x@ 11 remy  staff   374 25 Aug 21:56 ala
drwxr-xr-x@ 13 remy  staff   442 25 Aug 21:58 tmp
 master±  ~/Dropbox/Writing/cli-book
›
```

FIG 1.2: iTerm2 running my own customized shell. The *shell* is a text-based interface that gives you access to your operating system; it processes commands and returns output. We'll look at customizing the shell in Chapter 5.

- In Keys, check "Show/hide iTerm2 with a system-wide hotkey" and give yourself a shortcut. My personal favorite is cmd+esc—it really has become part of my muscle memory .

Windows "cmd.exe" terminal

Command Prompt is the official name for the Windows terminal, but you'll often hear it referred to in conversation as "command-dot-ex-ee." It provides a view on what DOS used to be like. Including Command Prompt in this book as a terminal is almost unfair, because it doesn't really hold a candle to the features and CLI tools of other terminals. PowerShell is way more powerful (and complicated)—arguably better than the Linux-type shells we'll use in this book—but it's beyond the scope of this brief volume.

If you're a Windows user, I recommend you get your hands on Git BASH. It comes with Git (the version control system), but you don't have to use Git if you don't want to (**FIG 1.3**).

Now you've got the same commands and navigation methods as you would on a Linux or Mac machine. This is a win for consistency.

THE PROMPT

There's a certain amount of jargon involved in working with the terminal, some of which we've touched on already. One of the first things you'll have to familiarize yourself with is the *prompt*. The prompt is where you'll enter commands.

Though usually represented by a `$` symbol, the prompt can really be anything (because you can customize it, as we'll see in Chapter 5). It's not uncommon to see blogs and online tutorials start a code block with a `$` symbol, which is shorthand for "You need to run everything after the `$` in the terminal." Note that you don't need to type this in; it's just a visual cue for the reader.

Now that you've fired up your terminal, you'll be greeted with...well, very little: a `$` symbol and a (mostly) blank screen. Yes, you'll need to know your way around—but fear not, that's why you're reading this book!

We're going to navigate around your hard drive to get a feel for how a path works. First, though, let's explore a little.

`ls`: listing files and directories

When you type `ls` (that's a lowercase *ell*, not a numeral one or an uppercase *I*) and hit Enter, the terminal will list the current working directory's files and subdirectories.

We want to *change directory*, or `cd`, into one of the directories listed. But it's entirely possible that the output from `ls` doesn't make it clear what is a directory and what is a file:

```
$ ls
chapter-outline.md  chapter1  chapter2  todo.md
```

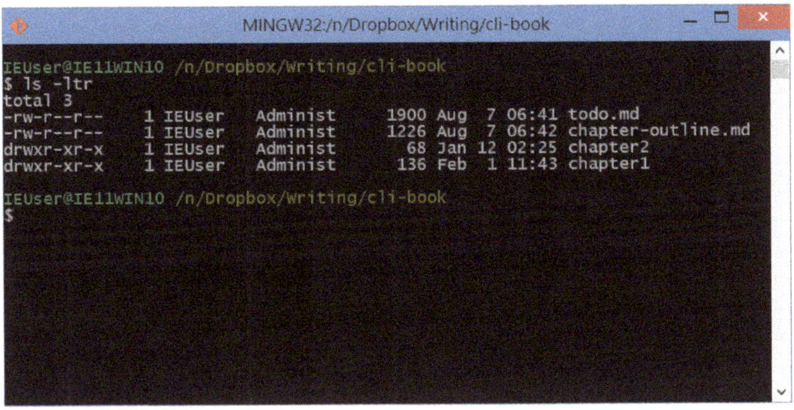

```
MINGW32:/n/Dropbox/Writing/cli-book
IEUser@IE11WIN10 /n/Dropbox/Writing/cli-book
$ ls -ltr
total 3
-rw-r--r--    1 IEUser   Administ     1900 Aug  7 06:41 todo.md
-rw-r--r--    1 IEUser   Administ     1226 Aug  7 06:42 chapter-outline.md
drwxr-xr-x    1 IEUser   Administ       68 Jan 12 02:25 chapter2
drwxr-xr-x    1 IEUser   Administ      136 Feb  1 11:43 chapter1

IEUser@IE11WIN10 /n/Dropbox/Writing/cli-book
$
```

FIG 1.3: Running Windows? Get some Git BASH to make your life a little easier.

In this case, we want to see clear distinctions between files and directories, and we want detailed information about each item in the current directory. Most commands can take *switches* (sometimes also called *options* or *flags*): arguments that modify how a command is carried out. So we'll repeat our `ls` command and add a couple of switches to it: `-l` (again, a lowercase *ell*) which gives us the details, plus `-F`, which adds a trailing slash to the directories. Note that single-character arguments can often be combined together—and here's what we get:

```
$ ls -lF
total 16
-rw-r--r--@ 1 remy  staff  1226  7 Aug 14:42
  chapter-outline.md
drwxr-xr-x@ 3 remy  staff   102 12 Jan 10:25
  chapter1/
drwxr-xr-x@ 2 remy  staff    68 12 Jan 10:25
  chapter2/
-rw-r--r--@ 1 remy  staff  1900  7 Aug 14:41 todo.md
```

Our output contains lots of information:

- **Total:** the first line will give you a *total* (16, in this case). Don't let this confuse you like it did me. *total*, here, means the total number of "blocks" used, not the total number of files. Just ignore this for the moment.
- **Permissions**: where you have access to read, write, or execute (i.e., run) the file.
- **Ownership**: which user owns the file.
- **File size:** given in bytes.
- **Timestamps:** the last time the content was modified.
- **Name:** of the file or directory.
- **Whether it's a directory or not:** indicated by the `d` preceding the permissions string and the trailing slash following the name.

Now we can tell directories from files. Let's pick a directory and change to it using `cd [directory name]`. In this case, I want to `cd` into chapter1:

```
$ cd chapter1
~/Dropbox/cli-book/chapter1
```

Quite often, I find I want to list the directory contents (so I use `-l`) by most recently modified. So I can use two more switches: the `-t` switch orders by time, showing newest contents first, while the `-r` switch reverses the order—so now the contents will display in ascending order, with the newest file is at the bottom. As the command lists the directory, the last file is likely to be the one I last worked on:

```
$ ls -ltr
total 264
-rw-r--r--@ 1 remy  staff  103726  1 Feb 19:43
  iterm2.png
-rw-r--r--@ 1 remy  staff   14749  1 Feb 19:50
  gitbash-for-windows.png
-rw-r--r--@ 1 remy  staff   12118  2 Feb 16:19
  chapter1.md
```

Once you have a directory listing, you'll want to start messing with the files. We'll do that in the chapters ahead. For now, though, let's just traverse the directories.

Directory shortcuts

We've already used `cd` to change directories. Navigating through those directories is easy once you understand how a directory is broken down, and made even easier once you know a few special shortcuts.

Here's a directory path: ~/Dropbox/cli-book/. Each directory is separated by a slash (similar to how a URL is structured).

The tilde indicates the user's home directory; in my case, if I type `cd ~`, I'll end up in /Users/remy. The home directory symbol is one of our special shortcuts. (Another way of going to the home directory is by typing `cd` and hitting Enter.)

Typing `cd -` will take you to whichever directory you were in last (a toggle back and forth between directories, if you will).

Here's how some of the directories are laid out in my Dropbox folder:

```
~/Dropbox
├── cli-book
├── introducing-html5
├── personal-stuff-n-stuff
└── zombies-and-rabbits
```

If I'm in the ~/Dropbox directory, I can run the following to move to the cli-book directory:

```
$ cd cli-book # moves to ~/Dropbox/cli-book
```

Note that the `#` symbol represents a comment that is valid to use on the command line (and you'll see this a few times in the book).

I can also use two periods to navigate to the parent directory: typing `cd ..` puts me back in ~/Dropbox. And I can *combine* this with directories, to move into the introducing-html5 directory:

```
$ cd ../introducing-html5 # moves to ~/Dropbox/
  introducing-html5
```

Typing one period instead of two means *this* directory, the one we're in now—also known as the current working directory. (We'll need this when we run our own scripts in later chapters.) You might understandably think that if I wanted to move up *two* directories, I'd use three dots, but that's not the case. Instead, I need to use multiple parent commands, like `cd ../../`, which means: move to the parent directory (the first two dots), then in that directory (the `/`), move to *its* parent directory (the second two dots):

```
$ cd ../../ # moves me to the parent of Dropbox,
  which is ~
```

Spaces in names

If you're using any kind of UI, like OS X or Windows, it's entirely possible that you have a folder or a file name with a space in it. If you try to just `cd` into that folder, it'll confuse the command:

```
$ cd my cool folder
cd: too many arguments
```

This doesn't only apply to `cd`; it applies to any command. That's okay, though—we've got ways to work around that limitation.

You can enclose the name of the file or directory in double or single quotes:

```
$ cd "my cool folder"
```

You can use an escape character (`\`) in front of the space:

```
$ cd my\ cool\ folder
```

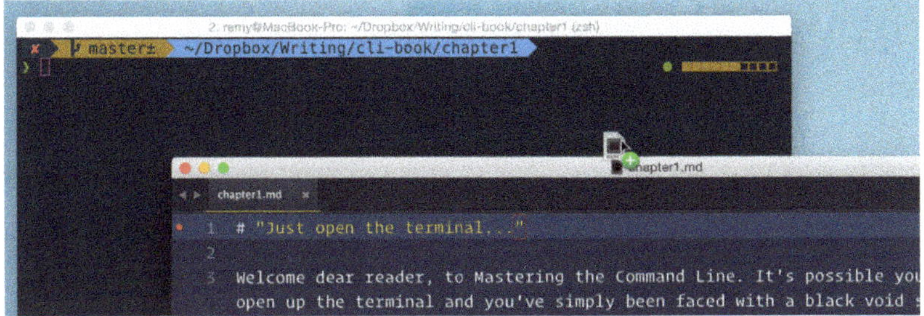

FIG 1.4: Dragging document icons into the terminal eases the pain of typing file names.

Or, if you're feeling super lazy and happen to have a Mac, you can drag the file onto the terminal and it'll insert the file name for you. Similarly, from a finder window, you can drag the icon in the title bar into the terminal, and it will insert the folder name for you (**FIG 1.4**).

USING YOUR HISTORY

As you use the shell, it keeps a record of your commands. (This record is private—particular to your account—and not accessible to anyone else who has their own login account on your machine.)

You can use the up/down cursor to cycle through your command history from the prompt, but there are also some shortcut commands you can use in the terminal that are especially powerful. Let's go through them.

`!!`

`!!`, known as *bang bang*, is shorthand for your last command.

So if you run a command, hit Enter, run `!!`, and then hit Enter again, it'll repeat that command:

```
$ echo "hello world"
hello world
$ !!
hello world
```

At first glance, it might seem like this is slightly more complicated than pushing the *up* cursor key, but the next chapter will show you how you can combine this command with other commands to powerful effect.

!$

`!$`, pronounced *bang dollar* or *pling dollar*, gives you the last argument of your previous command. In our `echo "hello world"` example, the last argument is the part in quotes (`"hello world"`).

On the Mac, there's also a command called `say`. We can use `!$` to say "hello world" after echoing it:

```
$ echo "hello world"
hello world
$ say !$
$
```

This causes your computer to say, out loud, "Hello world." Again, this gets even more interesting when you're able to "pipe" commands together. We'll talk more about piping commands in Chapter 3.

!n

Here, *n* refers to a number, specifically the *n*th entry in your history of commands. This number can mark a specific point in the history. A positive value works forward through the history, but you can also use a negative value to count from the end of the history. For example, you can use `!-1` to access the last command in your history:

```
$ echo "hello world"
hello world
$ !-1
hello world
```

You've already met the bang-bang (`!!`) command, which is an alias for `!-1`, but it also means that if you want to run the penultimate command, you can use `!-2` (not the last command, but the one before that) and so on, working backward from the last command.

If you run `history`, you'll get a complete list of all the commands you've run, with a history index beside it so that you can quickly reference a more complicated command. The history size can range depending on your operating system—500 items is typical, but some will be 1,000, and others 10,000. (If you want more information, search The Googles for "HISTSIZE".)

Here's my recent command history:

```
$ history
10161   boot2docker start
10169   cd test/a
10170   nodemon -w ../ a.js -V --dump
10171   z nodemon
10172   cd tmp
10175   docker images
10176   docker run -v ~/Sites/nodemon:/nodemon -t -i
  ubuntu/nvm:latest /bin/bash
10177   touch test/a/a.js
10178   touch test/b/b.js
10179   cd ..
10181   git diff
10182   docker run -v ~/Sites/nodemon:/nodemon -t -i
  node:0.10-slim /bin/bash
```

Notice that the numbers don't run exactly incrementally. This is the history for the *current* shell session. (If `10173` and `10174` are missing, it's because they were run in another terminal shell session.)

The index becomes useful if I want to rerun a command. I *can* rerun a command by copying and pasting the history item, like this:

```
$ docker run -v ~/Sites/nodemon:/nodemon -t -i
  ubuntu/nvm:latest /bin/bash
```

Or, I can save some time and energy by simply copying and pasting the index number:

```
$ !10176
```

This reran the 10,176th command, and dropped me into my Docker session (which is way beyond the scope of this book). Using the history index makes referring to historical commands really easy.

USING THE KEYBOARD

Although shortcuts aren't required, it's always handy to know a few power keyboard moves.

Tab

My favorite shortcut is the unsung *Tab*. All terminals have tab-completion support. So if you find yourself typing a command or directory name quite a lot, you only need to enter a bit of text, hit Tab, and your terminal will try to autocomplete it.

Different-flavored shells will do slightly different things. Some will complete the most common word you use, and hitting Tab again will cycle through to the next most common match.

Some will complete *up to* the point where there's more than one command that matches. For instance, if you have two applications, one called cowsay and one called cowthink, typing

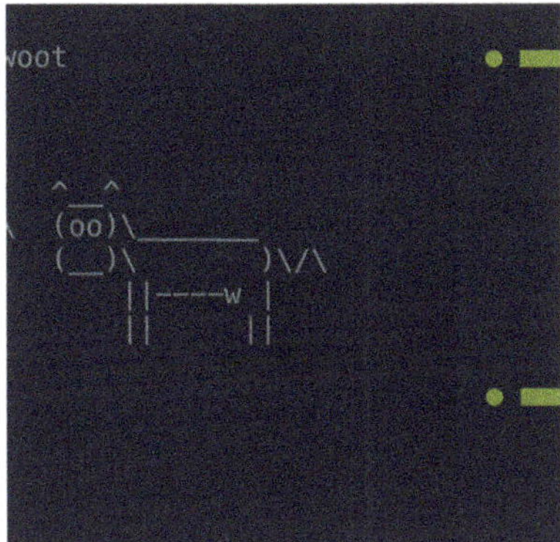

FIG 1.5: cowsay in all its glory.

"co" and hitting Tab would complete up to "cow"; then, if you added s and Tab, it would complete to "cowsay" (**FIG 1.5**).

Often, hitting Tab twice will list all possible matches. In our example, hitting Tab twice after typing "co" would show both "cowsay" and "cowthink," assuming these were the only commands in your *environment path* (a list of directories where the system can find programs) that started with "co". We'll go over paths in more detail in Chapter 2. (I'll show you how to install the obviously essential cowsay program there, too.)

Control-Left / Control-Right

Instead of using the left/right cursor keys to move through every character, you can use ctrl+left or ctrl+right to move by entire words. But! This will only work if you don't use multiple desktops on a system like Mac OS Yosemite, which uses these keys to switch desktops (though you can disable this in settings).

An alternative to ctrl+left / ctrl+right, albeit not one that is easy to use, is esc+b for backward and esc+f for forward.

Control-C

This means *abort*. It stops an application from running. If you try running `yes` in your terminal, it'll spew `y` over and over until you hit ctrl+c to abort.

You might also see this expressed as "^C". (Note that these shortcuts aren't case-sensitive; it's just the Control and C keys pressed together.)

Control-D

This means *end transmission*, which is basically like saying "GTFO." Instead of exiting your terminal using the mouse (or `logout` command), you can use ctrl+d and it'll close your terminal session.

Control-R

This is a bit of a power-user shortcut, but since we're reaching the end of Chapter 1, I think you deserve it.

Control-R lets you search for the most recent command matching your search term. Using my terminal history from earlier, if I hit ctrl+r, I'll be presented with this:

```
$
bck-i-search: _
```

Now if I type "no", it'll show the most recent command I ran containing the characters *n* and *o* together. If I wanted to match the `nodemon -w ../ a.js -V --dump` command, I'd need to type something unique to that command, like `mon -w`. Then the full command would come up and, if I hit Enter, it would run for me.

If you want to abort out of this mode, just hit ctrl+c.

OUT OF THE ABYSS

As this first chapter draws to a close, you should be proud. You've stared into the void— the terminal—and you've nailed down the fundamentals of navigating the CLI. Heck, you can even throw the words "pling dollar" into a conversation.

With these essentials in hand, let's look at how we can install third-party tools onto our machines and use them in the terminal.

INSTALL ALL THE THINGS

YOU KNOW THE STORY: you're following along with a tutorial when you run smack into a dependency on an existing application. I'm not talking about installable applications via the iTunes Store (or via a CD, if you're rocking it old school). I mean *terminal* applications.

It starts innocently enough: someone you follow on Twitter, let's say the formidable Mr. Paul Irish, posts a tweet about something you think would be useful (**FIG 2.1**).

You think to yourself: *That looks useful; I'd better install it!* And you dutifully follow the link. Now you've landed on a GitHub page. Okay, not a problem. Scroll, scroll, "usage," keep scrolling, "examples," cool, keep scrolling, YES! "Installation."

Copy, paste, BOOM! Not the cool "boom" that Steve Jobs used to drop, but the boom of failure (**FIG 2.2**).

It's a pretty unhappy experience: "Command not found," "No such file or directory." You have to start at the beginning and try to fix each problem one by one.

APPLICATION INSTALLERS

Most operating systems come with some core applications. Ruby is one of these; if you have a modern PC, you'll likely have Ruby installed, but it's not guaranteed. There are also built-in commands like `cd`, `ls`, and `echo`.

But beyond those, how do you install applications like Wget—or more important, cowsay? (Note that I'm just using cowsay as a simple, silly example of a program. I know, I know—this is the second time I'm asking you to install cowsay, and I won't be offended if you don't. But you should know that it does have an option to change the cow to a koala dressed as Darth Vader. Because *Star Wars*.)

Before I go any further, a disclaimer: this book is mainly aimed at beginners, front-end developers, and designers. And because there's a strong hint of "Mac user" among that particular audience, most of my examples of installing applications will use Mac methods.

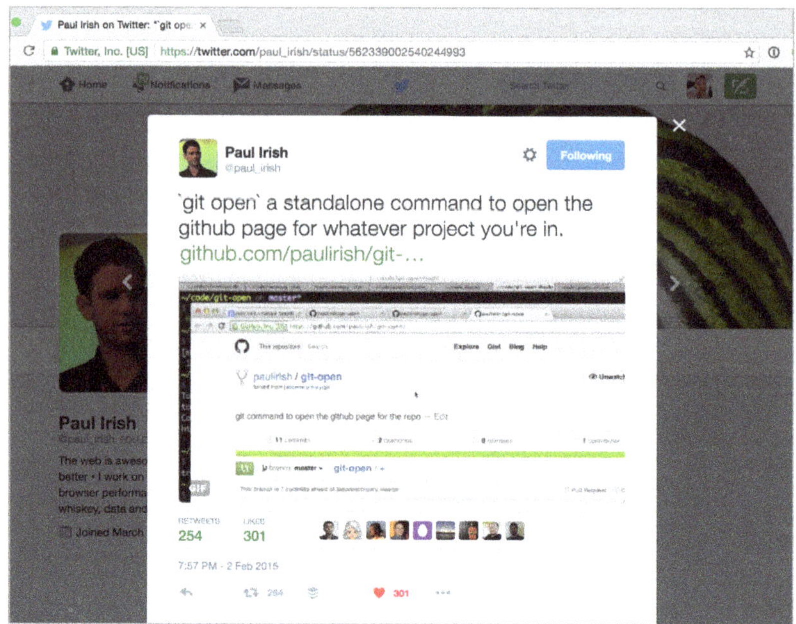

FIG 2.1: When Paul Irish tweets, I listen.

Mac users can skip the following two sections. Everyone else, read on and bear with me—most of the rest of this chapter should apply to you, too!

Linux

Linux comes in many flavors, and installing new applications differs slightly with each flavor. Google is your friend here—once you've found the application installer, it's smooth sailing.

If you're using Ubuntu, you need to run `apt-get install [package]`. Often you'll need root privileges to run this, but if you don't have root privileges, you can just prepend the command with `sudo`. (I'll go into more detail about root privileges and `sudo` in Chapter 4.) You'll be prompted for your password, and then the program will go ahead and install:

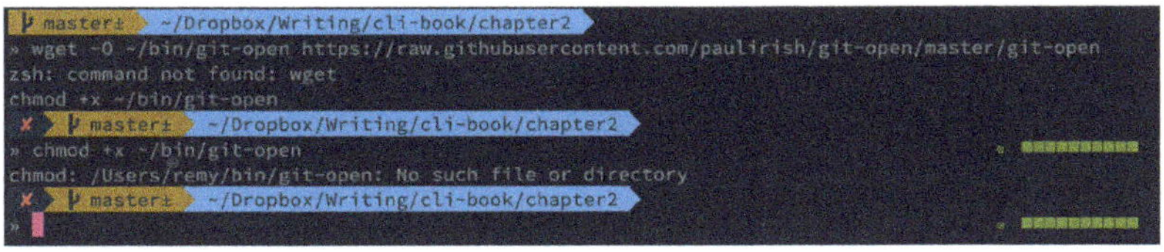

```
master± ~/Dropbox/Writing/cli-book/chapter2
» wget -O ~/bin/git-open https://raw.githubusercontent.com/paulirish/git-open/master/git-open
zsh: command not found: wget
chmod +x ~/bin/git-open
✘ master± ~/Dropbox/Writing/cli-book/chapter2
» chmod +x ~/bin/git-open
chmod: /Users/remy/bin/git-open: No such file or directory
✘ master± ~/Dropbox/Writing/cli-book/chapter2
»
```

FIG 2.2: Uh-oh...just when things were going so well! Looks like Wget needs to be installed.

```
remy@ubuntu:/# sudo apt-get install cowsay
Reading package lists... Done
[code omitted for brevity]
Setting up cowsay (3.03+dfsg1-6)
remy@ubuntu:/# /usr/games/cowsay woot
 ______
< woot >
 ------
        \   ^__^
         \  (oo)\_______
            (__)\       )\/\
                ||----w |
                ||     ||
remy@ubuntu:/#
```

Note that the prompt on Linux is `remy@ubuntu:/#`. On a Mac, you're more likely to have a `$` character as your prompt.

Windows

Windows is an odd creature. It doesn't natively have a terminal-like shell, but hopefully you're using Git BASH (introduced in Chapter 1), which is pretty close.

To install external shell applications, though, you'll need a tool called Chocolatey, which dubs itself the "apt-get for Windows" (also known as the "Brew for Windows"—we'll meet Brew next). The gotcha here is that all of your install processes need to happen in an administrative `cmd.exe` command prompt. Yes, it's turtles all the way down (**FIG 2.3**).

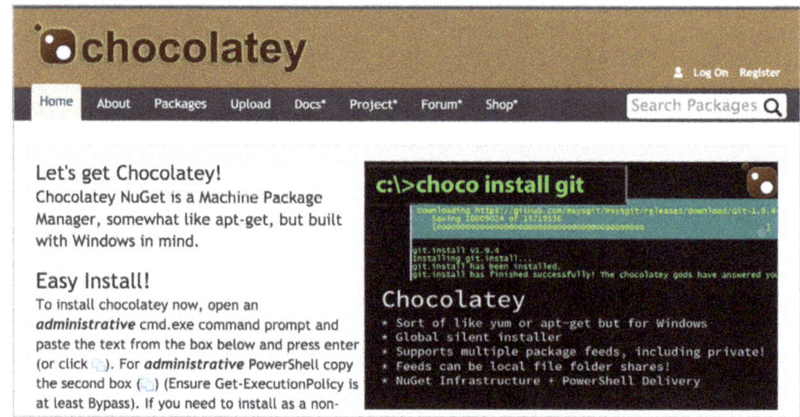

FIG 2.3: Chocolatey is the Windows method for installing terminal applications.

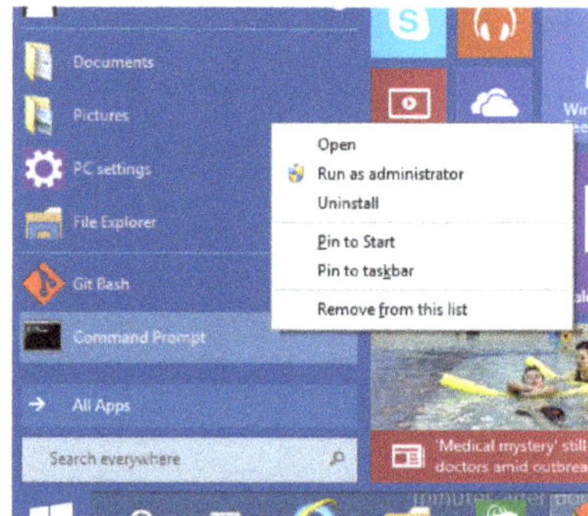

FIG 2.4: To install Chocolatey, you need to run `cmd.exe` as the administrator.

```
» brew install cowsay
==> Downloading http://ftp.acc.umu.se/mirror/cdimage/snapshot/Debian/pool/main/c/cowsay/cowsay_3.03.orig.tar.gz
Already downloaded: /Library/Caches/Homebrew/cowsay-3.03.tar.gz
==> /bin/sh install.sh /usr/local/Cellar/cowsay/3.03
🍺 /usr/local/Cellar/cowsay/3.03: 53 files, 228K, built in 2 seconds
```

FIG 2.5: The Brew installation process.

Installation isn't obvious (at least not to the naked eye), but take some time to read the documentation. You'll need to run `cmd.exe` as the administrator. To do this, hit the Start key to open the Start menu; then type "cmd". Don't hit Enter just yet:

instead of starting the command prompt, right-click and select "Run as administrator" (**FIG 2.4**).

Then, from the Chocolatey website, run the commands they provide for installing and paste them into the command line. You'll *also* need the admin command prompt to install applications.

Sadly, there's no cowsay on Chocolatey—but don't worry, dear Windows user, we'll fix that later in this chapter. For now, let's install Wget instead:

```
C:\Windows\system32>choco install wget
Chocolatey (v0.9.8.32) is installing 'wget' and
  dependencies. By installing you accept the license
  for 'wget' and each dependency you are installing.

Wget v1.11.4.1
Downloading Wget 32 bit
  from 'http://users.ugent.be/~bpuype/wget/wget.exe'
Added C:\ProgramData\chocolatey\bin\wget.exe shim
  pointed to '..\lib\wget.1.11.4.1\tools\wget.exe'.
Finished installing 'wget' and dependencies—if
  errors not shown in console, none detected. Check
  log for errors if unsure.
```

Now you can run Wget from your Git BASH terminal (or the regular cmd.exe).

Mac

There are a number of application installers for Mac, but I recommend Brew. It's comprehensive and reliable. Visit the Brew site and scroll down to the "Install Homebrew" section, where you'll see a command. Literally just copy it and paste it into your terminal, and you're done: Brew is installed.

Now you can install applications using `brew install [package]` (**FIG 2.5**).

If your installation is successful, you'll see a beer emoji.

How the heck do I run my own commands?

In this chapter, we've been installing *global commands*. When you run global commands, your environment path is searched until the program to execute is found. But what if the program lives in your current directory rather than in your environment path?

It's an easy fix, though not obvious if you've never done it before. Assuming that your program file is executable (I'll talk more about what that means in Chapter 4), simply prefix the file name with `./`, which refers to files in the directory you're currently in:

```
$ ./my-script
```

If the file isn't executable, you'll get an error like this when you run the script:

```
$ ./my-script
bash: ./my-script: Permission denied
```

In this case, you'll need to use the appropriate program (or *runner*) in front of it, like so:

```
$ ruby my-cool-thing.rb
$ node my-even-cooler-thing.js
$ php -f not-even-cool-enough-for-school.php
$ sh my-script.sh
```

The program file immediately following the prompt (`ruby`, `node`, and so forth) is the command; to the right of that is what you're applying the command *to* (`my-cool-thing.rb`). It's also worth noting that the file-name extension is only a hint to you, the author, about what program is needed to run the file. In fact, there doesn't even have to be an extension—so sometimes a little exploration or good old trial and error is required on your part.

RUBY, PYTHON, OR NODE?

Anna Debenham, this book's technical editor, wisely asked me, "How does someone know which is the right type of application to use?" An excellent question, and a complicated one that I would frankly rather sidestep—but I won't.

First of all, there are no hard-and-fast rules about which language is best. Personally, I gravitate toward Node: I find the installation of individual programs uncomplicated (using the package manager npm, which I'll come back to in a bit), and the support across different operating systems is absolutely superb.

Some people like Ruby, others like Python. There is no absolute right way—what matters most is how comfortable you are with a given language. Once you've set things up the way you want on your machine and have your workflow nailed down, you're good to go.

Occasionally, though, specific applications are only available under one language or another—so you really have no choice. Over the years, I've learned that I need to be able to install from the three major languages: Ruby, Python, and Node.

Ruby applications and gems

This is when it gets serious. You've read the latest cool thing, and you "just have to install" a Ruby *gem* (a bit of reusable code, also called a *package* or a *module* in other contexts).

I consider myself pretty comfortable with the terminal, but installing gems seems to be a dark art requiring all kinds of arcane rites. The real problem (in my experience) is that when you find a great application that says "just install the gem," it rarely tells you *how* to install the gem.

On the optimistic side, when you encounter this scenario, it's always worth trying to run the `gem install` command first. If that doesn't work, you'll need to update parts of your system (more about this later).

Let's start by installing lolcommits, a project that uses your webcam to capture your picture right after you commit to Git:

FIG 2.6: An optimistic Remy has just made a commit! (By the way, if you want to deepen your understanding of Git, consider reading David Demaree's excellent *Git for Humans*.)

```
$ gem install lolcommits
```

If this works, you'll see a torrent of install messages ending with something like this:

```
$ gem install lolcommits
Fetching: unf_ext-0.0.7.2.gem (100%)
Building native extensions.  This could take a while...
[code omitted for brevity]
35 gems installed
```

And if you follow the setup instructions, you'll be graced with some lovely photos whenever you make a commit (**FIG 2.6**).

When gems don't work

If Ruby hates you as much as it hates me, then you might need to update a few things to get gems to install properly. And honestly, it's entirely possible that you'll hit a wall after updating, and find that *still* nothing happens. I run into this all the time. The solution isn't to throw your machine through the window, as I have nearly done. Instead, calmly walk away, and accept that this particular gem shall not be part of your growing collection of command-line tools.

Here's a list of things you can do to *try* to get gems to install if you're having problems:

1. Try running the install as root (using `sudo`, which we met earlier): `sudo gem install lolcommits`.
2. Try updating the gem system: `sudo gem update --system`.
3. Install the latest Xcode command-line tools: `xcode-select --install`.
4. Upgrade to the latest version of your operating system.
5. Buy a new computer. Yeah, I'd give up before this point, too.

Steps 1-3 are the ones I would try, but I have also experienced a machine that needed step 4 to install a gem (it was two versions behind the latest OS X). Other times, I've had to abort—but this book is an introduction, so if you're getting stuck in gem black holes, it might be worth consulting your nearest ops engineer!

Python applications

Python has a package manager, but it's pretty hairy. There are a lot of moving parts to keep track of—like `pip`, `easy_install`, and `virtualenv`.

One place you can find packages for Python is pypi.python.org. In my own experience, though (as someone who has very little experience with Python packages), I found it tricky to get the right combination of installers. In fact, most of the Python-based applications I've installed in the past have been installed via Brew (which we met earlier). This might spare you a little pain in the future. Or, it might not.

Swiftly moving on...

Node applications

Because my background is in JavaScript, I tend to turn to Node-based applications as my go-to solution; Node, after all, is what is used to execute JavaScript.

Another thing that draws me to Node modules over Ruby gems or Python modules is, as I mentioned earlier, the very excellent cross-platform support they enjoy. Most of the time, the Node utility you install will work the same on Mac, Windows, and Linux.

The only prerequisite is installing Node, which is wrapped up in a nice application installer you can download from nodejs.org. Hit the big Install button, follow the prompts, and you're done.

Now, when you open your terminal, you can install Node modules via npm. ("npm" doesn't stand for "node package manager," by the way. It doesn't stand for anything.)

We typically use npm to install packages (also sometimes referred to as modules) into software we're writing. However, we can also use npm to install globally—that is, to install a command-line utility that's accessible from anywhere in the terminal.

Let's install our friend cowsay, since someone ported it to JavaScript. To do this, we'll type `npm` on the command line and tell it to `install` a package. Note that to install it globally, we need to use the `-g` flag:

```
$ npm install -g cowsay
/usr/local/bin/cowsay ->
/usr/local/lib/node_modules/cowsay/cli.js
/usr/local/bin/cowthink ->
/usr/local/lib/node_modules/cowsay/cli.js
cowsay@1.0.3 /usr/local/lib/node_modules/cowsay
└─ optimist@0.3.7 (wordwrap@0.0.2)
```

You can also use npm to install tools like Grunt, Gulp, Yeoman, or PhoneGap. And there's a huge community of developers contributing new and updated npm packages by the ~~day~~ hour.

In some situations, you *may* need to use `sudo npm install -g [package]`, but I recommend not using `sudo` and trying a regular install first. Installing packages with `sudo` can unintentionally inherit some of root's permissions, which results in the program having different permissions than your user when it runs. Bottom line: things can get gnarly. (I'll go into more detail about `sudo` in Chapter 4.)

Over the course of this chapter, you've learned how to install a wealth of applications for your new command-line skills—not only "classic" Unix-type applications like Wget, but also utterly awesome applications like cowsay and even (wait for it) ponysay. (Yes, as if a cow weren't enough, you can also get a brightly colored pony to say all the things.) Beyond `brew install`, you can now install all of the bespoke applications that pop up in your news and Twitter feeds via Ruby gems or npm packages.

If you want to find a program that does a particular thing, I recommend starting with Google (rather than with package-specific sites). Some initial, general research will give you an idea of whether the program is available in your preferred language, or will point you toward an alternative you perhaps hadn't thought of.

Armed with your new knowledge, you're ready to start remixing your command line applications. We'll do that next.

TOOLS OF THE TERMINAL TRADE

IF YOU'VE SPENT ANY TIME rummaging through tutorials, or perhaps shoulder-surfed a friend as they cruised around the terminal like a fish in water, then it's likely you've come across the *pipe*. The pipe typically occurs between two commands, like `echo "Hello Remy"` and `say`, which will make the machine speak and welcome me, like this:

```
$ echo "Hello Remy" | say
```

The pipe is a magic and integral part of the command line. It's super powerful and damn useful. What it does is take the *output* from the first command (on the left side) and "pipe" it to the second command (on the right side).

If you want an analogy, imagine a cartoon factory conveyor belt running through two big machines. Maybe we send a tree trunk down the conveyer belt and into the first machine (our first command), which eats it up, rumbles a bit, and spits out a carefully carved statue of a pony. The wooden pony continues along the conveyor belt (this is our "pipe"), and makes its way into a second machine (our second command), only to come out painted gloriously pink!

The key is that *anything* can be sent into that second machine, and it will come out bright pink—it doesn't just accept wooden ponies.

It's a pretty simple concept: you can use the output of one command as the input to another, and in fact you can *keep* piping commands together—this can go on, and on, and on, and on.

So which commands support this behavior? Most. In fact, if a command expects text as input (and most generally do), then it would be fair to expect the command to support piping of content. As a rule of thumb, if I installed an application via `brew install`, I'd expect it to support piping.

One caveat: Ruby gems, Node modules and utilities, Python scripts, and so forth might *not* support this. There are a lot of Unix commands available to you on the command line, but the third party command-line applications I just mentioned may not have written-in support for piping content.

Okay, so now you know the superpower that the command line offers. But what can you do with it? Lots.

STRING MANIPULATION

I'm going to cover a handful of core commands that let you do string manipulation. That may not sound very fancy, but once you know what you can do with these commands, they become the bread and butter of using the command line.

grep

grep is a tool that searches for an expression and prints matches to the screen. *Expressions* can be *regular strings* (like `foo`) or *regular expressions* (like `^foo`, which means "lines starting with 'foo'").

Regular expressions are way beyond the scope of this book. But if you're not familiar with them, don't worry—there's many a book on the topic. And Lea Verou has given an excellent talk on regular expressions.

Here's a simple example. I'm writing this book using Markdown. To create headings, I use hash symbols (`#`): one for a level-one heading, two for a level-two heading, and so on. If I want to find all the headings in Chapter 1, I can use `grep`; note that everything after the first line constitutes the output of the command:

```
$ grep '#' chapter1.md
# "Just Open the Terminal…"
## Why Use the Terminal?
## Terminal Applications
### Mac terminal
### Windows "cmd.exe" terminal
## The Prompt
### ls: list
### Spaces in names
## Using Your History
```

```
### !!
### !$
### !n
root@a1ed91d61306:/#
## Using the Keyboard
### Tab
### Control-left / control-right
### Control-c
### Control-d
### Control-r
## Out of the Abyss
```

See how I've put the # between quotes in the command line? That's because a hash symbolizes the start of a comment, so unless it's between quotes, it messes up the grep command. You typically won't need to quote the expression you're searching for. Also notice that my output includes the line *root@a1ed91d61306:/#*. That's because the line contains a hash symbol.

What if I'm really only interested in level-two headings (indicated by ##)? To find only those, I can use a regular expression: a caret (^), which means "starts with"; then two hash marks (##); and finally a space (since my Markdown titles are preceded by a space):

```
$ grep '^## ' chapter1.md
## Introduction
## Chapter 1
## Why Use the Terminal?
## Terminal Applications
## The Prompt
## Using History
## Using the Keyboard
## Out of the Abyss
```

The grep command by itself is helpful, but it can also be used to grep the output from another command.

Say you want to search your history. We encountered the history command in Chapter 1, but rather than simply listing thousands of entries, maybe you want to search your history for a *particular* command.

In my case, I want to retrieve a command that used `curl` (a command for getting and sending to URLs). So I'll pipe the output from `history` to `grep` and search for the word "curl":

```
$ history | grep curl
  210  curl http://jsbin.dev:8080/help
  220  curl -i https://jsbin.dev/
  260  curl http://localhost:3000/\?url\
  =emberjs.jsbin.com > emberjs-jsbin.com
  300  curl -i https://api.github.com/repos/octocat/
  Hello-World/hooks
  317  curl -i http://jsbin.dev/help
[code omitted for brevity]
 9855  curl rem.io/install
 9923  curl -H 'accept: application/json'
  http://jsbin.ff-platform.local/user/
  twitter\|648873/
```

That's a lot of matches. It's pretty hard for humans to process.

Adding `less`: "Less is more, more or less."

`less` is a command that lets us page through output. There's a similar command called `more`, but `less` is better because it allows us to page forward *and* backward (unlike `more`, which only goes forward).

I can use `less` to page through (and even search) the output of my history search:

```
$ history | grep curl | less
```

Now that I'm inside the `less` command, I can use the keyboard to cursor up and down; I can page forward (by pressing the Space key) or backward (by typing B). Significantly, I can search while I'm inside `less` by hitting the Slash key. I can enter an expression like `-H` (which is an argument to `curl`); `less` will highlight the matches and allow me to move through the *next* matches by typing N.

less has one oddity that I should note here: ctrl+c won't quit out of it. Type Q to quit.

Variations on history searching

For going through our history, there are a few extra things we can try out. What if we want to, say, find the last five items? A command called tail will show the tail end of a file (or stream of text), and the `-[number] option returns a specific number of entries:

```
$ history | grep curl | tail -5
 9651  curl jsbin.ff-platform.local:8000
 9652  curl localhost:8888
 9921  curl http://jsbin.ff-platform.local/user/
  twitter\|648873/
 9923  curl -H 'accept: application/json'
  http://jsbin.ff-platform.local/user/
  twitter\|648873/
10227  history | grep curl
```

But, since we ran it a number of times, our original command also turns up in the history. So we can pipe grep to another grep to remove matched expressions.

Or say we want to find the last five items matching curl but not history. We can use grep -v to remove all occurrences of a term in the results:

```
$ history | grep curl | grep -v history | tail -5
 9649  curl -I jsbin.ff-platform.local
 9651  curl jsbin.ff-platform.local:8000
 9652  curl localhost:8888
 9921  curl http://jsbin.ff-platform.local/user/
  twitter\|648873/
 9923  curl -H 'accept: application/json'
  http://jsbin.ff-platform.local/user/
  twitter\|648873/
```

SORTING AND PICKING

Sometimes you'll have a file from which you want to pick out some particular lines or pieces of data.

I used to find myself writing weird jQuery scripts and then putting all my data in an array and basically jumping through more hoops than a frog on speed. These days, though, the command line is my friend, because it offers tools like these:

- `grep`: to find lines (as we've just seen)
- `sort`: to sort lines
- `uniq`: to find unique lines
- `cut`, `sed`, and `awk`: to break a line into columns and pick a particular column

There are tons of things you can do by combining these tools, so let me present the following problem as an illustration of their range and flexibility.

Let's say I have an unusually high number of requests coming into my server, but I can't figure out what the source of the issue is. The access logs from my server typically follow a consistent format (but might appear slightly different depending on the situation):

```
IP - user [day/month/year:hour:minute:second zone]
  "GET /url HTTP/1.1" status_code bytes "referring_
  url" "user_agent"
```

Each entry shows us a lot of information:

```
127.0.0.1 - remy [24/Feb/2015:16:14:56 +0000] "POST
  /foobar/save HTTP/1.1" 200 34 "http://jsbin.
  local/foobar/edit" "Mozilla/5.0 (Windows NT 6.3;
  Win64; x64) AppleWebKit/537.36 (KHTML, like Gecko)
  Chrome/40.0.2214.115 Safari/537.36"
```

I can pipe commands together to search, sort, and separate the information in the access logs in an attempt to understand the problem.

1. Get the last 1,000 lines

I need to count the number of unique IP addresses that appear in the log—and, since my log file is pretty large, I'm only interested in the last 1,000 requests.

When I start off, I need to be in the directory that contains the logs. The `tail` command lets me look at the last 1,000 lines:

```
$ tail -1000 access.log
```

You can also use `tail` in combination with the `-f` option to continuously print lines as new lines are written to a file. This command shows each web request as it gets written to an access log:

```
$ tail -f access.log.*
```

2. Split the lines only showing the IP

A few tools split lines up. One such tool is `cut`; another is `awk`. `awk` is incredibly powerful (and, in fact, a programming language unto itself), but to keep things simple, I'm just going to stick with `cut`.

With `cut`, you have to specify the *delimiter* character (using `-d' '` to separate on spaces) and the field (using `-f[field number]`) you want:

```
$ tail -1000 access.log | cut -d' ' -f1
217.128.174.115
82.2.191.64
62.90.202.184
[code omitted for brevity]
```

In the command above, `tail` is feeding `cut` one line at a time and `cut` is printing out the first field on our split line.

3. Find the unique IP

For this, I'll use the uniq command. However, uniq is quirky in that it only works with lines that repeat (specifically, lines that are adjacent). This means uniq only works on a list like *a a b b*, and not on *a b a b*. So we need to combine uniq with a sort tool.

So first I'll need to sort the list of IPs:

```
$ tail -1000 access.log | cut -d' ' -f1 | sort
173.15.252.198
194.199.90.161
194.199.90.161
217.128.174.111
41.105.206.139
50.249.99.201
62.90.202.182
85.115.60.181
85.115.60.181
88.128.80.106
[code omitted for brevity]
```

It doesn't matter that it's sorted alphanumerically; the important thing is that the common entries are next to each other. Now I can pipe to uniq, and I'll add an argument (-c) that gives me a count of times the IP appears in the output (which I've snipped in the interest of brevity):

```
$ tail -1000 access.log  | cut -d' ' -f1 | sort |
  uniq -c
[code omitted for brevity]
  2 64.22.242.77
  1 66.249.64.146
  1 66.249.64.182
  2 66.37.35.161
 14 66.7.226.139
 12 68.45.20.22
 13 69.116.182.57
```

```
  1 70.88.199.14
  7 71.197.194.82
  3 72.226.11.1
[code omitted for brevity]
```

The output is still long, and it's also not sorted by number of occurrences, so I'm going to fix that, too.

4. Numerical sorting

The `sort` command uses alphanumerical order by default, but if you use `-n`, it will sort numerically. Since the output from the `uniq -c` command consists of numbers, this is perfect. In addition, I only want the top five requesting IPs, so I'm going to pipe this (again) to `tail` to get just the last five lines:

```
$ tail -1000 access.log  | cut -d' ' -f1 | sort |
  uniq -c | sort -n | tail -5
  33 77.57.124.151
  36 77.232.10.182
  38 109.70.40.211
  39 122.133.158.35
 152 198.21.21.22
```

Now I can see that there's a significant number of requests coming from a single IP: 198.21.21.22. From there, I can use this IP to search the logs to see what they've been requesting, or perhaps ban the IP for a set amount of time, or something else.

It's important to note that all of the commands I've used here come with Unix-based systems. So you don't have to install any of these separately.

The most important lesson to take away from this chapter is that commands can have their output piped to the input of another program using the `|` symbol. Putting commands together embodies the Unix philosophy mentioned at the start of this book; most programs support it. Mixing and remixing commands allows any number of combinations of manipulations—and that's powerful stuff.

HOW (NOT) TO SHOOT YOURSELF IN THE FOOT

NOW THAT YOU'RE FRESHLY EQUIPPED with a little bit of knowledge, I think it's time I show you just enough to do some *real* damage.

Or, put another way, I'm going to show you some commands that will help you get out of a pickle when an application goes haywire or your machine gets hammered.

You can achieve most, if not all, of these commands through a *graphical user interface* (GUI) if you're using a Mac (for instance), but as you grow more comfortable with the command line, you'll find that it becomes easier just to use that to remove files or to check your system health. And if you go on to tinker with remote servers, there won't be any visual UI for you to rely on; you'll be forced to stare into the void and will have no choice but to resort to the commands I describe here.

DELETING FILES: `rm`

...because who needs files when you can have DISK SPACE? Older PC users out there will appreciate this (and younger users perhaps won't believe it): when I started messing around with PCs (I think it was in 1991), I had an Intel 286, and there were these strange files taking up my precious 40-MB hard drive: `config.sys` and `autoexec.bat`. So I deleted them. Which taught me how PCs worked by plunging me into the deep end of recovering super-important configuration settings.

Suffice it to say: be careful about deleting. Today's systems go to great lengths to protect you from yourself, but since this is the foot-shooting chapter, I'm going to show you how to work around some of that.

Deleting regular files

It's probably easier to do this in a desktop application, like Finder, but to remove a single file or multiple files (either named or using a pattern), you can do the following (assuming, for the purposes of this discussion, that you're in a directory containing text files with the names I made up here):

```
$ rm my-file.txt
$ rm *.txt
```

Fun fact: the `*` is a wildcard character, and `*.txt` is called a *glob*.

This is all pretty straightforward. You might be presented with a tricky question, though:

```
$ rm not-my-file.txt
rm: remove write-protected regular file
  'not-my-file.txt'? y
$
```

A simple `y` back at your machine obliterates the file.

Directories aren't quite as simple: `rm` isn't really made to be used on them (though I'll explain in a bit how to get around that constraint). If you try to delete a directory, you get a quasi-tautological response:

```
$ rm chapter6/
rm: chapter6/: is a directory
```

Huh?

Deleting directories

Directories have a *special* command, `rmdir`:

```
$ rmdir chapter6/
$
```

That works—as long as the directory is entirely empty. Which, let's face it, is unlikely. Also, if you're using a Mac, you may have noticed .DS_Store files littered all over the place—or, you may not have, since *dotfiles* (files preceded by a dot) are hidden by default. Sometimes, a directory that looks empty may not be. (You may want to consider changing your system preferences to show hidden files.)

So let's try deleting a directory that isn't empty:

FIG 4.1: No, I couldn't get the license for a picture of Tom Cruise in an F-14 Tomcat. You'll have to settle for this amazing Photoshop effort.

```
$ rmdir chapter4
rmdir: chapter4: Directory not empty
```

In the face of "Directory not empty," you can go ahead and remove individual files one at a time—major boring—or *blow everything away in one fell swoop*! Welcome to the danger zone, cue music (**FIG 4.1**).

Ultimate delete!

The command `rm -rf` is usually my go-to answer to any fences the system wants to put in my way. Using `rm` with these two flags (`-r`, which recursively works through any subdirectories, and `-f`, which forcibly removes files without any prompts) will delete without any prompting and destroy any subdirectories.

For example, should I decide to nuke this book at any point, running the following would destroy all my hard work with a single quiet command:

```
$ rm -rf cli-book
$
```

No prompting to check if I'm sure, or if I've been drinking, or to warn me that Chapters 1 through 5 are about to go down the drain. Nothing.

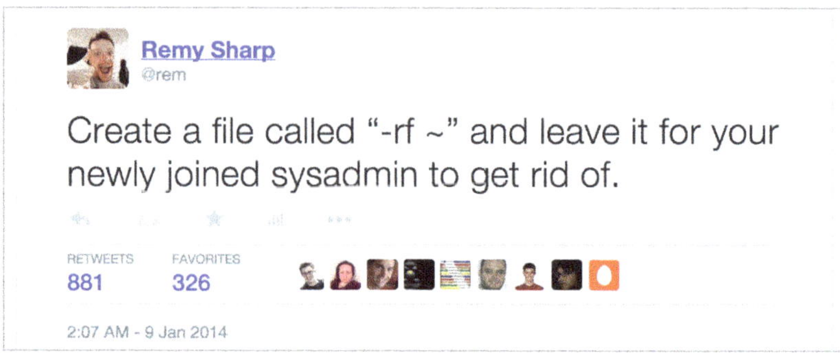

FIG 4.2: My `rm -rf ~` "joke."

Personally, I tend to use this command rather too quickly. I admit that, yes, in the years I've worked on the terminal, I have accidentally deleted the wrong directory because of trigger-happy fingers.

My most retweeted tweet involved a joke that would lead someone to run `rm -rf ~`, which means "delete my home directory, and don't worry about any warnings." I view my tweet's popularity as evidence that people are inherently evil (**FIG 4.2**).

But wait. `rm -rf` only works on files you have permission to write to. What about the files you don't own?

WHEN YOU DON'T HAVE PERMISSION: sudo

`sudo` stands for *Super User Do*. It's kind of like "Simon Says" for your terminal. We've already met `sudo` a number of times, and now I need to make good on my promise to tell you more about it.

Why is `sudo` necessary? Because computers have a user permission system. If you're using a Unix-based machine (again, this includes Mac), the user with the most privilege is root.

The almighty root can do absolutely anything, ranging from deleting all your files (without needing your permission), to rebooting, to deleting every file on the operating system (a.k.a. "real damage").

When you're logged into your machine, you're likely to be—and in fact should be—logged in under your own username. (Mine is "remy.") It is entirely possible that you don't actually perform the act of logging in, but you *do* have a user (and you're automatically logged in as that user). Your user has some privileges, but it's not as all-powerful as root.

If you share your computer with another person, you probably don't have access to read and write or execute that other person's files. This is the basis of the permission system. We'll look more closely at permissions in a moment, but first: what happens if you come across a monstrously large file that someone else has created, but that *you* need to remove?

Deleting the file won't work, because you don't have permission. Enter `sudo`.

As a rule, always try to proceed without `sudo` first, because using it is sometimes like taking a sledgehammer to a nail: it certainly works, but isn't always the right tool. With that in mind, let's add `sudo` to your toolbox.

Using sudo

You can prefix any command in the terminal with `sudo`. This will run your command with *superuser* (a.k.a. root) privileges. Since root can delete anything without asking permission, here's how we would `rm` another user's file:

```
$ sudo rm /User/jack/boring-pony.jpg
Password:
```

Enter your password, and that's it.

Almost. To be able to do things with `sudo`, you need to be a *sudoer*. On a Mac, if you're in the group called "admin," you're a sudoer by default.

However, if you find that the `sudo` command doesn't work, you'll need to manually add yourself as a sudoer. This will give you permission to use `sudo`. Do this by adding a line to a system file called /etc/sudoers (sudoers is the file name in the etc system directory, which is important because it holds your computer's configuration files):

```
remy  ALL=(ALL) ALL
```

Swap `remy` out for your username. This will allow you to run everything root can run if you prefix your command with `sudo`. You can customize the control you give to users in /etc/sudoers, but that's another story for another book. For now, let's focus on the fact that you have the first superpower to do some *real* damage.

Why not run as root all the time?

The short answer is that it's a bad practice, kind of like driving a tank around a quiet neighborhood—and no one wants that on their personal report card. Just because you *can* doesn't mean you *should*.

That's why most operating systems these days (like Mac and Windows) ask you to create your own user. The user you create doesn't have the same permissions as root. (When you're prompted for your password, it's because under the hood, your OS is trying to do something that requires more permissions, similar to using `sudo`.)

PERMISSIONS

Now that you know how to bulldoze right through permissions, it might be useful to know what permissions look like, what they mean, and how they function.

My directory list for this book currently looks like this:

```
$ ls -ltr
total 2608
-rw-r--r--@  1 remy  staff     1226  7 Aug  2014
  chapter-outline.md
drwxr-xr-x@ 11 remy  staff      374 11 Feb 10:05
  chapter2
drwxr-xr-x@  6 remy  staff      204 11 Feb 10:08
  chapter1
drwxr-xr-x@  3 remy  staff      102 11 Feb 13:46
  chapter3
-rw-r--r--@  1 remy  staff     2583 11 Feb 13:47
  todo.md
drwxr-xr-x@  4 remy  staff      136  4 Mar 16:03
  chapter4
-rwxr-xr-x@  1 remy  staff       30  4 Mar 17:46
  pony
```

Here you can see each file's permissions (far left), followed by the "link count" (which you can safely ignore), then the owner of the file, and, finally, the group the file is part of. My Mac has put me in an oddly named group called *staff*. I don't know why. Next comes the byte size of the file (including the byte size for the directory—note that this isn't the aggregate size), the timestamp, and the file name.

Changing permissions

Numbers appearing next to Read, Write, and Execute indicate that there are a couple of ways to change a permission (**FIG 4.3**). The first method is easier to learn, but the second method will let you show off your newly learned l33t haxor skillz (that's probably the most "leetspeak" I've used in two decades, by the way).

File ownership is broken into three sections:

FIG 4.3: drxwrxwrxw represents the range of permissions you can see on files. The first cluster of rxw characters is the most useful because it tells you whether the file is readable, executable, or writable by the owner (you).

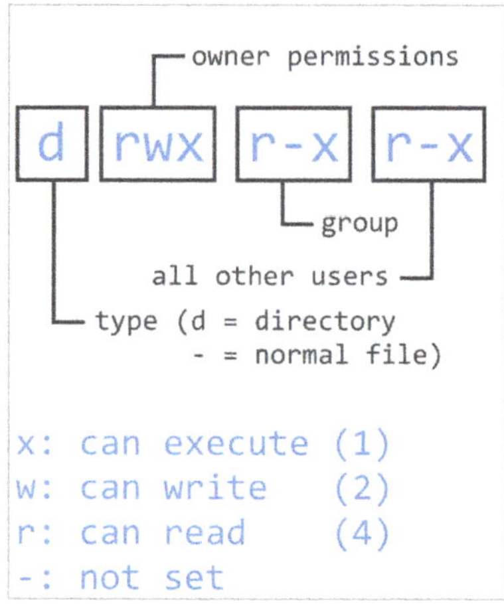

- **Owner**: you
- **Group**: you and anyone else in your "group" (useful if you share a machine or server)
- **Other**: anyone who *isn't* in your group

Why would we want to change file permissions? One reason might be to make a file executable. Another might be to allow a group member to access a file.

The command we use to do this is called chmod (short for *change mode*).

With chmod, we type the first letters for user (u), group (g), or other (o); then a plus operator (+) for adding permissions or a minus operator (-) for removing permissions; and finally the permission letters for read (r), write (w), or execute (x).

Let's look at this in action. To change a file so that it's executable by the user and the group, we'd run the following:

```
$ chmod ug+x my-script
```

This sets the user and group permissions to *executable*.

If I want all users to be able to read my-script, I could either type ugo+r or use a shortcut for "all" (a):

```
$ chmod a+r my-script
```

As long as you can remember how to communicate User, Group, and Other, and Read, Write, and Execute, you should be able to remember the modes and flags.

As we saw earlier, permissions can also have numerical values: `4` = read, `2` = write, and `1` = execute (**FIG 4.3**). Occasionally, when you run across `chmod` in a tutorial, you'll see it expressed as something like `chmod 110 my-script` or `chmod 744 my-script`. This is the second method I alluded to, and it's frankly a tad confusing and not particularly easy to remember.

The first digit represents the user permissions, the second the group permissions, and the third the permissions of all other users. To set the user permissions to *read-only*, make the first digit 4. To set the user permissions to *read and write*, make the first digit 6 (i.e., 4 + 2). To make a file executable for all users, readable and writable for the owner, and readable for everyone else, the values are 7 (4 + 2 + 1), 5 (4 + 0 + 1) and 5:

```
$ chmod 755 my-script
```

It's common to make a file readable for other users, but not writable: since you're the owner of the program, you don't want anyone else messing with it.

Changing ownership

Along with changing permissions, you may also want to change the ownership of a file—either from yourself to another user, or from another user to yourself. I've needed to do that in the past when I've had more than one login for my machine and wanted to move a file from the other user to myself so that I could edit it.

On a Mac, if the situation is simple enough, the Finder can do that work for you (and can also handle some permission changes). However, I've found it useful to know how to perform such tasks on the command line because the Finder UI isn't always available, particularly when working with remote machines.

The command to change ownership is `chown` (short for, appropriately enough, "change ownership"), followed by the new owner's name (`anna`, in this case). Here's how you might change the owner of a file:

```
$ chown anna my-script
```

You can also use `chown` to change all the files in a directory simultaneously by specifying the `-R` (short for "apply recursively") flag:

```
$ chown -R anna cli-book/
```

You can explore additional flags and usages of `chown` on your own, but these two commands should be enough to get you out of trouble.

What is a group, and when did I join one?

Every user is automatically part of *group*, even if it's just a group of one. Your user is already part of a group. On a Mountain Lion Mac, you are part of the "staff" group, and, if you're sharing your machine, so are the other users.

If you want to add a user to the admin group, you need a special command. On a Mac, run:

```
$ dscl . -append /Groups/admin GroupMembership remy
```

Note that the group name is preceded by /Groups/.

On a Linux machine, you need a different command entirely:

```
$ useradd -G admin remy
```

Groups are a good way to manage user permissions when you're collaborating with multiple people deploying to a server (and similar sysops ninjafoo).

PROCESSES

A *process* refers to an application running on your operating system. If you use Sublime Text 2, for instance, there is a process called—wait for it—Sublime Text 2.

If you're a Mac user, take a look at the Activity Monitor program, which lists the processes currently running. PC users can use the trusty Task Manager for the same view.

ps (short for "process status") is the command-line equivalent of Activity Monitor. Here's what happens when I run ps on my machine right now:

```
$ ps
  PID TTY           TIME CMD
95218 ttys000    0:04.06 -zsh
61075 ttys001    0:00.21 -zsh
77196 ttys002    0:00.60 -zsh
  509 ttys003    0:04.94 -zsh
  525 ttys004    0:02.52 -zsh
```

This output doesn't really represent what's happening on my machine, though. The list above shows five zsh (*Z shell*) commands. Z shell refers to my shell, a text-based interface that runs in my terminal, processes commands, and returns output. (We'll look more closely at what the shell is, and Z shell in particular, in Chapter 5.)

Notice that Sublime Text doesn't appear here, even though I'm using it *right now* to write this chapter. In fact, ps by itself only lists processes that have a terminal attached.

But we want to list *all* processes, with the full command used and the process owner (which is also linked to who has permission to terminate the process, but more on that later).

It's a mouthful, but using the ps auxww command (the order of the flags doesn't matter) gives us lots of ps goodness. I've cropped the screenshot because it was reams of lines (**FIG 4.4**).

The output from ps becomes more manageable when you pipe the output into a tool like grep to search for a particular

FIG 4.4: Plain output from ps can be a bit unwieldy, but using grep will help us narrow down what we're looking for.

command—perhaps to make sure it's running as you expected, perhaps to kill it. Here, I'm piping the output of `ps auxww` to `grep -i [term]` (the `-i` on `grep` means *case insensitive*):

```
$ ps uaxww | grep -i sublime
remy              59329   0.0  1.5  3308128 260008
  ?? S      8Mar15  48:43.56 /Applications/
  Sublime Text 2.app/Contents/MacOS/Sublime Text 2
  -psn_0_18747872
remy              66220   0.0  0.0  2432780    428
  s000  R+    1:00pm   0:00.00 grep -i sublime
```

What's strange is that this returns *two* results. Why? Because when we grepped, the grep command with the term we were looking for was currently running, so it appears in the ps list. *Inception*, anyone?

If that bothers you, remember that we learned in Chapter 3 how to use `grep -v [term]` to *exclude* the term from your results (the `-v` stands for "invert-match"):

```
$ ps uaxww | grep -i sublime | grep -v grep
remy    59329   0.0   1.6   3311748 262020   ??  S
  8Mar15  49:04.37 /Applications/Sublime Text 2.app/
  Contents/MacOS/Sublime Text 2 -psn_0_18747872
```

There's a lot of information here, but most relevant for us are the first, second, and last columns: the user who started the process (and who therefore owns it), the *process ID* (PID), and the full command running.

Kill kill kill!

If When a process goes haywire, you'll probably first notice by it hanging. If Sublime hangs for me, I can't enter any text. Sometimes my machine will kill the process automatically; other times, more aggressive action is required.

First, let's locate the process ID. In this example, it's *59329*:

```
$ ps uaxww | grep -i sublime | grep -v grep
remy    59329   0.0   1.6   3311748 262020   ??  S
  8Mar15  49:04.37 /Applications/Sublime Text 2.app/
  Contents/MacOS/Sublime Text 2 -psn_0_18747872
```

If you know part of the process name, you can also try using `pidof [term]` to find the "process ID of" the given term. (Mac users may have to `brew install pidof` first).

Now we use the command `kill` to stop the process dead in its tracks:

```
$ kill 59329
```

Remy reopens Sublime to continue writing.

FIG 4.5: The `kill -9` command deals a fatal blow to all running programs. It asks no questions and grants no mercy.

For me, Sublime just terminated. No warnings. No "Do you want to save your carefully crafted prose?" Nothing. Just killed.

But what if the process doesn't belong to you? What if you don't have permission to kill it? That's right, `sudo` to the rescue (as you blow away some poor sap's program):

```
$ sudo kill 59329
```

Sometimes, though—just sometimes—a kill isn't enough. You have to kill *harder*. The kill command says to the process, "Would you mind gracefully shutting down?" Typically, the program will behave politely and exit, but once in a while you have use some force.

The `kill -KILL [pid]` and `kill -9 [pid]` commands mean the same thing: kill the process and don't wait for the process to respond.

When using `-9` to kill, you may also need to add `sudo` to the mix. But it will get the job done. It's the fatality move of the command line (**FIG 4.5**).

DIAGNOSING PROBLEMS

Now that you have the knowledge to completely ruin your machine, it's also worth learning about a handful of command-line tools that will help you quickly diagnose simple problems.

top

`top` will show you a live, constantly updating view of processes running. You can order the list by CPU usage (`P`) or memory (uppercase `M`)—very helpful if you have a process hog. A word of warning, though: `top` on a Mac can be a little hard to deal with because it delivers a barrage of way too much information. (The Linux flavor of `top` differs from the Mac version, and is, frankly, more useful.)

A viable alternative to `top` is `htop`, which is consistent across platforms and generally looks nicer than `top`. It supports the same keyboard shortcuts that I use to sort `top` with, but also features quick searching using the `/` character. You can install `htop` on a Mac by typing `brew install htop`.

Both `top` and `htop` provide information very much akin to that of the activity monitor or task manager you may already be familiar with. Consider making `top` or `htop` your go-to tool for quick health analysis.

uptime

`uptime` offers a quick overview of your machine's health (also shown at the top of `top`). The values returned by `uptime` include how long your machine has been running (handy if you suspect the machine has recently restarted) and *load averages*:

```
$ uptime
13:38  up 48 days, 22:40, 9 users, load averages:
  1.37 1.62 1.78
```

The load averages show numerical values for the current load, the average over five minutes, and the average over fifteen

```
$ df -kh
Filesystem      Size   Used  Avail Capacity  iused     ifree %iused  Mounted on
/dev/disk0s2   931Gi  271Gi  659Gi    30% 71191372 172874989   29%   /
devfs          191Ki  191Ki    0Bi   100%      662         0  100%   /dev
map -hosts       0Bi    0Bi    0Bi   100%        0         0  100%   /net
map auto_home    0Bi    0Bi    0Bi   100%        0         0  100%   /home
```

FIG 4.6: Running the df -kh command results in a list of available disk space.

minutes. This is a vaguely useful metric: if it's around 1, then it's okay; if it's 10 or above, the machine is probably struggling and something might be wrong.

df -kh

If your server appears to have a normal load but things are nevertheless going very wrong, it's entirely possible that you've run out of disk space. Understandably, machines get rather weird about having no disk space.

The `df -kh` command lists the available disk space on the machine (**FIG 4.6**). Depending on whom you ask, `df` stands for either "display free (disk space)" or "disk free"; `-k` indicates kilobytes and `-h` means (importantly) "human readable."

The important columns to note here are `Size`, `Used`, `Available`, and `Mounted on`.

`Mounted on` tells you which path is the problem. In the above `df`, it's including some funky virtual drives (I can see they read a size of `0`). I'm ignoring those values and focusing on the row that's mounted on `/`: that's the root of my operating system, and where all my files live. I can use this information to get a sense of how much disk space I have left (and whether I should start removing some files).

You've basically learned how to completely destroy your machine. `rm -rf` will blast away files without prompts, `sudo` will let you do anything to anyone's files or processes, and `kill -9` will terminate a program in mid-execution.

Rumor had it that you could do `sudo kill -9 1` and it would shut down a machine in one go. As I mentioned earlier, systems protect themselves from such stupidity nowadays, but one can only try!

You now know some seriously dangerous moves. But if you want to be a hero, you have a few tools to check on your system's health, too.

5

MAKING THE SHELL YOUR OWN

IN CHAPTER 1, I showed you how to replace your default terminal with an alternative. The terminal is the application that runs your shell. You've already met and used the shell—it's where you actually run commands and see the output. The shell, irrespective of the terminal application you choose, can have its own customizations.

Let's look at some of those, now that you have a little more experience under your belt. Although most shell customization offers only modest power-ups, I'd argue that it's quite important: customization is what makes a thing feel like it belongs to you. Potentially, at least, there are as many shells as there are users (**FIG 5.1**).

Terminal customization follows a certain hierarchy: first, there's the terminal application itself; then, within the terminal, is the shell; inside the shell is the prompt; and, finally, there are aliases and shortcuts. We'll look at each in turn (**FIG 5.2**).

THE TERMINAL

As I mentioned at the beginning of this book, iTerm2 is far and away my favorite terminal emulator. Like most other terminal applications, iTerm2 accepts a wealth of customizations. Let's take a look at the preferences for my keyboard shortcuts (**FIG 5.3**).

As I mentioned in Chapter 1, split windows can be quite useful. In iTerm2, you can type cmd+d to split your terminal vertically (so you have two terminals side by side), or cmd+shift+d for a horizontal split. Then you can keep splitting to your heart's content. This is a feature of the application; your mileage may vary (**FIG 5.4**).

You'll also find in the preferences the theme (or "profile") for your terminal, which allows you to customize the colors and the font. Iterm2-color-schemes is a good place to start browsing around for themes. Some people prefer a dark theme, some prefer a light theme, others have images in the background of their terminal, and still others use a semitransparent background. My extra pro-user tweak is that I use a hot-pink (#d13a82) cursor combined with a dark theme.

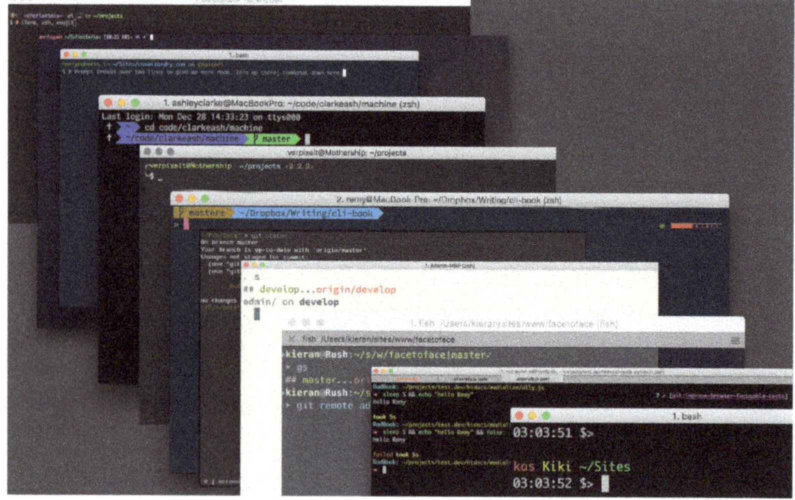

FIG 5.1: A smattering of terminal customizations from my Twitter followers.

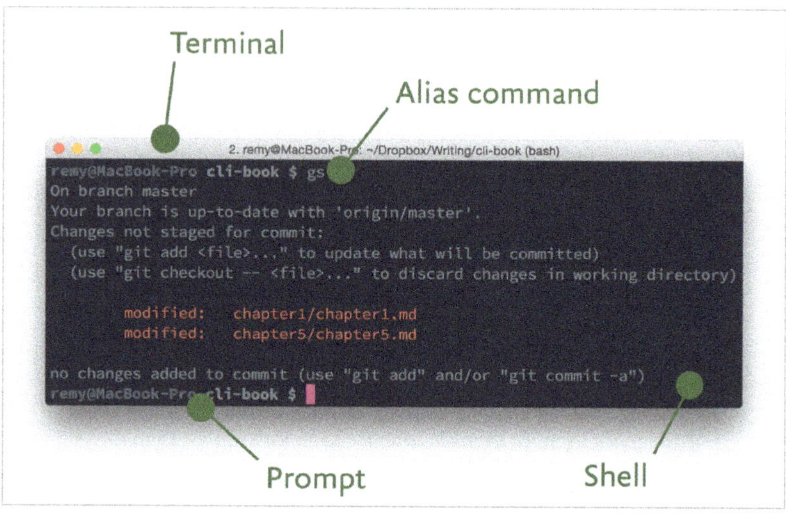

FIG 5.2: Areas of the terminal that can be personalized.

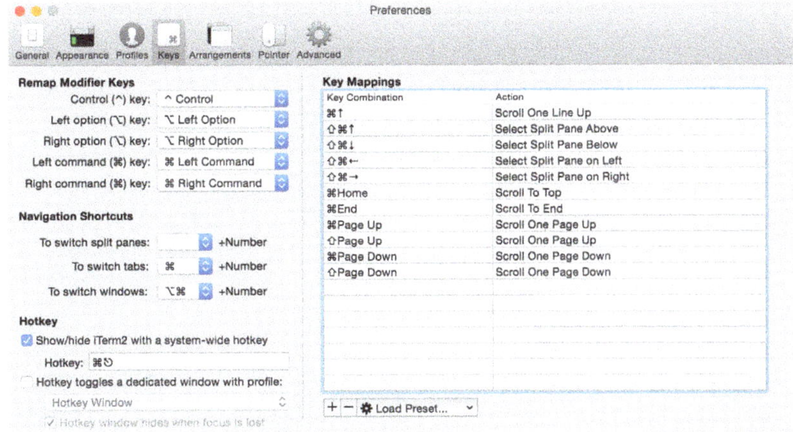

FIG 5.3: My iTerm2 keyboard preferences. In particular, I've changed the shortcut for navigating from one split panel to another, and (most important, because it's my favorite keyboard shortcut) the system-wide shortcut to bring iTerm2 to the front: cmd+esc.

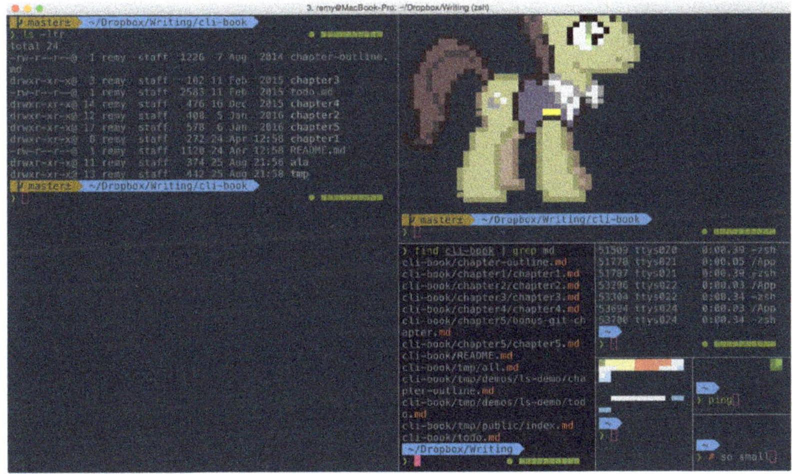

FIG 5.4: Ordinarily I split a window only a few times, but if you want to go wild, you can split your terminal into the golden ratio.

THE SHELL

There are a number of different shells available with varying customizations, but in all likelihood, assuming that you're on a Mac, your machine will come with a shell called Bash. Bash is a good go-to shell if you're managing servers, but if you use your own machine for development, you might want to go for something a little more powerful.

Fish

Fish Shell is an option with at least one nice advantage: it makes it easy to get started by including installers for all platforms, and even includes a standalone app for OS X, which is a nice way to preview it.

I don't use Fish myself, but I mention it here because it includes a lot of features by default: autocomplete, tab completion, highlighting, and a web configuration interface for customizing the theme and prompt (you have to run `fish_config` in the shell). If ease of configuration is what you need, this is a good option.

Z shell

Z shell, or zsh, has some great features—but if you really want to get the most from it (with the least amount of effort), you'll also want to install Oh My Zsh, a community-driven framework for managing zsh. I like Oh My Zsh because it gives me a bunch of plugins and makes theming my shell really easy.

My terminal uses the features of zsh to give me a rather special and informative prompt: it includes the current directory, Git status, battery power, and whether I have a connection to the internet (**FIG 5.5**).

Installing zsh is a bit more involved than Fish, but it's certainly worth the extra work. To install it, you'll use Brew; while you're at it, go ahead and install the Oh My Zsh manager, too:

FIG 5.5: Here's what my zsh prompt looks like today.

```
$ # install zsh
$ brew install zsh zsh-completions
$ # add oh-my-zsh
$ curl -L https://github.com/robbyrussell/oh-my-zsh/
  raw/master/tools/install.sh | sh
$ # make zsh your default
$ chsh -s /bin/zsh
```

Windows users will need an alternative way to get zsh. A project called Babun looks promising—it includes zsh as the default shell, with Oh My Zsh also included by default. The shell is preconfigured and doesn't require admin rights to run. This could be a nice alternative to the GitBash shell that you may already be using.

Security of `curl ... | sh`

It's worth noting that you should be cautious of anything that asks you to run `curl -L [URL] | sh`. This command effectively runs a remote script on your local machine with the same privileges as you have. Potentially (worst-case scenario), the remote script could remove your entire home directory. If you're familiar with JavaScript, the equivalent would be like including a remote `<script src="...unknown.js">` on a web page. It could be perfectly harmless; it could also be malicious.

Z shell themes

Now that you have zsh installed and set as your default shell, you can select a theme and add some plugins to make the shell super awesome.

There are tons of themes to choose from. Z shell's default theme is called "robbyrussell" (named after the author of Oh My Zsh). Agnoster is a popular theme, but it requires custom fonts. My prompt is a modification of the Agnoster theme—mainly a riff on its prompt. I'll explain the prompt in the next section so that you can create your own perfect fit.

A complete list of preinstalled themes is available on the Oh My Zsh wiki page, with screenshots for each. There are also external themes that do not come bundled with Oh My Zsh, but the links include directions on how to install them.

To select your theme, you need to edit the **.zshrc** file in your home directory. If you can do this in your favorite editor, then go ahead and open the file. If you're using Sublime Text like me, though, the file will be hidden (since dotfiles are hidden by default).

One thing you can do to get around this is to use `open` (if you're on a Mac) and hope that the file opens in an editor:

```
$ open ~/.zshrc
```

Otherwise, you can try using a terminal editor program called nano by typing `nano ~/.zshrc`. The commands to save and exit run along the bottom of the window, so it's pretty self-explanatory (**FIG 5.6**).

Find the line that contains `ZSH_THEME="robbyrussell"` and update it to any name you like. Once you're done, save the file and restart your session (which may close the entire terminal window).

Quick history searching with zsh

If you've familiarized yourself with the cursor keys enough to navigate the history on the CLI, then zsh adds something incredibly useful.

Before zsh, if you were looking for a recent command—say, `wc`, to get the word count of a document—you would `grep` the `history` output looking for `wc`, and then run that particular history item again (either by copying and pasting the command or by running `![n]`—where `n` is the history number).

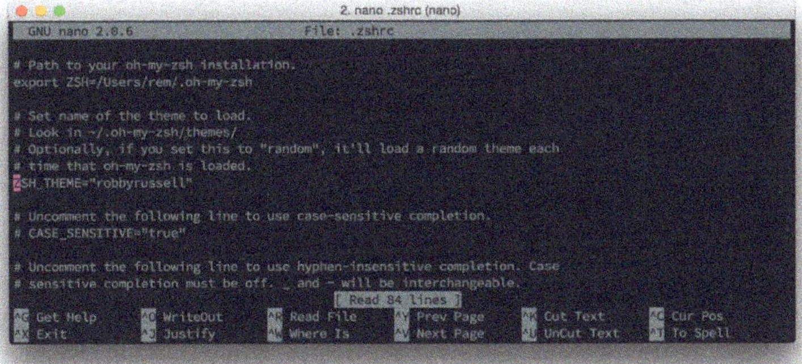

FIG 5.6: The nano editor isn't as handsome as Sublime Text, but it does the job. Just remember that `^` means the Control key on your keyboard!

But with zsh, you can type the start of the command (`wc`) and then cursor up—and the cursor will cycle through every command that *starts with* `wc`. In most cases, you can immediately find the command you want and rerun it.

Plugins

One of the key features of Oh My Zsh is the plugin ecosystem. I can't cover all of the plugins here, but I can show you how to enable a few that I personally find very useful, and where to find more.

By default, Oh My Zsh comes with a large number of plugins listed in detail on its plugin overview wiki page. I highly recommend browsing through them once you're comfortable adding plugins to see if there's anything that captures your interest.

If you want a plugin that's outside of the default collection, you can often find installation directions in the plugin's readme file. Unfortunately, the "simplest" installation method often requires Git on the command line.

Oh My Zsh makes enabling plugins easy: you need to edit the .zshrc file (as you did earlier for the theme). Find the line that starts with `plugins=(`. From there, add the names of the plugins you want to make available in your shell, separating each with a space.

At this writing, my list of plugins reads as follows:

```
plugins=(sublime z zsh-syntax-highlighting)
```

It's worth noting that all of the plugins I'm using are part of the default plugins shipped with Oh My Zsh, except for `zsh-syntax-highlighting`, which I'll explain in a moment.

As a user of Sublime Text, I find myself navigating directories and editing hidden files via my terminal. I'm handy with CLI editors (Vim in particular, and also nano, which I touched on earlier), but I'm much more comfortable editing in Sublime Text.

From the terminal, I can use the Sublime Text plugin that adds an `st` command to my shell to open a file or directory in Sublime Text:

```
$ st cli-book # opens the cli-book directory in
  sublime
$ st cli-book/chapter5/chapter5.md # opens the
  individual file
```

If you're a TextMate user, there's also a plugin for that; just use `mate` in place of the `st` command.

Next up is `z`, which is possibly the command I use the most in my daily workflow. It allows me to jump to any directory using just a fragment of the name (if I've been there before), the `z` in this list of plugins:

```
plugins=(sublime z zsh-syntax-highlighting)
```

Say I navigate to the cli-book directory in my terminal. After I've changed to that directory for the first time, I can use the `z` command with any part of the directory name to quickly jump to it.

```
» daate
zsh: command not found: daate
 ✗  ~
» date
Mon  4 Jan 2016 15:46:46 GMT
 ~
»
```

FIG 5.7: The zsh-syntax-highlighting plugin shows you in real time if a command exists or not (or if you've made a typo). That way, you don't have to memorize all of the programs on your computer.

```
$ z cli # takes me to ~/Dropbox/writing/cli-book/
$ z book # takes me to ~/Dropbox/writing/cli-book/
$ z writing # takes me to ~/Dropbox/writing/
```

Running `z` alone will result in the full list of directories and their frequency of use. The highest-frequency directories take priority in matching the argument you give to the `z` command.

There are a few alternatives to this command, including `autojump`, `jump`, and `wd` (all provided by Oh My Zsh's default plugins). I personally haven't tried any of these alternatives, since z does the job just fine for me, and I suspect there's no advantage to having more than one installed.

Finally, I'd like to mention zsh-syntax-highlighting. This plugin is really handy. It colors your command green if it exists and red if it does not, in real time, *as you type*. This makes it easy to catch errors in commands: if the text turns red, you'll know that either the program doesn't exist or you've made a typo (**FIG 5.7**).

There are a number of ways to install zsh-syntax-highlighting, as the install page explains, but I find that the cleanest method is to use Git to copy it directly into your plugins:

```
$ git clone git://github.com/zsh-users/
  zsh-syntax-highlighting.git ~/.oh-my-zsh/custom/
  plugins/zsh-syntax-highlighting
```

Then edit your ~/.zshrc file (perhaps using `st ~/.zshrc`) and add `zsh-syntax-highlighting` to the end of your plugins.

(Note that the plugin must be the last plugin in the list as per the installation instructions.)

Now when you restart your shell session, the zsh-syntax-highlighting plugin will be enabled. If you don't want to keep exiting and restarting your session, you can load the .zshrc file using the following command:

```
$ source ~/.zshrc
```

The `source` command runs the given file, and thus reloads your entire shell configuration. Super-pro tip: the `source` command is interchangeable with `.`, so you could run `. ~/.zshrc` if you really wanted to impress someone.

Installing the Git CLI tools

As we saw in Chapter 2, there's always a way to install stuff via the CLI. If you're using Windows and Git BASH, then you have Git on the command line already. If you're on a Mac, you probably have Git, but it's likely to be out of date (because Git is released more frequently than new operating systems), so you'll need to update it.

```
$ brew install git
$ git --version
```

Now you'll be able to use the directions that might require you to `git clone` the plugin into your Oh My Zsh plugins directory.

THE PROMPT

You've already met the prompt. It often looks like this: `$`. Maybe it includes your machine name and username: `MacBook-Pro:~ remy$`. Which is fine, but you probably don't care about the machine name if it's your own machine, and I hope you know your own username. (These names can be useful if you're connecting remotely, though.)

```
→ ~ z cli
→ cli-book git:(master)
```

FIG 5.8: The default zsh prompt. Pretty fancy, eh?

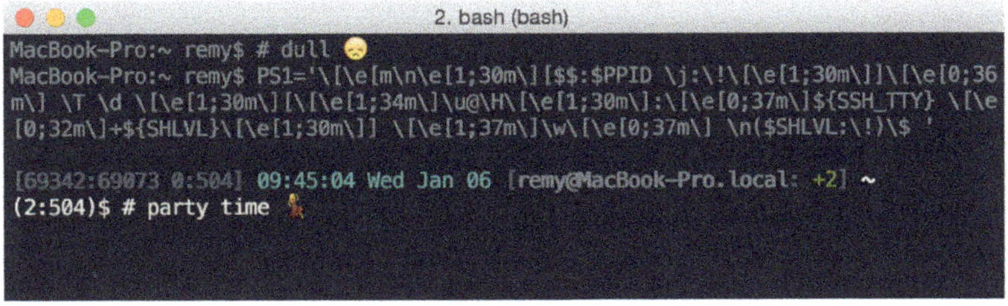

```
2. bash (bash)
MacBook-Pro:~ remy$ # dull
MacBook-Pro:~ remy$ PS1='\[\e[m\n\e[1;30m\][$$:$PPID \j:\!\[\e[1;30m\]]\[\e[0;36
m\] \T \d \[\e[1;30m\][\[\e[1;34m\]\u@\H\[\e[1;30m\]:\[\e[0;37m\]${SSH_TTY} \[\e
[0;32m\]+${SHLVL}\[\e[1;30m\]] \[\e[1;37m\]\w\[\e[0;37m\] \n($SHLVL:\!)\$ '

[69342:69073 0:504] 09:45:04 Wed Jan 06 [remy@MacBook-Pro.local: +2] ~
(2:504)$ # party time
```

FIG 5.9: Prompt overkill.

If you've switched to zsh already, you're more likely to have a very sleek prompt (FIG 5.8).

If we break this down, what we see in this prompt is an arrow (➜) followed by the current directory name (not the full path). When we're in the Git repository, it says `git` and notes which branch is active.

Prompts can get fairly complicated. If they get too complicated, they look like garbage. If I set Bash custom shell (PS1) to a new value, it modifies my prompt—but, wow, that's some horrible code (FIG 5.9).

Fortunately, much progress has been made in the area of sharing prompts and making them slightly more readable. Sharing prompts is important because it helps people experiment, learn, and improve.

My general recommendation is to take a theme you like from zsh, copy it, and tweak it to make it your own. Let's say you've decided to use the robbyrussell theme and want to customize it a little. First you will need to make a copy of it, so let's call the new theme my.zsh-theme and put it in the themes directory:

```
$ cp ~/.oh-my-zsh/themes/robbyrussell.zsh-theme
  ~/.oh-my-zsh/themes/my.zsh-theme
```

Now open the my.zsh-theme file in your favorite editor. Try not to let it bamboozle you too much (like I did the first time I encountered it). What interests us here is the first line, in particular the arrow (➜) character, which appears in the file twice:

```
local ret_status="%(?:%{$fg_bold[green]%}➜
  :%{$fg_bold[red]%}➜ %s)"
PROMPT='${ret_status}%{$fg_bold[green]%}%p
  %{$fg[cyan]%}%c %{$fg_bold[blue]%}$
  (git_prompt_info)%{$fg_bold[blue]%} %
  %{$reset_color%}'
```

The variable `ret_status` changes the arrow icon depending on whether the last command exited successfully: a bold green arrow(`$fg_bold[green]`) if so, and a bold red arrow (`$fg_bold[red]`) if there was an error. The second line sets the magic value of `PROMPT`, creating the prompt you'll use.

Now, let's change the arrow to a snowman (☃). (This isn't necessarily very practical, but it will do for the exercise at hand.) We'll also show the full path, but on a line of its own, above the prompt.

Swapping the arrow out for the snowman is simple, but since the emoji won't change color if there's an error, we'll use an alien emoji for errors instead (and drop the color information). Furthermore, getting the full path in the prompt will require moving some elements around in the `PROMPT` value. It's also perfectly legitimate to put a line break in the value of `PROMPT`, which is how we'll get our multiline prompt:

```
local ret_status="%(?:☃ :👾 %s)"
PROMPT='%{$fg[cyan]%}%d
${ret_status}%{$fg_bold[green]%}%p
  %{$fg_bold[blue]%}$(git_prompt_info)
  %{$fg_bold[blue]%} % %{$reset_color%}'
```

Now we'll be able to see when we get a random error; our prompt will switch to the alien until there's a successful command (**FIG 5.10**).

```
/Users/remy/Dropbox/Writing/cli-book
☃ git:(master) ✗ random error
zsh: command not found: random
/Users/remy/Dropbox/Writing/cli-book
👾 git:(master) ✗
```

FIG 5.10: Huzzah. Our prompt now features a snowman when things are okay, and an alien when the last command failed.

There's also a right-hand prompt with zsh; this can be set using the `RPROMPT` value. You can do all sorts of things with this value, like add the current time (or perhaps something more creative).

Or let's say you want to add the current time in square brackets and in blue, just for the heck of it. Simply add the following to your my.zsh-theme file:

```
RPROMPT="%{$fg[blue]%}[%*]"
```

The 24-hour time with seconds is represented by `%*`, so the final prompt is a bit of a visual mess of curly braces and percent signs. For that I apologize, but once you've got your prompt, you probably won't change it again...ever.

The full list of prompt variables is listed in the zsh prompt expansion documentation. It's a little dry, but it contains all the values you can use. If you're after a more approachable account, you can read about my entire prompt setup on my blog.

ALIASES

Aliases are just alternatives to existing CLI commands. To create an alias, use the `alias` command. For instance, you might alias the command ll to ls -ltrFa (a shortcut to list all files with hidden files included, ordered so that the most recently changed appears at the end of the output):

```
$ alias ll='ls -ltrFa'
```

However, running this in the shell means that you only have the alias for as long as the session lasts and, crucially, that the alias won't work in other sessions. Not cool. So let's fix that.

To make your aliases easy to manage and add to later on, it can be useful to create a file called .aliases in your home directory (cd ~) containing all your aliases. That way you can effortlessly pull in your .aliases file by adding the following line to your .zshrc file:

```
source ~/.aliases
```

Because this is part of your .zshrc file, it means that every new session will include all of your aliases. Many developers have published their own aliases, which I highly recommend checking out; they are amazing resources that you can add to your own aliases to make your workflow more efficient.

Aliases can be simple (as we've just seen), or they can combine commands. Remember how we learned to navigate to parent directories in Chapter 1? You can use aliases to do that work much more efficiently:

```
alias ..="cd .."
alias ...="cd ../.."
alias ....="cd ../../.."
alias .....="cd ../../../.."
```

These commands will allow you to type `..` in the shell to get it to move to the parent directory. Three dots will take you to the parent's parent directory, and so on.

Aliases are useful for commands that you may not find easy to remember. For instance, if you can't remember the exact command to run each time you might want to clear the DNS cache on your Mac, you can use this alias:

```
alias flush="dscacheutil -flushcache"
```

Or for example, I can never remember the series of commands to show and hide the desktop icons on my mac, so I use two aliases to make my life easier:

```
alias hidedesktop="defaults write com.apple.finder
  CreateDesktop -bool false && killall Finder"
alias showdesktop="defaults write com.apple.finder
  CreateDesktop -bool true && killall Finder"
```

I'd love to reel off all of my aliases here and now, but that would spoil all the fun you'll have browsing other people's ideas on your own. Plus, it would likely take up oodles of pages in this book and wouldn't copy and paste very well. I *will* point you toward Mathias Bynens, though, who has compiled an excellent repository of dotfiles (including aliases, his shell setup, and more), where he also references the sources that have inspired him. It's well worth a look to spur your motivation, and to start flexing your copy-and-paste muscles.

Functions

Aliases have one limitation: you can't insert an argument. For instance, if you want to get the base64 data URL for a file, you can't quite do that with an alias; you need a function. You can run function names in your terminal the same way you run aliases.

Here's the code required to generate a base64 URL for any file:

```
function dataurl() {
  local mimeType=$(file -b --mime-type "$1");
  if [[ $mimeType == text/* ]]; then
    mimeType="${mimeType};charset=utf-8";
  fi
  echo "data:${mimeType};base64,$(openssl base64 -in
    "$1" | tr -d '\n')";
}
```

This lets you get the data URL for an image from the terminal:

```
$ dataurl book-cover.png
data:image/jpeg;base64,/9j/4AAQSkZJRgABAQAAAQABA...
```

We've just covered a lot of ground, but now you know how to customize your terminal to suit your personal style. You've learned about, and hopefully converted to, Z shell and the awesome Oh My Zsh project. You'll have a few personal aliases to make your workflow a little sleeker, and finally you'll have your very own customized prompt—designed by you, for you.

YOUR TURN

Hm. All endings are more or less arbitrary, I suppose, but I can't just close this book by showing you how to add functions to your prompt, can I? So let me bid you farewell and wish you the best of luck with your continued journey into the void.

In these pages, I've tried to spill a little of my knowledge into your head and have shared my recommendations for worthwhile terminal features (tabs, split windows, and so on). You now know how to install all kinds of CLI utilities, and since they're so tiny, you'll soon have—lucky you—thousands of single-use programs at your disposal. The tools of the terminal, I suspect, will become your go-to programs on the command line. I have no doubt that with time, you'll be using these to manipulate text and commands as you see fit.

Above all, my hope is that this book has given you enough nerve not to run away screaming from the inevitable: "Just open the terminal..."

RESOURCES

Here are a few essential resources to help you take on the command line.

Configuration and dotfiles

- Remy's terminal setup. A look at how I've configured my terminal, which you've seen in various screenshots throughout this book.
- GitHub's guide to dotfiles. A great starting point to discover other people's *dotfiles* (the configuration files for your prompt, aliases, and functions). Includes some useful links to help enhance the zsh.
- Some popular dotfiles by Mathias Bynens, Ben Alman, Paul Irish, and me.

Useful shell command browsing sites

- Ask HN: Share your favorite bash/zsh aliases. Here people share their favorite aliases. A good place to pinch a few ideas.
- Bash one-liners. A vast collection of little bash commands, useful for browsing and learning a new trick here and there.
- alias.sh. Although the site is now retired, it still hosts lots of great aliases and explanations about how they work.

Bonus: pretty much the best feature of my terminal

- ponysay. An alternative to cowsay, ponysay brightens up my terminal every day!

ACKNOWLEDGMENTS

I'd like to extend special thanks to a few people who helped usher this book into existence.

First, to Mark, who chucked me into the deep end of the terminal long before I'd ever published anything on the web. To Craig, for inviting me to write a book on the CLI. And to Anna, for strong-arming me into finishing the last half of this project after it had started to languish. I'm pretty sure this book never would have been finished had it not been for our conversations.

Thanks to Katel and Caren for all of their help, especially to Caren for making sense of my sometimes roundabout way of saying things.

Finally, a special thank-you to my family for their support and to Julie for for letting me write when we really could have used two parents to wrestle our children's attention and imaginations.

REFERENCES: WORKING THE COMMAND LINE

Shortened URLs are numbered sequentially; the related long URLs are listed below for reference.

Chapter 1

01-01 http://www.linfo.org/unix_philosophy.html

01-02 http://iterm2.com/

01-03 https://git-for-windows.github.io/

01-04 https://web.archive.org/web/20120225123719/http://www.nog.net/~tony/warez/cowsay.shtml

Chapter 2

02-01 https://chocolatey.org/

02-02 https://chocolatey.org/docs

02-03 https://chocolatey.org/install

02-04 http://brew.sh/

02-05 https://github.com/mroth/lolcommits

02-06 https://abookapart.com/products/git-for-humans

02-07 https://pypi.python.org/pypi

02-08 https://nodejs.org/en/

02-09 https://github.com/npm/npm/blob/7fe6950b44d241bb4d90857a44d89d750af1e2b3/doc/misc/npm-faq.md#if-npm-is-an-acronym-why-is-it-never-capitalized

02-10 https://www.npmjs.com/package/cowsay

Chapter 3

03-01 https://www.youtube.com/watch?v=EkluES9Rvak&feature=youtu.be

03-02 http://daringfireball.net/projects/markdown/

03-03 https://en.wikipedia.org/wiki/Less_%28Unix%29#Frequently_used_commands

Chapter 5

05-01 http://iterm2colorschemes.com/

05-02 http://fishshell.com/

05-03 https://github.com/robbyrussell/oh-my-zsh/wiki/themes
05-04 https://github.com/robbyrussell/oh-my-zsh/wiki/External-themes
05-05 https://github.com/robbyrussell/oh-my-zsh/wiki/Plugins-Overview
05-06 http://zsh.sourceforge.net/Doc/Release/Prompt-Expansion.html
05-07 https://remysharp.com/2013/07/25/my-terminal-setup
05-08 https://github.com/mathiasbynens/dotfiles
05-09 https://github.com/mathiasbynens/dotfiles#thanks-to

Resources

06-01 https://dotfiles.github.io/
06-02 https://github.com/cowboy/dotfiles
06-03 https://github.com/paulirish/dotfiles
06-04 https://github.com/remy/dotfiles
06-05 https://news.ycombinator.com/item?id=9869231
06-06 http://www.bashoneliners.com/
06-07 https://web.archive.org/web/20141216192521/http://alias.sh/
06-08 https://github.com/erkin/ponysay

INDEX: WORKING THE COMMAND LINE

ABOUT THE AUTHOR

Remy Sharp has been working commercially on the web since 1999 and blogging for over a decade. He runs his own consultancy, has been writing JavaScript long before it was cool, and founded the web conference ffconf in 2009. Remy tends to attract bugs and he enjoys squishing them. He uses the terminal daily.

8

IMAGE PERFORMANCE

MAT MARQUIS

FOREWORD BY
ETHAN MARCOTTE

BRIEFS

Publisher: Jeffrey Zeldman
Designer: Jason Santa Maria
Editor-in-Chief: Katel LeDû
Managing Editor: Lisa Maria Martin
Technical Editor: Eric Portis
Copyeditor: Katel LeDû
Proofreader: Caren Litherland
Book Producer: Ron Bilodeau

ISBN: 978-1-937557-77-5

A Book Apart
New York, New York
http://abookapart.com

TABLE OF CONTENTS: IMAGE PERFORMANCE

To the members of the RICG.

FOREWORD

WE WORK IN A DIGITAL MEDIUM, but there's a *weight* to our work. Over the years, the screens we design for have gotten considerably sharper. But as the quality of those screens has increased, so too have the images we've served to them. And, as you'll see in the pages ahead, those images are one of the chief reasons our websites have ballooned in size. Our websites may be prettier, but they're far, far slower.

our responsive designs have long made fine use of *flexible images*—by slapping `img { max-width: 100%; }` into our stylesheets, we have images as flexible as the fluid grids in which they're placed. But simply resizing an image with CSS won't help users on high-resolution screens; and delivering a huge, crisp image won't help users on punishingly constrained data plans. If we want to reach more devices, more *people*, with our responsive designs, `img { max-width: 100%; }` is a start—but it isn't enough.

Thankfully, the the Responsive Issues Community Group (RICG) was formed to address that dilemma. Lead in part by Mat Marquis, author of the little book you're about to read, the RICG developed a responsive images *standard*—a standard that allows us to deliver the most appropriate images to our users, based on any number of criteria. In other words, our images can now be as responsive as our layouts.

Now, that standard can appear intimidating at first, filled with obtuse-looking markup patterns. But if you're searching for a guide, you couldn't have picked a better one than Mat Marquis. Mat was responsible for shepherding this nebulous "responsive images" idea through the specification process, and he understands it better than most. In the pages ahead, Mat will use his indefatigable humor and wit to break down even the thorniest topic. Thanks to Mat's words, you'll be slinging responsive images in no time.

I'm glad you're about to read this funny, insightful, *powerful* little book. And I bet your users will be, too.

—Ethan Marcotte

INTRODUCTION

THAT FACT THAT YOU'RE reading this tells me something about you. It tells me that you're different from the way I once was.

I've been doing this—making websites—for a little more than a decade now. I like to think I've grown up some during that time. I don't mind saying I took some things for granted early on.

I've been incredibly fortunate, that much I've always known—and I'd appreciate it if you'd knock on wood for me here, reader. I've received way more than my fair share of help from friends, family, and total strangers alike. I've had—and have—the benefit of immense privilege. I've always tried my damnedest not to take any of *that* for granted.

What I took for granted were the *mechanics* of this work—at least at the start. If I made an element show up in the right place, on the right page, in the right browsers—no small feat, oftentimes—then my work was done. I'd never dig deeper than that surface level. I didn't know what I didn't know: that making a `div` show up in roughly the same place as a square in a `.psd` was just the tip of the web-development iceberg.

Below the surface—that's where the *meaning* is. To build a page that can be easily parsed by assistive technologies is to contribute to a more inclusive web; to render a page more performantly is to broaden the web's reach. To think too shallowly about a project means nudging the larger web in the same direction: toward something meant not for all, but for some; toward something meant only for those who experience it the way *we* do.

But I don't think that's who *you* are. Not now—not today, as you read this. You're ready to dive headfirst into a book about a subject that's easy to take for granted: putting images on the web.

At the risk of spoilers: any ol' image format in an `img` tag styled with `max-width: 100%` will get the job done. If all you were after was a passing grade, you wouldn't need to read any further. It might not be fast, it might not be accessible—it might not even *work* in some browsing contexts, depending on a set of factors you'd never come to know. But the job would, technically, be done. "*D* is for *diploma*" was my constant refrain in high school.

I can tell, though: scraping by isn't enough for you. Maybe you've been at this long enough to gain a healthy respect for your element, long enough that you don't take a single CSS property or markup pattern as a given. Maybe you're just starting out, sharp-eyed and voracious, looking to learn all you can about the web's inner workings. Maybe you're somewhere in between, starting to wonder what details lie beneath the surface of your workplace and your medium, the web.

Regardless of where you are in your understanding of the web, you know you want to make it work *better*. You want to play a part in building something faster, more reliable, and more inclusive.

If you believe that anything worth doing is worth doing well—hell, maybe even worth overdoing a little—then I've written this book for you.

Making the case

Listen: images do *damage*. The median webpage's total transfer size is huge: 1.7 MB, as of May 2018. Images alone accounted for roughly half of that.

It's not hard to see how the trouble started. Ultra-high-resolution displays feel ubiquitous now—I'm using one to write this, and I have more than one on my person as we speak. With the advent of Retina displays came the need for Retina-ready image sources—and that was just the beginning. Retina on the iPhone 4 begat Retina HD on the iPhone 6-8, then *Super* Retina HD Display on the iPhone X, and—if the pattern holds—we can expect Super Retina HD Display 2 Turbo: Tournament Edition in the near future. Of course, not to be outdone, manufacturers of countless mobile devices have continually upped the resolution stakes with each new iteration, in the exact same way.

That means trouble, for us and for users. It's no secret that there's a direct relationship between a site's performance and a user's willingness to, well, *use* it. Putting a bandwidth-obliterating wall of images—no matter how nice they are—between your users and the thing they came to your site to do will absolutely drive them away. An experiment done by Etsy a few years back saw an increased bounce rate of 12 percent from users on mobile devices when they added just 160 KB of images to a page.

This isn't an isolated incident. Check out any of the statistics on wpostats.com, a site dedicated to collecting this data, and you'll see the same results: from a business-case standpoint, you can very literally draw a line between users' time and their attention.

Web development is a game of inches. A stray comma breaks a build; a missing semicolon prevents a page from rendering. There's a lot of resiliency built into the web platform, but, ultimately, it does what we developers tell it to do. In aggregate, the web isn't a terribly opinionated platform—it isn't hard to think of the technology itself as neutral.

But nothing is ever neutral where people are involved—not technology, and not the tiny, seemingly inconsequential development decisions we make during the course of an average, boring workday.

I can't speak for you, reader, but in my day-to-day browsing context, an extra 160 KB here and there doesn't even register. As developers, we tend to occupy a position of privilege when it comes to using the web we're building. As a matter of occupational necessity, we have fast computers, modern browsers, and bandwidth to burn. That browsing privilege, unexamined, will skew what we build; unquestioned, it will lead us to unconscious bias. And our biases can have very real costs for others.

As of this year, according to Pew Research Center, one in five Americans owns a smartphone, but doesn't have a home broadband connection—up from 13 percent in 2015, and 8 percent in 2013. Likewise, a full 31 percent of adults making less than $30,000 a year have access to a smartphone, but no broadband connections in their homes, up from 20 percent in 2015. And 39 percent of adults with a high school diploma or less—a demographic I am part of—have a smartphone, but no home broadband.

These are all users who only experience the web by way of metered connections. Even users with an "unlimited" mobile data plan will have their connection speed throttled beyond a certain cap.

To reduce the browsing experience for these users is to limit their options—on the web and in their daily lives:

Among Americans who have looked for work in the last two years, 79% utilized online resources in their most recent job search and 34% say these online resources were the most important tool available to them.

Very few of us are likely to have built a job-search website. But maybe we built the site a user visited the day before they lost their job, the one that drained their prepaid data plan. Maybe it was something that could be justified in an early meeting: it was a site about art, so users should expect heavy images. It was a shopping site, so we figured nobody would be using it on their phone. It was a site for games, a luxury—but maybe that user gave their phone to their kid because they needed a little peace and quiet on the day they lost their job—a little time to think about what to do next.

A study conducted by Ericsson (PDF) in early 2016 found that delays in loading a mobile website caused, on average, a 38 percent increase in heart rate, and an increased stress level roughly on par with watching a horror movie or answering math problems. Honestly, that sounds right to me—you'd be hard-pressed to find anyone in any browsing context who isn't frustrated by a seemingly never-ending loading spinner.

But I don't mind admitting, here, to having recently experienced a *uniquely* exasperating "loading" animation during the process of checking my bank account balance while standing in a supermarket checkout line. I ended up losing my race against the cashier—or at least, my phone did. I was fortunate enough to have a declined card not cost me much more than my pride (*itself* a cost I'm not willing to foist upon anyone in a vulnerable position). But for a family that has to make every last dollar count, an unexpected overdraft fee could cost them a meal as well.

Building performant websites is a vast and ever-evolving discipline, ranging from tasks as large as compiling a web server to as small as optimizing the contents of a stylesheet. But it isn't a stretch to say that, on any given project, optimizing image assets and their delivery may be the single largest performance optimization we can make. If you care about building a more performant web, images are the place to start.

IMAGE FORMATS AND COMPRESSION

OVER THE COURSE OF THE NEXT FEW CHAPTERS, we're going to cover a surprising amount of ground. But before digging into responsive image use cases and syntaxes—before combing through the nuances of browsers' speculative preparsers and how requests for image sources are made—we have to start with a little groundwork.

Choosing the right image format is a topic I'm betting will be familiar to more than a few of you. It might be a bit of a refresher for some, but I won't mince words: getting this part right can be far more important than any flashy new "responsive image" technique. An image source that is only a few hundred kilobytes as a JPEG might be several megabytes as a PNG-24, without any discernable difference in quality to the end user.

In making decisions about formats, encodings, compression levels, and so on, we need to consider the contents of the image: is it a real-world photo or an illustration? We have to decide one level higher than JPEG versus PNG: we have to look at vector versus raster formats.

VECTOR FORMATS

When we talk about vector images on the web, we're talking about Scalable Vector Graphics (SVG). I don't mind admitting I was a little resistant to SVG at first, even as it was becoming more and more commonplace. SVGs are made of *math*—and that alone was enough to bias me against it conceptually. I lived and breathed raster, and "vector" conjured up images of ill-fated forays out of my Photoshop comfort zone and into the uncanny valley of Illustrator—where my muscle-memory for key commands was just wrong enough to be frustrating, and where there were no comforting little squares to zoom in on.

But upon opening an SVG in my code editor for the first time—by accident, knowing me—I was presented with something immediately recognizable and deeply comforting: *markup*.

```
<?xml version="1.0" encoding="utf-8"?>
<svg xmlns="http://www.w3.org/2000/svg" width="400"
  height="400">
```

FIG 1.1: These three shapes use the same SVG markup—but their fill colors are controlled through CSS, the same way we'd style any other element on the page.

```
  <circle cx="100" cy="100" r="50" fill="red" />
</svg>
```

Granted, it isn't HTML markup—but it's close enough to make sense at a glance. Those of you who have been in the industry for a while might recognize it as our old friend XML.

For simple edits, like changing the opacity or color of an icon, we don't have to fire up Adobe Illustrator—we can make those changes in the SVG itself. We can style them and animate them with real CSS, both in the SVG file and from the page that contains them (**FIG 1.1**).

We can even add custom *scripting* to an SVG, in order to bake behaviors and interactions into the images themselves (**FIG 1.2**).

And as much as that might appeal to us as designers and developers, SVG is also an *incredibly* powerful format in terms of the end user experience. It is, by any practical measure, an image format built for the modern web.

The most critical difference between vector and raster formats is—as the SVG name implies—*scalability*. To oversimplify, SVG is a method of communicating a series of coordinates to a browser's rendering engine, a set of instructions for how shapes should be drawn. The task of connecting these points is left to the browser—so when that set of coordinates is scaled up or down, the lines and shapes connecting them are redrawn to scale (**FIG 1.3**).

Raster images are more fixed: pixel-by-pixel instructions for rendering, with no fill-in-the-blanks for the browser in between. When scaled up—well, odds are you've seen the results in the

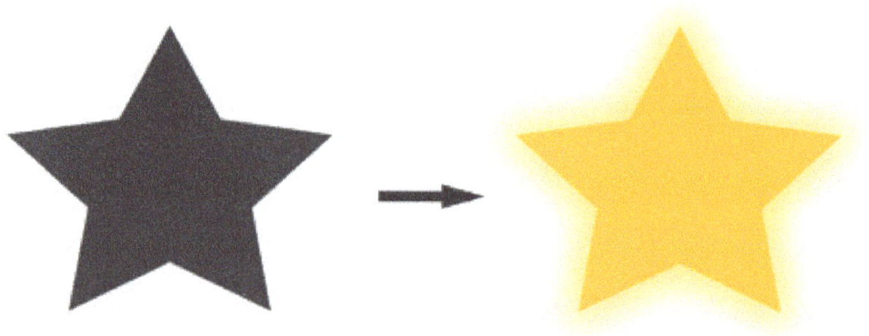

FIG 1.2: We can use JavaScript to add behaviors and interactions to an embedded SVG—such as toggling this star icon on and off with a click.

FIG 1.3: A resized vector image will be redrawn with sharp lines.

past, possibly by mistake. A raster image source scaled beyond its inherent dimensions tends to appear distorted, blocky, or blurred (**FIG 1.4**).

SVG doesn't suffer from this issue—a smooth curve between two points, drawn by the browser, will be redrawn just as smoothly at any size. We're going to spend a lot of time on the topic of ensuring that users receive viewport- and display-den-

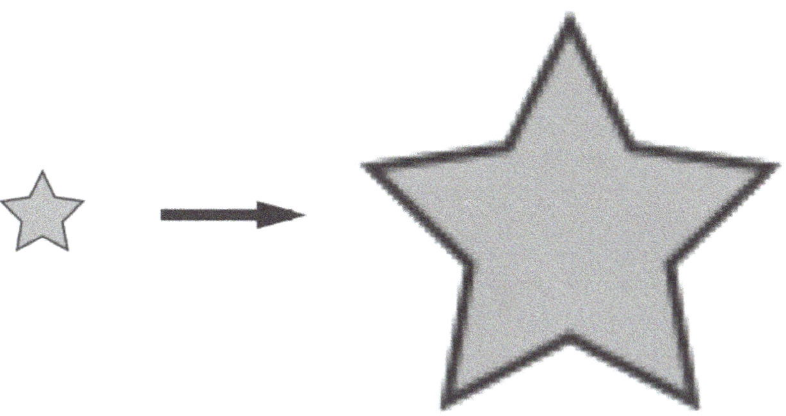

FIG 1.4: A raster image scales proportionally, and the result looks blurry at the edges.

sity-appropriate raster images—but with SVG, it's a given. And as you saw in the earlier example, the markup powering an infinitely scalable SVG source can be incredibly compact.

All that said, though, there are a few caveats to consider. Browser support for SVG is very good, but not guaranteed—not in the way that support for common raster formats can be universally assumed. Leaving a user without images in some contexts could very well mean leaving them with a website they can't navigate—so, depending on your project and how SVGs are being used, you might need to provide a fallback in the form of a better-supported raster version of the image source. All told, though, this is fairly easy to automate—projects like Grunticon handle generation of raster fallbacks for us, and there's a simple method for serving the correct asset to the end user. We'll talk more about that in the next chapter.

There's another catch with SVG, and this one is a key part of the decision between raster and vector for a given application: complexity. By nature of its function, the SVG format needs a little more active interpretation from the browser than raster formats—SVG's "draw a smooth curve connecting this point to that point" involves more thinking than raster's "draw a blue pixel, then a dark blue pixel, then a darker blue pixel, etc." For this reason, complex SVGs can be more taxing to render—and potentially larger, over-the-wire, than raster images.

There's no hard-and-fast rule there; it may take a little trial and error before you're able to instantly recognize an image source candidate as better served by SVG versus a conventional raster format. There are a few guidelines, though. For my money, I can say that interface elements—such as icons—are almost always better served by SVG than raster image sources. In fact, anywhere the icon fonts of yesteryear might have felt appropriate is likely to be a strong candidate for SVG.

For artwork containing multiple gradients, photo-realism, or intricate detail, though—when only pixel perfection will do—raster images are still the right tool for the job.

RASTER FORMATS

The lion's share of your content images—from photographs to animated GIFs—are going to be raster images. There's plenty more to discuss on this subject—and we will—but for now: think of a raster image as a two-dimensional grid made up of pixels, like so many brothers Mario.

When we break raster images down into formats—JPEG versus GIF versus PNG, and so on—what we're really talking about are the compression methods (or lack thereof) we're applying. Ultimately, choosing the appropriate raster-image format is about striking a balance between fidelity and file size.

Now, I'm the first to admit I don't have much of a mind for algorithms. But as a web developer—or maybe as the product of a Nintendo-centric childhood—I definitely have a mind for little pictures made of squares. So, in thinking about image formats, it helps to keep a pixel grid in mind (**FIG 1.5**).

Imagine this is the entirety of our source image. Choosing an image format effectively means choosing the method by which we're describing the contents of the file. For example, the top row of our grid could be described as:

- Row one, column one is blue.
- Row one, column two is blue.

FIG 1.5: Think of this as a close-up view of a raster image's pixels.

- Row one, column three is blue.
- Row one, column four is red.

But it could also be described as:

- Row one, columns one through three are blue.
- Row one, column four is red.

Assume you're playing the role of a web browser. You're ready—crayons and paper in hand—to render an image. I'm playing the role of a web server, and as such, I communicate in much the same way I do here in the text: I can't convey *an image*; I can only describe it.

If I were to ask you to draw a grid, and I read either of the previous descriptions to you, you'd end up with the same result—the same information is conveyed in either case. The first method does so absent any sort of compression: one "pixel" at a time. The second method, however, manages to describe the same image with far fewer characters. Or, in more practical terms: fewer bytes transferred over the wire, from the server (me) to the rendering engine (you).

Now, as you've probably guessed, this method of "encoding" and "decoding" an image doesn't resemble most actual formats in a meaningful way—there are often much more efficient ways to describe a grid, computationally speaking, than row-by-row and column-by-column. But it does come pretty close to describing one format: our old friend the GIF, animated or otherwise.

GIF

Saving an image as a GIF almost always means irrevocably reducing the fidelity of the original image.

That might sound scary on the surface, but it's worth keeping in mind that our eyes, well, they don't have the best fidelity either. Fine-tuning image compression is about striking a balance between the level of detail we're able to perceive and the level of detail being passed along to the computer rendering that image.

Think back to our raster image grid, and how that information is passed from server to browser. This time around, let's add a little more detail: a single darker pixel (**FIG 1.6**).

As simple as this image is, it wouldn't take many characters to break this down into something human-readable:

- Row one, columns one through three are blue. Row one, column four is red.
- Row two, column one is blue. Row two, column two is dark blue. Row two, column three is blue. Row two, column four is red.
- Row three, columns one through three are blue. Row three, column four is red.
- Row four, columns one through three are blue. Row four, column four is red.

Assuming you and I have the same definition of "blue," "dark blue," and "red," that description would allow you to render a pixel-perfect interpretation of the original image. Think of this as a *lossless* method of compressing the image data for transfer from me to you. We've managed to condense the pixel-by-pixel description in a few places ("columns one through three are..."), but with no change to the visual fidelity.

Now, suppose we take a *lossy* approach to that description:

FIG 1.6: Adding a small detail to our pixel grid can add a lot of complexity to its encoding.

- Row one, columns one through three are blue. Row one, column four is red.
- Row two, columns one through three are blue. Row two, column four is red.
- Row three, columns one through three are blue. Row three, column four is red.
- Row four, columns one through three are blue. Row four, column four is red.

I've simplified the description of our original image, and the end result is that we've sacrificed pixel-perfection—as the rendering engine, you've rendered the image exactly as I've encoded it—but I left out the detail of the darker blue cell in my encoding, for the sake of a smaller transfer size. This specific lossy compression technique is called *quantization*, where a range of values are reduced to a smaller, approximated set of output values.

Reducing three colors to two across the span of a whopping twelve "pixels" makes for an obvious change (**FIG 1.7**). Across a larger and more detailed image, however, the effects might not be as noticeable—to a point. As we increase the lossyness of a GIF, the smooth gradients of the original image are replaced by a mottled effect (**FIG 1.8**). The file size plummets from around 318 KB to around 54 KB, and it—well—it becomes more pixel-y.

FIG 1.7: A lossy approach to compressing the previous image data means we've lost the dark blue detail.

We can reduce file sizes even further by manually restricting the color palette. What we end up with, then, is an image that retains the basic shape and hue of our original, but in a barely recognizable form (**FIG 1.9**). It would be smaller (weighing in at only 23 KB or so), but not terribly useful.

In practice, all of this means that GIFs are suited for a slim number of applications:

- limited color palettes and hard edges
- binary transparency (as in: a pixel is either 100 percent transparent, or 100 percent opaque)
- animation

All told, I don't find much call for an old-fashioned GIF in my day-to-day work, not anymore. Images with limited color palettes and hard edges—icons, line art, stylized flat-color illustrations—are almost always better served by SVG.

And I don't have much need for GIF-style binary transparency, either—not when PNG-24 handles transparency so much better.

As for animation, well...that's where I can't help but feel a little conflicted. I am, I don't mind admitting, something of an animated GIF enthusiast.

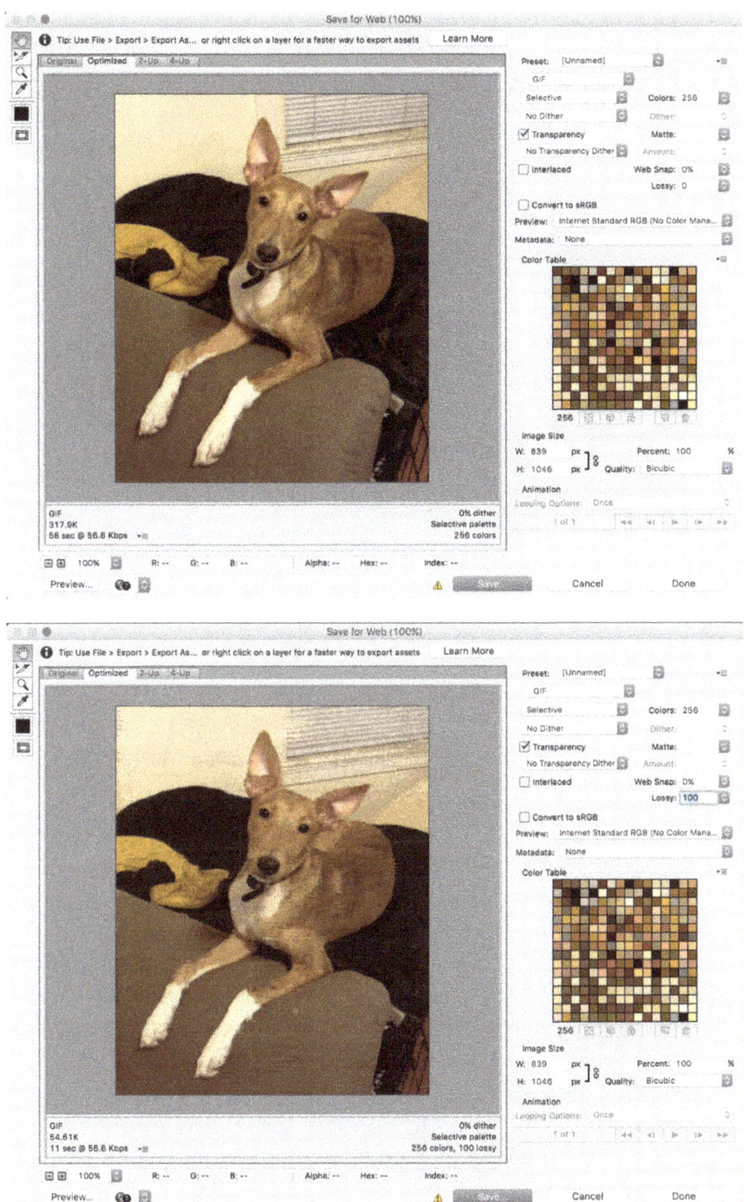

FIG 1.8: The more we increase the lossy compression, the more conspicuous it becomes.

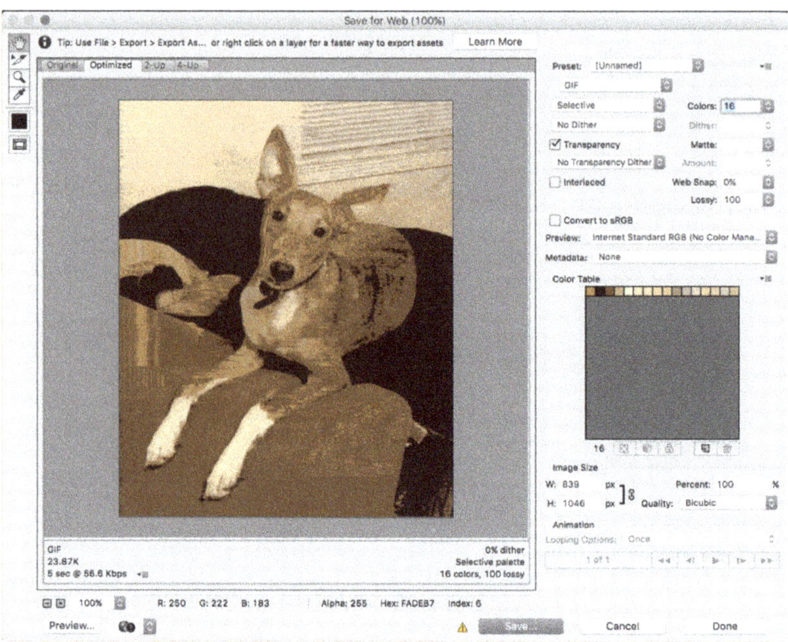

FIG 1.9: Taken to its extreme, we have a barely recognizable—if much smaller—image.

Animated GIF

For all intents and purposes, animated GIFs behave like self-contained flipbooks of individual GIF stills.

They're refreshingly simple, in both composition and use. If you see an animated GIF you like, you can grab it and throw it in a bukkit. You can open it up in an image editor, edit it, remix it, and resave it as a new GIF—Photoshop, for example, opens an animated GIF as a set of layers, each of which contains one frame of the animation. You can upload it to an incredible number of venues, with a click or a drag: chat clients, social media networks, text message conversations, whatever—and the process repeats.

Animated GIF *feels* almost analog, harkening back to the early days of the web itself—a little clunky, but made to be pulled apart and understood.

In every user-facing way, though, animated GIFs are practically indefensible.

They're slow to render, and excruciating in terms of file size. From an accessibility standpoint, it's difficult—at times, impossible—to sum up the contents of a complex animation in a single, terse `alt` attribute. The role of animated GIFs is almost invariably better served by short video clips—and video formats have the potential for richer accessibility features, like captioning and audio description tracks, more than an `alt` could ever hope to provide.

As such, animated GIFs are becoming less common. In fact, in order to retain the long-honed performance optimizations of the `img` element *and* make use of the reduced file sizes of video formats, several browsers have expanded the `img` element's `src` attribute to accept video source files—you can see this in Safari, at the time of writing, and Chrome isn't far behind. By any measurable metric, that's a win. Services like Twitter now convert animated GIF uploads to MP4 video, behind the scenes, before the associated tweet is posted, and that's a win too—it's great for performance and usability.

At my least generous, though, I can't help but notice that it provides Twitter with fertile new ground for advertisements. And those animations are now siloed—the generated files aren't something that a layperson can easily save, edit, or share on other services. Users can, of course, share a link to the tweet on Twitter dot com, and boost those engagement numbers.

Animated GIF—and maybe the GIF format itself—might just end up going the way of the carburetor and the record player. They're impractical, sure; nobody would argue that a record beats an MP3 for portability, or that an electronic fuel injection system is less reliable than a carburetor.

But still. There's just something warmer about analog.

PNG

PNG (Portable Network Graphics) comes in three variants:

- *grayscale* PNG, which is limited to black and white (or shades of gray)

- *indexed color* PNG (Photoshop calls it "PNG-8"), which can contain up to 256 colors
- *truecolor* PNG (a.k.a. "PNG-24"), which can contain many, many more colors—up to 16 million

There are a few things that set PNG apart from other formats. First, it was built for *lossless compression*, meaning that the encoding *itself* can be compressed—the way you might convert a huge text file to a ZIP to shave off a few bytes—but none of the actual image data will be reduced. In practical terms, that means that saving a source image as a lossless, truecolor PNG will never result in a drop in visual quality—but it *will* result in much larger files.

Second, while GIF handles transparency as sort of a binary proposition—either a pixel is 100 percent transparent or 100 percent opaque—PNG supports semi-transparency.

Between its large color palettes and its lossless compression methods, PNG-24 is a good choice for the canonical source version of an image—but rarely, if ever, the right choice. The use cases for PNG are similar to those of GIF: images with limited color palettes and sharp lines—cases where, more often than not, an SVG is the better choice.

You'll really only require a PNG when you need one specific feature: a raster-formatted image with transparency. Because PNG was designed to solve use cases that are now better served by SVG, you'll often see PNG used as the fallback version of UI elements in browsers that don't support SVG. Truth be told, that's almost the only time I use PNGs anymore.

JPEG

JPEG is far and away the most common image format used throughout the web, and with good reason: it's almost invariably the right choice for photographs. In fact, the use case is right there in the name, if a little obscured—"JPEG" itself stands for Joint Photographic Experts Group, the committee responsible for issuing the standard way back in 1992. You'll see the file extension for a JPEG as either .jpg or .jpeg, interchangeably.

JPEG is the poster format for lossy compression. Just like GIF, saving an image as JPEG means reducing the quality of that image. But unlike GIF, JPEG compression operates in a number of ways beyond quantization.

Let me get this out of the way right up front: unlike the refreshingly simple pixel-by-pixel encoding that GIF uses, JPEG compression is based on algorithms with names like "discrete cosine transform," which—to quote Wikipedia directly—"expresses a finite sequence of data points in terms of a sum of cosine functions oscillating at different frequencies."

Now, if this sentence has awakened in you a burning need to learn more about the dark and arcane math that powers images on the web, you have my blessing. However—and I cannot stress this enough—you *also* have my blessing to forget this information forever. Personally, I've never met an MIT URL that made a whole lot of sense to me.

So, in this section, I'm going to take a few liberties with the way a JPEG might be encoded into human-readable language. As you might expect from a format built around one computer communicating to another as efficiently as possible, it doesn't translate well to the written word.

Downsampling

Remember when I said our eyes are a little lossy in and of themselves? In terms of processing visual information, there's a lot we humans can't do very well. We're not great at processing "high-frequency detail"—we're able to recognize a tree, tell it apart from other trees, and even see a forest for said trees on a good day. But what we don't see—or we do *see*, I suppose, but don't fully *process* at a glance—are the positions of each leaf on the tree. We can seek out this information, for sure—but driving past a row of trees, we're not looking for each individual leaf in relation to those around them.

Likewise, come autumn, we see that the leaves on that tree have turned yellow—we can quickly absorb that there are different shades of yellow, the colors changing along gradients, the ambient lighting and shadow. We don't capture the precise hue of each individual leaf in comparison to the one beside it.

To put it in what I hope are increasingly familiar terms: we just don't have that kind of bandwidth. Mentally, we round things off, so we're not constantly overwhelmed by details.

JPEG compression attempts to compress an image source in a way that (loosely) matches the way our own psychovisual systems "compress" an image source. In effect, JPEG tries to throw away details we weren't likely to notice anyway so it can sneak the compression past us.

At its core, that isn't too different from a GIF; simply reducing the fidelity of a photograph ever so slightly might not register to our eyes, but it does reduce file size. With a GIF, removing a few colors from a photograph can mean a big reduction in quality for a relatively minor reduction in file size. With a JPEG, we can round down the level of detail in a way that might not register at all to our lossy eyes, if done within reason—*and* introduce far more opportunities for bandwidth savings.

JPEG does that rounding down—*downsampling,* it's called—in a particularly interesting way. It takes advantage of the fact that humans are more sensitive to differences in brightness than to differences in hue. As with GIF, color details (or *chroma*) can be reduced. Unlike with GIF, though, luminance details (or *luma*) are retained.

You can think of luma as a separate light/dark layer superimposed over our colors. For example, this photograph of a handsome dog—one who could *never* be mistaken for a deer—has been broken down into its luma and chroma layers (**FIG 1.10**). Superimpose those two layers again, and you have your source image (**FIG 1.11**).

It might seem like an academic distinction, as though GIF describes part of an image as "dark blue," while JPEG describes part of an image as "blue, dark." But by separating chroma and luma, JPEG is able to leverage one of our major psychovisual weaknesses: our eyes aren't as good at noticing slight differences in chroma as they are at noticing slight differences in luma. By throwing away detail from the layer we can't process as well but leaving the luma layer untouched, more opportunities for compression are created without causing noticeable degradation in the result. Slight differences in the *hue* of blue

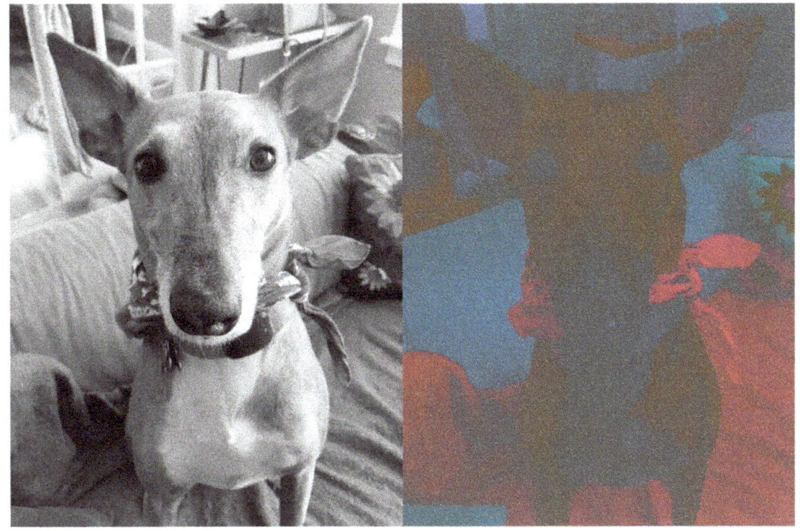

FIG 1.10: A photograph separated into luma (luminance) and chroma (color) layers.

FIG 1.11: While not explicitly encoded in the image, it can be assumed that the subject of the photograph is a very good boy.

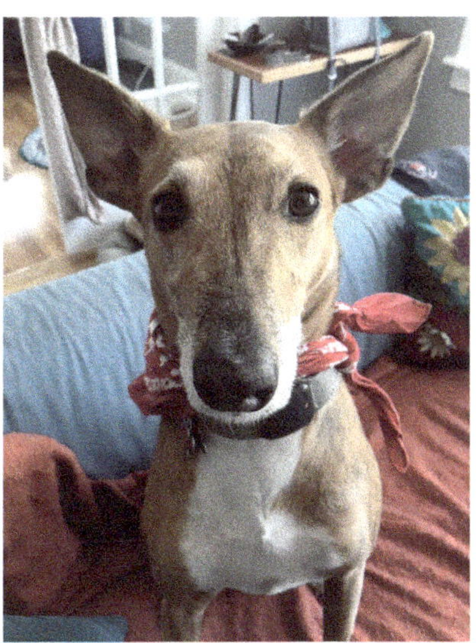

might be rounded down, but its brightness will be retained—and we likely won't notice.

Now, I mentioned before that JPEG has complicated, math-heavy methods of encoding images—we're not going to dig into those, but suffice to say that JPEG encoding doesn't encode images one pixel at a time the way GIF does. While "one pixel at a time, left to right, top to bottom" is easy for us humans to understand, it isn't a terribly efficient way to describe a source. So, instead, JPEG encodes the image as eight-by-eight blocks of pixels and describes the *blocks*—not the individual pixels inside them—algorithmically.

Consider that an image transfer is a computer communicating to another computer, and that sorting through information is something computers excel at doing efficiently, but in ways that aren't necessarily scrutable in writing. So, a grain of salt: I'm taking a few liberties as I convert aspects of JPEG encoding into human-readable language.

In terms of relayed instructions, you can think of JPEG downsampling as turning an image source into two sets of instructions. One encodes chroma:

- All blocks are blue.

The other encodes luma:

- The first half of the block at row two, column two is darker (**FIG 1.12**).

This may not seem like much of a win over GIF-style encoding, especially with this example—an image with flat colors and sharp lines. But JPEG is well suited to a much more common use case for images: gradients (**FIG 1.13**).

Describing a gradient using GIF-style encoding would be extremely verbose. Compressing it using GIF-style lossy compression would reduce the transfer size—but not without a pretty noticeable change in the rendered result. In restricting the color palette, we'd lose detail; the resulting image would have a sharp line between the light and dark shades of blue (**FIG 1.14**).

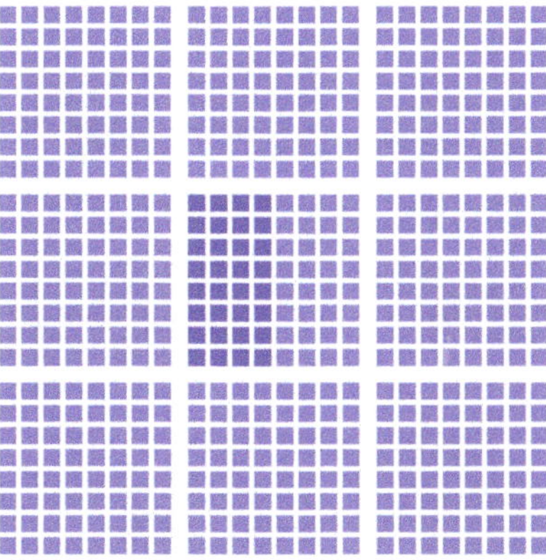

FIG 1.12: Rather than describing each individual pixel, JPEG encoding describes blocks of pixels.

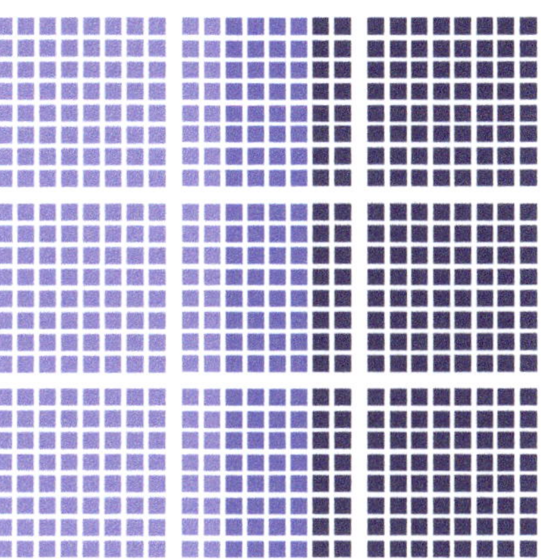

FIG 1.13: A pixel grid showing a light-to-dark-blue gradient.

FIG 1.14: Our gradient pixel grid with GIF-style lossy compression applied.

FIG 1.15: An uncompressed image of the White Mountains in Vermont, weighing in at 1.54 MB.

A gradient isn't a strong use case for GIF, no matter how you look at it. But using JPEG's method of encoding our blue gradient source image would give us a very simple chroma:

- All blocks are blue.

It would yield a similarly terse luma:

- All blocks in column one are light.
- All blocks in column two follow a gradient from light to dark.
- All blocks in column three are dark.

Before we apply any compression, JPEG-style encoding gives us a small transfer for a pixel-perfect representation of our image source—so we know JPEG is the right choice.

Now, imagine this writ much, much larger—for example, with a photograph of the sky (**FIG 1.15**). GIF-style encoding barely halves the file size and creates perceptible stripes of blue across the sky (**FIG 1.16**). But with JPEG encoding, and a little quantization of the details—something our lossy psychovisual systems might not even recognize—the savings potential is huge (**FIG 1.17**).

FIG 1.16: Encoded as GIF and using a high level of compression, our file size is reduced to 38 KB, with a marked drop in quality. Notice the streaks across the sky, and the lack of detail in the foreground trees.

FIG 1.17: With moderate JPEG compression, the reduction in detail isn't apparent—and the file size is reduced all the way down to 26 KB.

Even if we only factored in this one approach to compression, you can see where JPEG is almost invariably the right choice for photographs: the real world is made up of gradients. You can likely also see where it isn't as well suited to the pixel-perfect use cases for GIF, like sharp text and hard lines—situations where pixel-perfection is necessary, even if it means sacrificing some algorithmic efficiency.

Artifacts

We could quite literally spend the remainder of this book going over JPEG alone. It would make for some dry reading, though, and steer us way into academic territory. I'd be remiss, however, if I didn't take a moment to mention the most infamous side effect of JPEG compression: artifacts.

You may not know them by name, but you almost certainly know them by appearance (**FIG 1.18**). JPEG *artifacts* result from JPEG compression taken to the extreme. Because JPEG compression samples and applies high-frequency detail-reduction in eight-by-eight pixel squares, we get—in strict technical terms—a blocky, glitchy version of our image.

Determining the ideal level of compression for your images is a finesse game, given the complexity involved in JPEG compression. When we're compressing images individually, we might be able to trust our gut—and our eyes. But summing up such a complex set of instructions with a single "quality" or "compression" number can be a fraught prospect. When it comes to setting sensible defaults—for example, automatically applying compression to user-uploaded images, the way WordPress does—what might work invisibly for one image *could* be noticeable in another.

There are tools that help remove some of the guesswork from the process—for instance, DSSIM allows us to introduce an intermediary step in our build or upload processes, analyzing each of our images for the optimal balance of perceptual fidelity and file size. That comes at the cost of higher processing overhead—paving the way for hyperoptimized content delivery services like Cloudinary.

FIG 1.18: A heavily compressed JPEG. The blurry, blocky, discolored effects are artifacts of the compression process.

But don't let that potential source of overhead discourage you. With a sensible default level of JPEG compression applied to all of our images, you and I might still be able to spot an artifact here and there. We know what we're looking for, after all, and we're focused on it—we're looking for the individual leaves on the tree, so to speak. But most users will just see a tree, with any faint artifacts blending in with the tiny details that their lossy psychovisual systems gloss over.

In fact, odds are you and I won't notice most of them either, even though we're wise to the tricks JPEG tries to play on us. For that reason, it's almost always a safe bet to nudge JPEG compression just a *little* lower than you think might be noticeable. You'll see it when you're looking for it, there in the JPEG compression options dialog, but when you're not—when *you're* the user—you'll likely fall for it, too.

Progressive JPEG

Progressive JPEG (PJPEG) effectively parallelizes the process of rendering a JPEG. Rather than the incremental rendering of a baseline JPEG (**FIG 1.19**), progressive JPEG breaks rendering into a set of full-sized "scans," with each scan increasing the quality of the image (**FIG 1.20**).

FIG 1.19: A baseline JPEG loads in gradually.

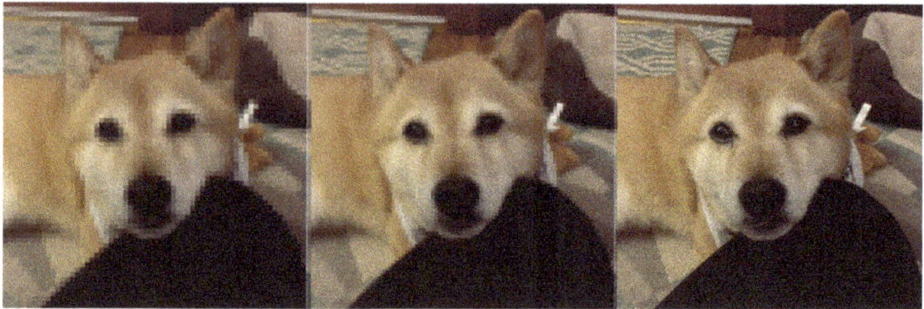

FIG 1.20: In modern browsers, PJPEG renders a low-quality version of an image first, then makes multiple passes at sharpening it.

The benefit is mostly perceptual. By delivering a full-size version of the image right away—albeit a blurry one—instead of empty space, PJPEG can *feel* faster to the end user.

That said, PJPEG isn't *strictly* a matter of user-facing smoke and mirrors. With the exception of *very* small image sources, PJPEG often means a smaller file size as well.

Browser support for rendering PJPEG isn't guaranteed, but it's very good. Worst-case scenario, the PJPEG renders all at once rather than, well, progressively. You'd lose the perceptual performance gains, but at no user-facing cost.

There is one trade-off: decoding PJPEG is more complex than plain ol' JPEG, and that means putting more strain on the browser—and a device's hardware—during rendering. That rendering overhead is difficult—but not impossible—to quantify in exact terms, but suffice to say that it likely won't be noticeable outside of severely underpowered devices. So, as in countless other web-development matters, I can't leave you with much more than a hearty "it depends"—but I will say I reach for PJPEG more often than not in my own work.

FORMATS OF THE FUTURE

Given that JPEG approaches compression in a handful of algorithmically intensive ways, you can probably see where there's nearly endless potential for improvement. The humble JPEG has given way to a number of slight variations, all of which aim to improve both image quality and transfer size by tweaking encoding and compression methods.

Once we start tinkering with encoding, however, there be dragons: even though some of these formats share the JPEG name, they're as fundamentally dissimilar as Java is to JavaScript. In order for those files to render, the browser has to be able to "speak" that new encoding. If we're not careful about how they're used, we run the risk of serving users an image file their browser can't render.

Some formats, like JPEG 2000—currently only supported in Safari—are intended to fulfill all of the same use cases as a baseline JPEG, but improve on the standard compression methods to deliver a visually similar but much smaller image. Other formats, like FLIF—not yet supported in any browser—aim to provide more efficient solutions to GIF-like animation and PNG-like transparency.

WebP is one of the more exciting formats, thanks in part to the level of interest it's seeing from browsers. This smaller, better-featured version of JPEG is currently only supported in Chrome and Opera, but Safari, Firefox, and Edge have all started experimenting with it as well—and, thanks to the responsive image patterns we'll discuss in the next chapter, we can use it responsibly right away.

RESPONSIVE IMAGES

I COME HERE NOT TO BURY `img`, but to praise it.

Well, mostly.

Historically, I like `img` just fine. It's refreshingly uncomplicated, on the surface: it fires off a request for the file in its `src` attribute, renders the contents of that file, and provides assistive technologies with an alternative narration. It does so quickly, efficiently, and seamlessly. For most of the web's life, that's all `img` has ever had to do—and thanks to years and years of browsers competing on rendering performance, it keeps getting better at it.

But there's a fine line between "reliable" and "stubborn," and I've known `img` to come down on both sides of it.

Though I admit to inadvertently hedging my bets a *little* by contributing to the jQuery Mobile Project—a framework originally dedicated to helping produce "mobile sites"—I've always come down squarely in the responsive web design (RWD) camp. For me, the appeal of RWD wasn't in building a layout that adapted to any viewport—though I *do* still think that's pretty cool. The real appeal was in finding a technique that could adapt to the unknown-unknowns. RWD felt—and still feels—like a logical and ongoing extension of the web's strengths: resilience, flexibility, and unpredictability.

That said, I would like to call attention to one thing that m-dot sites (dedicated mobile versions of sites, usually found at a URL beginning with the letter *m* followed by a dot) did have over responsively designed websites, back in the day: specially tailored assets.

TAILORING ASSETS

In a responsive layout, just setting a `max-width: 100%` in your CSS ensures that your images will always *look* right—but it also means using image sources that are at least as large as the largest size at which they'll be displayed. If an image is meant to be displayed anywhere from 300 pixels wide to 2000 pixels wide, that same 2000-pixel-wide image is getting served up to users in all contexts. A user on a small, low-resolution display gets saddled with all of the bandwidth costs of massive, high-resolution images, but ends up with none of the benefits. A high-resolution image on a low-resolution display looks like any other low-resolution image; it just costs more to transfer and takes longer to appear.

Even beyond optimization, it wasn't uncommon to show or hide entire blocks of content, depending on the current viewport size, during those early days of RWD. Though the practice became less common as we collectively got the hang of working responsively, `img` came with unique concerns when serving disparate content across breakpoints: our markup was likely to be parsed long before our CSS, so an `img` would have no way of knowing whether it would be displayed at the current viewport size. Even an `img` (or its container) set to `display: none` would trigger a request, by design. More bandwidth wasted, with no user-facing benefit.

Our earliest attempts

I am fortunate enough to have played a tiny part in the history of RWD, having worked alongside Filament Group and Ethan Marcotte on the *Boston Globe* website back in 2011.

It was, by any measure, a project with *weight*. The *Globe* website redesign gave us an opportunity to prove that responsive web design was not only a viable approach to development, but that it could scale beyond the "it might be fine for a personal blog" trope—it could work for a massive news organization's website. It's hard to imagine that idea has ever needed proving, looking back on it now, but this was a time when standalone m-dot sites were widely considered a best practice.

While working on the *Globe*, we tried developing a means of delivering larger images to devices with larger screens, beginning with the philosophy that the technique should err on the side of mobile: start with a mobile-sized and -formatted image, then swap that with a larger version depending on the user's screen size. This way, if anything should break down, we're still erring on the side of caution. A smaller—but still perfectly representative—image.

The key to this was getting the screen's width in JavaScript, in the `head` of the document, and relaying that information to the server in time to defer requests for images farther down the page. At the time, that JavaScript would be executed prior to any requests in `body` being made; we used that script to set a cookie about the user's viewport size, which would be carried along with those `img` requests on the same page load. A bit of server-side scripting would read the cookie and determine which asset to send in response.

It worked well, but it was squarely in the realm of "clever hack"—that parsing behavior wasn't explicitly defined in any specifications. And in the end, as even the cleverest hacks are wont to do, it broke.

Believe it or not, that was good news.

Prefetching—or "speculative preparsing"—is a huge part of what makes browsers feel fast: before we can even see the page, the browser starts requesting assets so they're closer to "ready" by the time the page appears. Around the time the *Globe*'s site launched, several major browsers made changes to the way they handled prefetching. Part of those changes meant that an image source might be requested before we had a chance to apply any of our custom logic.

Now, when browsers compete on performance, users win—those improvements to speculative preparsing were great news for performance, improving load times by as much as 20 percent. But there was a disconnect here—the *fastest* request is the one that never gets made. Good ol' reliable `img` was single-mindedly requesting the contents of its `src` faster than ever, but often the contents of those requests were inefficient from the outset, no matter how quickly the browser managed to request, parse, and render them—the assets were bigger than they'd ever need to be. The harm was being done over the wire.

So we set out to find a new hack. What followed was a sordid tale of `noscript` tags and dynamically injected `base` tags, of `document.write` and `eval`—of *rendering all of our page's markup in a* `head` *element, to break preparsing altogether*.

For some of you, the preceding lines will require no explanation, and for that you have my sincerest condolences. For everyone else: know that it was the stuff of scary developer campfire stories (or, I guess, scary GIF-of-a-campfire stories). Messy, hard-to-maintain hacks all the way down, relying entirely on undocumented, unreliable browser quirks.

Worse than those means, though, were the ends: none of it really *worked*. We were always left with compromises we'd be foisting on a whole swath of users—wasted requests for some, blurry images for others. It was a problem we simply couldn't solve with sufficiently clever JavaScript; even if we had been able to, it would've meant working *around* browser-level optimizations rather than taking advantage of them. We were trying to subvert browsers' improvements, rather than work with them. Nothing felt like the way forward.

We began hashing out ideas for a native solution: if HTML5 offered us a way to solve this, what would that way look like?

A native solution

What began in a shared text file eventually evolved into one of the first and largest of the W3C's Community Groups—places where developers could build consensus and offer feedback on evolving specifications. Under the banner of the "Responsive Images Community Group," we—well, at the risk of ruining the dramatic narrative, we argued on mailing lists.

One such email, from Bruce Lawson, proposed a markup pattern for delivering context-appropriate images that fell in line with the existing rich-media elements in HTML5—like the `video` tag—even borrowing the `media` attribute. He called it `picture`; `image` was already taken as an ancient alias of `img`, after all.

What made this proposal special was the way it used our reliable old friend `img`. Rather than a standalone element, `picture` came to exist as a wrapper—and a decision engine—for an inner `img` element:

```
<picture>
  <source …>
  <img src="source.jpg" alt="…">
</picture>
```

That `img` inside `picture` would give us an incredibly powerful fallback pattern—it wouldn't be the sort of standard where we have to wait for browser support to catch up before we could make use of it. Browsers that didn't understand `picture` and its `source` elements would ignore it and still render the inner `img`. Browsers that *did* understand `picture` could use criteria attached to `source` elements to tell the inner `img` which source file to request.

Most important of all, though, it meant we didn't have to recreate all of the features of `img` on a brand-new element: because `picture` didn't render anything in and of itself, we'd still be leaning on the performance and accessibility features of that `img`.

This made a lot of sense to us, so we took it to the Web Hypertext Application Technology Working Group (WHATWG), one of the two groups responsible for the ongoing development of HTML.

If you've been in the industry for a few years, this part of the story may sound a little familiar. Some of you may have caught whispers of a fight between the WHATWG's `srcset` and the `picture` element put forth by a scrappy band of web-standards rebels and their handsome, charismatic, and endlessly humble Chair. Some of you read the various calls to arms, or donated when we raised funds to hire Yoav Weiss to work full-time on native implementations. Some of you have RICG T-shirts, which—I don't mind saying—were *rad*.

A lot of dust needed to settle, and when it finally did, we found ourselves with more than just one new element; edge cases begat use cases, and we discovered that `picture` alone wouldn't be enough to suit all of the image needs of our increasingly complex responsive layouts. We got an entire suite of enhancements to the `img` element as well: native options for dealing with high-resolution displays, with the size of an image in a layout, with alternate image formats—things we had never been able to do natively, prior to that point.

THE FOUR USE CASES

Ultimately, those years of experimenting, prototyping, iterating, and ~~arguing with each other~~ impassioned discourse on various mailing lists gave us four mix-and-match use cases—four key problems with image delivery that any proposed solution (or solutions) *must* solve to be considered viable.

In sum, the term "responsive images" refers to any combination of the following use cases:

- **Art direction:** requesting visually distinct source files at specific viewport sizes.
- **Image types:** requesting new image formats with responsible fallbacks.
- **Display density:** requesting image sources appropriate for high-density displays only when necessary.
- **Flexible images:** providing the browser with information about a set of image sources and how they'll be used in a page's layout, so it can make the most appropriate request for a user's browsing context.

Let's take a closer look at each of these use cases.

Art direction

The art-direction use case comes into play whenever

- you want to specify alternate versions of an image for different viewport sizes,
- you need explicit control over what sources appear when, or
- you need different cropping and zooming to best represent the subject of an image.

At any viewport size, the subjects of these images are the same—though their proportions may change across layout breakpoints (**FIG 2.1**). This sort of "cropping" can be achieved through CSS, certainly—but will still leave a user requesting hundreds of kilobytes of an image they might never end up seeing.

FIG 2.1: Different crops of the same image subjects are shown for different viewport sizes.

The markup for the `picture` element follows a precedent already set by HTML5's `audio` and `video` elements: a wrapper element containing `source` elements, each of which has an attribute defining the conditions for the use of that source (`media`) and the asset—or set of assets—to request if that condition is met (`srcset`):

```
<picture>
  <source media="(min-width: 800px)" srcset="pic-
  big.jpg">
  <source media="(min-width: 400px)" srcset="pic-
  med.jpg">
  <img src="small.jpg" alt="Cubes of tofu simmering
  in a fiery red sauce.">
</picture>
```

It's worth mentioning here that art direction does *not* apply to radically different image sources. A good rule of thumb is that you should be able to describe all of your sources with a single `alt` attribute—not least of all because you'll have to.

Similar to the pattern established by `video`, the `picture` element contains fallback content: an inner `img`. If the `picture` element isn't recognized by the user's browser, it's ignored. Its associated `source` elements are similarly discarded, since the browser doesn't have any context for them. That inner `img` element will be recognized, though—and rendered.

In addition to providing a robust built-in fallback pattern, `img` is the heart of the `picture` element in browsers that *do* support it. Rather than having `picture` recreate all of the accessibility features and performance optimizations of `img`—and adding a huge barrier to support for both browsers and assistive technologies alike—the `picture` element doesn't actually *render* anything on its own. Instead, it acts as a decision engine for the inner `img` element, telling it what to render.

The first `source` with a `media` attribute that matches the viewport size will be the one selected. There's precedent for this: the `video` element uses `source` elements, with `media` attributes, in the exact same way.

If we're using `min-width` media queries, we want to have our largest sources first, as illustrated in the example above. When we're using `max-width` media queries, we want to make sure our smallest sources come first:

```
<picture>
  <source media="(max-width: 400px)" srcset="small.
  jpg">
  <source media="(max-width: 800px)" srcset="pic-
  med.jpg">
  <img src="small.jpg" alt="Cubes of tofu simmering
  in a fiery red sauce.">
</picture>
```

We'll *always* want to specify the inner `img` last in the source order—it serves as our default source if `picture` is unsupported, or if *none* of our `source` elements match their `media` attribute criteria.

Image types

The image types use case isn't concerned with viewport size or resolution—it's concerned with the image *formats* supported by the user's browser. It allows us to use the single-request fallback pattern already built into `picture` so we can serve alternate image formats in smarter ways.

One of the most common suggestions we'd hear from people just joining the responsive-images conversation was that we "just" needed a new format—a single image containing all of the different sources we could possibly need. The browser then would only request the appropriate part of that source file—and, in a vacuum, it's hard to argue with the logic.

But to make this happen, we would need to not only invent that new format, but also invent a reliable way to serve it to users with browsers that supported it, *and* invent a way for browsers to know which specific byte range of the file to load *without* requesting the entire "package" of images. The last bit would likely mean throwing together a new protocol for the web to run on. That was usually about the end of those threads.

It did get us thinking, though: one of the less impossible stumbling blocks to the introduction of any new format would be to serve it responsibly. A new image format can't have a fallback pattern in and of itself—if the browser doesn't recognize a file at all, it can't take advantage of a baked-in fallback pattern.

At the time, the best solutions all involved requesting and transferring the new image file *before* determining whether to throw it away and load a fallback:

```
<img src="image.svg"
 data-fallback="image.png"
 onerror="this.src=this.getAttribute('data-
  fallback'); this.onerror=null;"
 alt="…">
```

We were using this approach to contend with spotty browser support for SVG years before formats like WebP caught on. With this pattern, the request for `image.svg` would still be made in every browser. Once a browser had the file, it could figure out whether or not it was capable of *rendering* it. Browsers that couldn't render the SVG would throw an error. That error would trigger a line of JavaScript that did two things: first, it copied the contents of the `data-fallback` attribute into the `src` attribute, triggering a new request and rendering the PNG instead. Then, the script overwrote itself, to prevent any further errors from creating a loop if the fallback couldn't be rendered for any reason.

If it sounds a little convoluted, well, that's because it was—but when it came to making these decisions on the front end, approaches like this one were the only game in town.

But with `picture`, we were already inventing a decision engine—one explicitly designed to let us avoid redundant requests. Granted, that decision-making could never be completely automated—short of us *telling* the browser about a source file, there's no way for it to recognize a format it doesn't support without requesting it. We still need to provide the browser with information about the file so it can decide whether or not to make a request in the first place.

We can do that by using a `type` attribute on one of our `source` elements. In that attribute, we provide the *Media Type* (formerly MIME type) of the source. These can look a little arcane, but they all follow a predictable `type/subtype` format. For example, the Media Type for a PNG is `image/png`; for a WebP, it's `image/webp`.

With this syntax in place, we tell the browser to disregard a source *unless* it recognizes the contents of a `type` attribute:

```
<picture>
  <source type="image/webp" srcset="pic.webp">
  <img src="pic.png" alt="…">
</picture>
```

That code, for instance, ensures that any browser that supports WebP will get the WebP source, while every other browser will get the PNG (**FIG 2.2**).

One request; no wasted bandwidth. And this is forward-thinking: as newer and more efficient file formats come along, they'll come with Media Types of their own, and we'll be able to take advantage of them thanks to `picture`—no scripts, no server-side dependencies. Just good ol' `img` doing what it does best, with a little help from us.

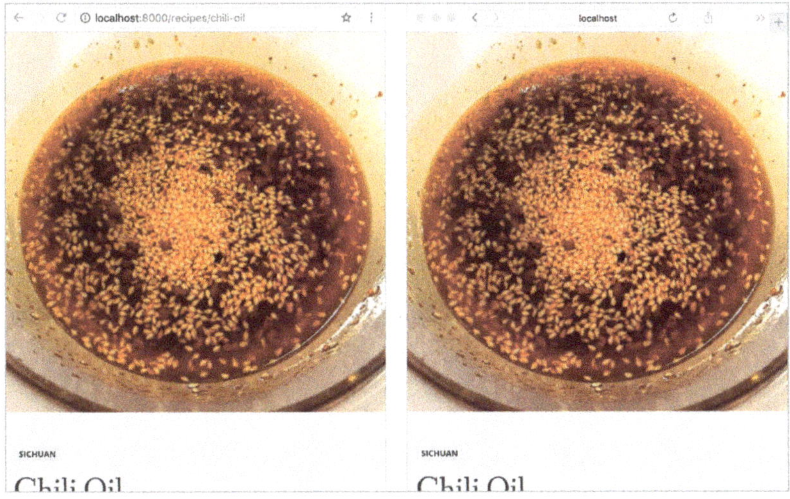

FIG 2.2: Users in Chrome (left) receive an 87 KB WebP, while users in Safari (right) receive a 132 KB JPEG.

Display density

The display density use case is about serving image sources that are appropriate to the hardware resolution of a device's screen—ensuring that only devices with high-resolution displays receive image sources large enough to look sharp, without passing that same bandwidth cost along to users with lower-resolution displays.

This determination hinges on a user's *device pixel ratio* (DPR). DPR is calculated by dividing a viewport's CSS pixels by the device's actual screen resolution, to get the number of real-world hardware pixels that make up a device's display.

For example, `@media(width: 320px)` will match on both an original, non-Retina iPhone and a Retina iPhone 5s—they both have a "normalized" viewport size of 320 × 568 CSS pixels. The actual resolution of the 5s *screen* is twice as high as that of the original iPhone, though: 640 × 1136. So, the original iPhone has a DPR of 1, while the Retina iPhone has a DPR of 2.

Likewise, the Samsung Galaxy S4 has a 1080 × 1920 display—but has a viewport of 360 × 640 CSS pixels. Because the Galaxy S4's actual resolution is three times higher than that of its resolution in CSS, it has a DPR of 3.

You can test this for yourself by opening the developer console of your browser and entering the following:

```
> window.devicePixelRatio
<- 2
```

In any browsing context, an `img` with a width of `100px` set via `width` attribute or CSS will occupy the same amount of the viewport—a normalized, CSS-pixel width of 100px. But in the devices with a DPR greater than 1, the rendered image has the potential to *look* sharper due to the resolution of the screen itself. In order to do so, the image being rendered has to have a natural width of at least 200 pixels. Once scaled down to fit in a 100-pixel space, that 200-pixel image source is rendered with double the pixel density. It won't look any different on a display with a DPR of 1, since that display can't make use of the increased density of the image. On a display with a DPR of 2, however, it'll look nice and sharp.

Once you've got the hang of DPR as a concept, the actual syntax that governs serving low-resolution versus high-resolution image sources is pretty straightforward:

```
<img src="sd.gif" srcset="hd.jpg 2x" alt="…">
```

This `x` syntax inside the `srcset` attribute acts as a suggestion to the browser, pointing out the source most appropriate to the real-world pixel density of the user's display. I say "suggestion" deliberately—but we'll get to that in a bit.

You'll notice that we also used this new attribute—`srcset`—inside the `picture` element, because this syntax can be used on those `source` elements as well:

```
<picture>
  <source media="(min-width: 60em)" srcset="big.jpg
  1x, big-hd.jpg 2x">
```

```
  <source media="(min-width: 25em)" srcset="med.jpg
  1x, med-hd.jpg 2x">
  <img src="small.jpg" srcset="small-hd.jpg 2x"
  alt="…">
</picture>
```

That's a *lot* of syntax, but before you panic: know that I've never actually needed to use this approach on a project. Not because there isn't an appeal to tailoring image assets to both viewport size *and* density—but because there's a much easier way. Weirder, maybe, but ultimately much easier: `sizes`.

Flexible images

So, we have a couple of options for explicit control over sources—and we'll need that sometimes, for sure. But in *most* cases, we want what we've always wanted in a responsive layout: an image that stretches to fit a viewport of any size, the way an `img` element with a single, gigantic source image would—we just want it to be more performant.

The flexible-images use case refers to these situations exactly—situations where we don't need explicit control over which source is shown when. The `sizes` syntax allows us to provide the browser with a couple of sources and some information about them, after which it completely takes the wheel and requests a single source. It's similar to the `type` attribute in that we're providing the browser with information about image sources up front, but different in that the browser uses a much fuzzier set of rules for determining what to do with that information.

Before we get into that syntax and how it works, a caveat: what we're going to cover here is a peek behind the curtain at the way the browser uses these attributes to make its decisions—it's not math you'll ever need to do. Fortunately, the *nature* of the math will be familiar to anyone working on a responsive layout: it ultimately comes down to "target divided by context," the same way we'd size an element in CSS.

But still, if you're as math-averse as I am, take heart: this syntax is strictly declarative. The `sizes` attribute is shorthand

FIG 2.3: These image sources are identical apart from their dimensions, which remain proportional.

for "here is the size of the rendered image in the layout," and the `srcset` attribute is shorthand for "here are the source files, and here are their inherent widths."

So, envision a 1600 × 1200-pixel image uploaded to a CMS, which then generates two more resized versions of that same image on the server: one that is 400 pixels wide, and another that is 800 pixels wide. These sources are identical in appearance, naturally, apart from their dimensions (**FIG 2.3**).

FIG 2.4: At this breakpoint, the largest space this image will ever need to occupy is roughly 25 percent of the viewport. Choosing an image source for this position based on viewport size alone would be tremendously wasteful.

The `sizes` attribute specifies the space the image will occupy in our layout—*not* the size of the user's viewport, as with media queries. After all, the size of the user's viewport doesn't really tell us anything about how an image is meant to be *displayed*, and that's how we want this decision to be made. Sizing an image meant to occupy 25 percent of a layout based on the width of the user's viewport would leave us with a much larger image source than the user will need (**FIG 2.4**).

Let's assume a fairly common instance: a "hero" image, up at the top of a page, occupying a space that spans the entire viewport (**FIG 2.5**). (It makes for easier math, for the sake of discussion.)

```
<img
  sizes="100vw"
  srcset="small.jpg 400w, medium.jpg 800w, large.jpg
  1600w"
  src="fallback.jpg"
  alt="…">
```

In this markup, we're saying *explicitly* that the space the image occupies in the layout has a width of `100vw`—100 percent of the viewport width.

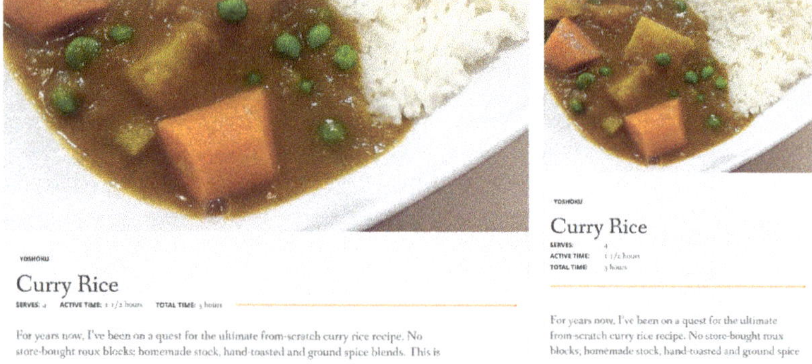

FIG 2.5: The hero image for this recipe page occupies 100 percent of the viewport—so `100vw`.

If we're looking at this markup on a device with a 320-pixel-wide viewport, 100 percent of that is, predictably enough, 320 pixels. That's our context. The browser takes that value—`320px`—and divides all the image-source sizes against it:

- Our smallest image has an inherent size of 400 pixels, so: 400 ÷ 320 = 1.25.
- Our medium image is 800 pixels wide: 800 ÷ 320 = 2.5.
- Our largest image is 1600 pixels wide: 1600 ÷ 320 = 5.

Those final calculations (1.25, 2.5, and 5) are, functionally-speaking, `devicePixelRatio` options—meaning that the browser is left with a set of source options that are *specific to the user's viewport size*. On a 320-pixel-wide viewport, `sizes="100vw"` is functionally equivalent to us writing out the following:

```
<img src="small.jpg 1.25x, medium.jpg 2.5x, large.
  jpg 5x" alt="…">
```

On a device with a `devicePixelRatio` of `2`, the browser would likely choose `medium.jpg`—the closest match to `2x` while erring on the side of not serving the user a blurry image. On a device with a `devicePixelRatio` of `1`, the browser would likely serve us `small.jpg`.

If we were to visit a page using that same `sizes`/`srcset` syntax, with a viewport 640 pixels wide, the result of all that math would be completely different: `100vw` is now `640px`. When we divide our sources' widths against that, we get .625, 1.25, and 2.5. Those newly calculated values would be functionally equivalent to us writing this:

```
<img srcset="small.jpg .625x, medium.jpg 1.25x,
  large.jpg 2.5x" alt="…">
```

On a 640-pixel-wide viewport, our smallest image source will never match; that source is too small for any 640-pixel-wide viewport. Instead, `medium.jpg` will be chosen on `1x` devices, and `large.jpg` will match on `2x` devices.

If that all makes sense on your first read-through, you're in better shape than I was the first time I tried to make sense of it—and I helped write the spec. But it's important to keep in mind that we didn't have to think any of this math through when we wrote that markup: we only had to know our source files, their sizes, and the amount of space the image would occupy in the page.

You can probably already see where that adds up to a more common use case than the explicit breakpoints of `picture` when we're just looking to optimize requests.

Handling breakpoints

There's a little more potential for complication, even when we're just passing information along to the browser and letting it drive our responsive image decisions: a full-width hero image isn't the *least* common use of an `img`, but there's a much better chance that the space our image occupies in a layout is going to change across our layout's breakpoints.

In that case, we need to pass a little more detail along to the browser—and since the size of the image is going to change based on the media queries we're using in our CSS, we'll use media queries here as well.

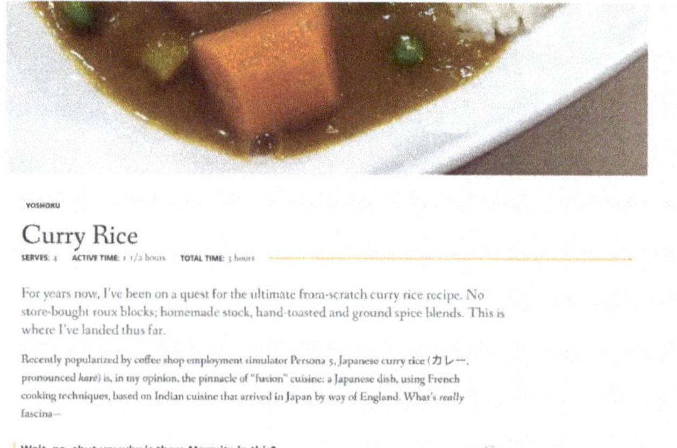

FIG 2.6: Our hero image occupies 100 percent of the available viewport width—until the viewport reaches 1200 pixels.

Let's imagine our hero image occupies 100 percent of the layout—but that layout has a `max-width` of `1200px` (**FIG 2.6**).

If we only used `sizes="100vw"` here, a user visiting the page with a 2000-pixel-wide viewport would get an image source appropriate for rendering *at* 2000 pixels wide. So, instead, we'll use `sizes` to tell the browser the following: on viewports up to 1200 pixels, this will occupy 100 percent of the viewport. On viewports at or above 1200 pixels, this image will occupy a space *exactly* 1200 pixels wide:

```
<img
  sizes="(min-width: 1200px) 1200px, 100vw"
  srcset="small.jpg 400w, medium.jpg 800w, large.jpg
  1600w, x-large.jpg 2400w"
  src="fallback.jpg"
  alt="…">
```

Let's break that value down step by step:

- `(min-width: 1200px)` we know well enough; in CSS, it means "the following applies on viewports wider than 1200 pixels," and that's what it means here.
- The `1200px` that follows is the size of the space our image will occupy on viewports larger than 1200 pixels: `1200px` of the viewport.
- The `100vw`, preceded by a comma, isn't scoped to any media query—and again, just like styles in our CSS that aren't scoped to a media query, these apply unless that `(min-width: 1200px)` criteria is met.

Now, it's important to keep in mind that these values are *first match*—if `(min-width: 1200px)` doesn't match, the browser moves on to the next comma-separated value.

Let's add additional conditions to our `sizes` attribute above and step through them the way a browser would:

```
sizes="(min-width: 1200px) 1200px, (min-width:
800px) 80vw, 100vw"
```

- For a 600-pixel viewport, the browser asks: "Does `(min-width: 1200px)` match? No, moving on. Does `(min-width: 800px)` match? No, moving on. No qualifier. This image will occupy `100vw`."
- For an 850-pixel viewport, the browser asks: "Does `(min-width: 1200px)` match? No, moving on. Does `(min-width: 800px)` match? Yes. This image will occupy `80vw`."
- For a 1400-pixel viewport, the browser asks: "Does `(min-width: 1200px)` match? Yes. This image will occupy a space that is `1200px` wide."

Now, if we had accidentally written that attribute the other way around, we'd have problems. An unqualified `sizes` value—one without a media query—is *always* going to match, at any viewport size. Once the browser encounters it, it throws the rest of the `sizes` attribute away:

```
sizes="100vw, (min-width: 800px) 80vw, (min-width:
1200px) 1200px"
```

- For a 600-pixel viewport, the browser says: "No qualifier. This image will occupy `100vw`."
- For an 850-pixel viewport, the browser says: "No qualifier. This image will occupy `100vw`."
- For a 1400-pixel viewport, the browser says: "No qualifier. This image will occupy `100vw`."

If we had put the `(min-width: 800px)` qualifier before `(min-width: 1200px)`, we'd run into the same sort of problem. A viewport smaller than 800 pixels wouldn't qualify for the values scoped to either `(min-width: 800px)` or `(min-width: 1200px)`, naturally. But a viewport wider than 1200 pixels is *also* going to match `(min-width: 800px)`—if we put that first, the browser stops there:

```
sizes="(min-width: 800px) 80vw, (min-width:
1200px) 1200px, 100vw"
```

- For a 600-pixel viewport, the browser asks: "Does `(min-width: 800px)` match? No, moving on. Does `(min-width: 1200px)` match? No, moving on. No qualifier. This image will occupy `100vw`."
- For an 850-pixel viewport, the browser asks: "Does `(min-width: 800px)` match? Yes. This image will occupy `80vw`."
- For a 1400-pixel viewport, the browser asks: "Does `(min-width: 800px)` match? Yes. This image will occupy `80vw`."

min-width versus max-width

When we use `min-width` media queries in a stylesheet, our unqualified styles represent our first breakpoint. We then override them with our smallest media query's styles, then override those with the next breakpoint up, and so on. Our unqualified styles apply on viewports *smaller* than the scope of our media queries.

We do the opposite when we use `max-width` media queries in a stylesheet: our first `max-width` media query is our first breakpoint, and we go upward from there. Our unqualified styles apply on viewports *larger* than the scope of our media queries.

Just like our CSS, `max-width` media queries in `sizes` will work the same way:

```
sizes="(max-width: 720px) 100vw, (max-width:
1250px) 80vw, 1500px"
```

- For a 600-pixel viewport, the browser asks: "Does `(max-width: 720px)` match? Yes. This image will occupy `100vw`."
- For an 850-pixel viewport, the browser asks: "Does `(max-width: 720px)` match? No, moving on. Does `(max-width: 1250px)` match? Yes. This image will occupy `80vw`."
- For a 1400-pixel viewport, the browser asks: "Does `(max-width: 720px)` match? No, moving on. Does `(max-width: 1250px)` match? No, moving on. No qualifier. This image will occupy `1500px`."

Now, I wouldn't fault you for asking why any of this is happening in an attribute at all. Markup feels like a strange place to encounter media queries, let alone write them—and presumably, the browser knows everything it needs to know about our layout on account of, you know, *rendering our layout*.

But at the time the browser initiates requests for images, it has no other information about the site—it may not have made requests for external stylesheets yet, or had a chance to apply them. Waiting until a page is fully rendered would mean introducing huge delays in requesting image sources—and once loaded, those images could then change the layout, causing a need for recalculation, and new requests for sources, and so on unto infinity.

In terms of `srcset`/`sizes`, we can safely say that the browser only knows a few things when it parses our markup and starts making external requests: the contents of that markup, the size of the viewport, and the pixel density of the display.

I wouldn't blame you for feeling a little wired after all that. These attributes pack an incredible amount of information into precious few characters. Once you learn the *rules* of `srcset` and `sizes`, though, you don't actually have to think much about how the browser makes decisions with those attributes. As a matter of fact, we *can't* know how the browser makes its decisions, given all this information. Believe it or not, that's by design—in fact, it might be the most exciting feature of responsive images.

The "explicitly vague" source-selection algorithm

You may have noticed that all of the responsive image solutions we've discussed only tangentially address the original problem we aimed to solve: serving bandwidth-appropriate assets to users.

From a syntax standpoint, telling the browser "use this source on a high-resolution display" or "here's some information, pick the right one for this viewport" is relatively easy—but knowing when a user *wants* high-resolution images is impossible. If I'm on a top-of-the-line MacBook but tethered to my phone's internet connection, using shaky airplane WiFi, or browsing the web by way of a metered connection, I might want to opt out of high-resolution image sources, regardless of my screen's capabilities.

These syntaxes can ensure that we're serving image assets more efficiently, but they can't do anything to address bandwidth concerns *directly*—and not for lack of trying. Members of the RICG and beyond spent a lot of time talking through how we could tailor assets to a user's bandwidth and what kind of syntax might make the most sense for that, revisiting the subject over and over. A server-side solution could give us an assumption based on the device, but a mobile device can be on anything from EDGE to WiFi.

We came up with what seemed like a perfectly sensible solution: a bandwidth media query. And after our initial excitement wore off, well—we came to hate our own idea.

We quickly realized we couldn't possibly ensure a consistent browsing experience for the user this way. Within the scope of a single project, sure—we could maintain a consistent bandwidth-based "breakpoint" for things like high-density images. But across the web, the browsing experience would be wildly inconsistent. Where *I* set that bandwidth breakpoint is different from where others might set it—a user could end up with high-resolution images on one site and low-resolution images on the next.

Worse still, we'd be making all of this optional: one more thing to test, one more thing to go wrong, one more thing for us developers to keep in mind—or to forget. In cases where that media query was omitted, or set too high, the web would still *feel* broken to end users—slow and inconsiderate about bandwidth usage. On other pages, the web would *look* broken: unaware of the compromise being made on their behalf, a user would only know that they were seeing grainy images on their high-density display—something that wouldn't be the case on sites that set their bandwidth breakpoint a little higher.

There's a technical problem, too. Media queries feel like the right fit for bandwidth considerations, seeing as they're already designed to respond to client-side concerns—viewport height and width, device orientation, hardware features like ambient light level, and OS-level accessibility settings. But media queries are designed to respond to *changes* on the client side, and bandwidth can be unpredictable.

For example, when a user first lands on a page, they might qualify for our high-resolution images, then have their bandwidth drop off as they go through a tunnel. Now we have to send them low-resolution images, because that media query told the browser to listen for client-side bandwidth changes. As their connection speeds back up, we have to send them the high-resolution images again.

The only way to work around this would be to change the expected behavior of media queries from a guarantee ("if the viewport is smaller than 600 pixels, this will happen") to a potentiality ("if the viewport is smaller than 600 pixels, this may or may not happen"). That guarantee was the very thing that made media queries a natural fit for the art-direction use case: the `source` element that matches the `media` attribute we specify is the one that has to be used, full stop. Otherwise, we might end up with an image source that's inappropriate for the current layout.

But `srcset` is a syntax that's brand-new to the web, with no expected behaviors to redefine. So, the HTML5 specification defines `srcset` as a set of *candidates*. Any and all decisions about their use are left up to the browser, due to a critical feature of the selection algorithm encoded in the specification: once all the math has been done, and the sources and their descriptors have been sorted, the browser is free to do whatever it wants.

The syntaxes certainly *seem* declarative, but in practice, we're saying, "here is a source visually appropriate for devices with a `devicePixelRatio` of `2`"—not "here is the source to use on devices with a `devicePixelRatio` of `2`." The difference is slight in print, but huge in implication: nothing we include in `srcset` is a *command*, only a *candidate*.

That lack of explicit control can sound a little scary at face value, but `srcset`—using either the `devicePixelRatio` or `sizes` syntaxes—ultimately comes down to requesting one from a list of identical-looking sources. Because of that, there's very little room for an experience to seem *broken*, regardless of the decisions made by the browser.

By acting as a list of suggestions, `srcset` allows browsers to introduce user settings like "always give me low-res images"—something mobile Chrome's "data saver" mode does today. It paves the way for settings like "give me high-res images as bandwidth permits"—instead of instructing browsers to frantically respond to changes in bandwidth from one site to another, the browser can take an average across a given time frame or browsing session. Instead of developers drawing the line between delivering high- or low-resolution assets, with each of us landing in different places, those decisions can be made *by* the user, not *for* them.

It also means there's room for the browser to get creative—for example, in some browsers, an `img` or `source` marked up with the `srcset`/`sizes` syntax will never fire a request for a smaller source than the user already has in their browser's cache. After all, what would be the point in making a new request for a source with smaller dimensions, when the browser already has an identical-looking image that works for those viewport sizes? If the user scales their viewport up to the point where a new image is needed, that request will still get made—we want things to look seamless for them, after all, and upscaling a too-small image would look wrong.

The fact that we can't know for certain how `srcset`/`sizes` will behave to the end user? That's this use case's strongest feature.

MIXING AND MATCHING

There's one last aspect of the four responsive-image use cases I want to go over: combining them. We touched on it briefly early on, with `picture` using `srcset`'s `devicePixelRatio` syntax on its `source` elements to provide both art direction *and* sources tailored to a user's display density.

Any and *all* of the four use cases can be used in concert:

```
<picture>
  <source
    media="(min-width: 1280px)"
    sizes="50vw"
    srcset="nomad-wide-200.webp 200w,
        nomad-wide-400.webp 400w,
        nomad-wide-800.webp 800w,
        nomad-wide-1200.webp 1200w,
        nomad-wide-1600.webp 1600w,
        nomad-wide-2000.webp 2000w"
    type="image/webp">
  <source
    sizes="(min-width: 640px) 60vw, 100vw"
    srcset="nomad-crop-200.webp 200w,
        nomad-crop-400.webp 400w,
        nomad-crop-800.webp 800w,
        nomad-crop-1200.webp 1200w,
        nomad-crop-1600.webp 1600w,
        nomad-crop-2000.webp 2000w"
    type="image/webp">
  <source
    media="(min-width: 1280px)"
    sizes="50vw"
    srcset="nomad-wide-200.jpg 200w,
        nomad-wide-400.jpg 400w,
```

```
            nomad-wide-800.jpg 800w,
            nomad-wide-1200.jpg 1200w,
            nomad-wide-1600.jpg 1600w,
            nomad-wide-2000.jpg 2000w">
      <img
        src="nomad-crop-400.jpg" alt="An orange-coated
      shiba inu in the snow."
        sizes="(min-width: 640px) 60vw, 100vw"
        srcset="nomad-crop-200.jpg 200w,
            nomad-crop-400.jpg 400w,
            nomad-crop-800.jpg 800w,
            nomad-crop-1200.jpg 1200w,
            nomad-crop-1600.jpg 1600w,
            nomad-crop-2000.jpg 2000w">
    </picture>
```

This monster of markup tells the browser:

- Using `type`, determine whether to use the `source` elements that reference WebP or standard JPEG images.
- Within each branch of that decision, use `media` as the selection criterion for each art-directed `source`.
- Once the final `source` has been selected, choose from a list of candidate sources inside the `srcset` attribute, with `sizes` describing the space the image will occupy within that range of viewport sizes.
- If none of the `source` elements apply due to the current viewport size and/or browser's WebP support, render the inner `img` as-is, using `srcset`/`sizes`.
- If none of the responsive-image markup patterns are supported by the user's browser, render the `src` of the inner `img` element.
- If the user is navigating by way of assistive technologies, narrate "an orange-coated shiba inu in the snow."

Now, I can say with some certainty that you'll never need to do this—I know I've never even come *close*. `srcset`/`sizes` on a single `img` is generally all I need, with only the occasional `picture` interlude.

I say all this to point out how much has changed in just a few short years: from a single method of showing a single image source, with no opportunity to apply any conditional logic, to an *incredible* number of mix-and-match options for smarter asset delivery, with all of the performance, accessibility, and reliability of our old friend `img`.

With so many options at our disposal—and with even the most common single use case being a little unintuitive—I wouldn't blame you for feeling a bit rattled. I certainly was, seeing the code snippet above for the very first time: not only would I be stuck *using* all of this in my day-to-day work, but I would know exactly whom to blame for such a sprawling syntax: me.

HOW I LEARNED TO STOP WORRYING AND LOVE RESPONSIVE IMAGES

I've mentioned a few times that some of these syntaxes aren't for *us*, so much as they're for computers. They're terse by necessity—that much was apparent early on in the specification process. Anything we might have done to make these syntaxes a little less dense—and more easily parsed by us humans—could have made them more complex for a browser to parse. Adding complexity to a parser translates to more potential for bugs, or for unintentional differences in behavior from one browser to another.

But as much as that density feels like a syntactical weakness when we're rooting through all this markup by hand, it reveals itself to be a strength in practice: a syntax more easily read by machines is a syntax more easily *written* by them.

Creating alternate cuts of an image, outside of manual art direction, is a task that content management systems (CMS) have been handling for us since time immemorial—you'd be hard-pressed to find a mainstream CMS that doesn't offer something in the way of "thumbnails" generated from uploaded images, whether natively or via plugin. It isn't much of a stretch to imagine that pattern extended just a little further, allowing the CMS to generate all of the images we could want to populate a `srcset` attribute, and—knowing all of the sizes it was told to generate—the syntax to match.

WordPress was one of the earliest adopters of native responsive-images markup, starting in version 4.4, and it does exactly that:

> *A new default intermediate size,* `medium_large`, *has been added to better take advantage of responsive image support. The new size is 768px wide by default, with no height limit, and can be used like any other size available in WordPress. As it is a standard size, it will only be generated when new images are uploaded or sizes are regenerated with third party plugins.*

Whether via CMS, a task runner like Grunt or Gulp, or even a third-party service like Cloudinary, `srcset` is a relatively simple case for automation.

`sizes` is a little harder. Since it should refer to the *displayed* size of the image, it doesn't lend itself well to defaults.

Now, this doesn't mean `sizes` doesn't have a default *behavior*. If that attribute is left empty, or omitted altogether, the browser will assume a `sizes` value of `100vw`, in order to err on the side of excessively large images rather than images that could appear distorted. This doesn't *prevent* potential visual issues, though: by telling the browser than an image is meant to occupy 100 percent of the available viewport width, the browser will attempt to use it as the image's natural width. Unless acted on by CSS—using a maximum `width` on either the `img` or its container—that image could be scaled beyond its source's maximum size.

This led to a default `sizes` attribute in the WordPress implementation:

```
(max-width: {{image-width}}px) 100vw, {{image-
  width}}px
```

In other words: "`100vw`, up to a viewport width equal to the width of the uploaded image; beyond that, a fixed width equal to the image's natural width." This ensures that the behavior of the `img` more or less matches the behavior of an `img` with a `src` pointing at the uploaded image. And, of course, the WordPress team provided an API hook that allows authors to supply their own `sizes` attributes within their templates.

That would still mean *writing* that attribute by hand, but tools have popped up to abstract that away, and with an efficiency we could never match by hand: the RespImageLint project, for example, provides you with a bookmarklet that vets your `sizes` attributes for accuracy and efficiency, and provides suggestions for potential improvements. Even as steeped as I am in this topic, I never leave home without it.

On a personal site, I recently encountered the following situation: I had written, manually, what I thought to be a perfectly respectable `sizes` attribute, based on a little back-of-napkin math, performed by my perfectly average human brain:

```
(min-width: 1480px) 935px, (min-width: 800px) 64vw,
  98vw
```

Close enough, I figured. A pass through RespImgLint, however, resulted in the following:

```
(min-width: 1560px) calc(-1.25vw + 358px), (min-
  width: 760px) calc(21.03vw + 14px), (min-width:
  500px) 47.5vw, 97.22vw
```

That's math I could never have hoped to reason through, considering the degree to which I struggle when it comes time to calculate a tip. But by simulating the resizing of a browser window and calculating the precise space each `img` element occupies in a page's layout at each viewport size, RespImageLint suggests an incredibly tailored `sizes` attribute—which, in terms of asset delivery, would no doubt be just a hair more efficient than mine. And with countless users loading countless pages, a kilobyte here or there can certainly add up.

But that's not the entire appeal for me. See, by not writing these attributes by hand—by using a tool like RespImgLint to generate a hyper-optimized `sizes` value, plus a task runner or CMS to generate alternate image cuts and a corresponding `srcset` value, and with a template engine to bind it all together for me—I barely have to think about responsive images at all these days.

They're no less important, of course. I still get to provide users with an experience that feels tailored, in a completely invisible way—they'll never know what responsive-image use cases I sought to address for them, or how I went about doing it. Nothing will look any different from any other site they've encountered over the years: their images will look as sharp as their display (and their eyes) will allow. Those images will be sized the way our layouts dictate—the way users have come to expect from a well-crafted website.

But our sites will feel faster. And as these techniques propagate more and more, the web *itself* will feel faster, with no cost to the people using it—no drawbacks, no compromises, no hacks, and no grainy images.

CONCLUSION

In a way, this book was to be my images-on-the-web swan song. The RICG's work on images has long since concluded, its members scattering to work on browsers and CDNs and CMSes, to write guides and tutorials, to give talks and lead workshops. Together, they're pushing the web toward something better, faster, and more inclusive, whether they're building the tools or teaching others how to use them.

I had this conclusion all mapped out in my head, because the contents of it were, sadly, already second nature. I was going to wrap things up the way I've concluded so many talks and blog posts about how images work on the web: with a plea. Try harder; do better. Websites keep getting larger, month after month, and image transfers are still responsible for most of the damage. The web is becoming more exclusive—something for the few, for those with the same browsing privilege as the people building it. We developers are *severing* peoples' connections to the web, rather than helping to build them. I'd sound the call-to-arms: we have to try harder. We have the tools; we need to use them. We can do better. We *have* to do better. Can't you see that we're *losing*?

But, in reviewing statistics from HTTP Archive, I saw something I've never seen before: during the course of 2018, the median image transfer size has been declining month to month.

We *are* doing better.

The momentum, finally, might just be on our side, thanks to countless hours of work by countless developers, designers, educators, and writers—and thanks to you. You're someone who believes that anything worth doing is worth doing well. You're someone who doesn't take anything for granted—not even a topic as "simple" as putting images on the web.

I wrote this book for you. But you—you're writing this ending for me.

ACKNOWLEDGMENTS

I can't believe they let me do this *again*.

The "they" in question is, of course, the team at A Book Apart. They're a "they" of incredible talent, patience, and—apart from *me*, the one glaring blemish on their otherwise impeccable record—taste in authors. Katel, Jeffrey, and Jason: thank you so, so much for this opportunity, and for so many others.

Lisa Maria Martin, my editor: thank you for so diligently holding me to account for deadlines. Lisa Maria Martin, my girlfriend: thank you for encouraging me to blow off those deadlines every once in a while. As always, and as in all things: I couldn't do it without you.

Finally, to the RICG:

To Eric Portis, my technical editor, whose writing on the subject of responsive images has always far eclipsed my own.

To Yoav Weiss and Marcos Caceres, who did all the heavy lifting from the very start.

To every one of you—every member of the nebulous, pirate-radio web standards group who managed to change the way the web is built through sheer determination.

And to you, reader, for fighting the good fight.

Thank you.

RESOURCES

Now what? Well, there are a couple pages you can turn to for the next step in your image-performance choose-your-own-adventure story.

If you want to dig even further into the topic of image formats, I've got good news: even with as much as we've covered here, we're still just *barely* scratching the surface. *High-Performance Images*—which counts a number of RICG members in its list of authors—will take you even further into the realm of encodings, algorithms, and quirks. Jeremy Wagner's *The WebP Manual* is absolutely required reading.

If you can't get enough of responsive images, well, who could blame you? Eric Portis, who was kind enough to provide technical editing for this book, is a prolific writer on the subject himself:

- "Responsive Images in Practice"
- "Srcset and Sizes"
- "Responsive Images Done Right"

It probably goes without saying, but Scott Jehl's *Responsible Responsive Web Design* and Ethan Marcotte's *Responsive Design: Patterns & Principles* are both absolutely essential reads, on the topic of images and so much more.

REFERENCES: IMAGE PERFORMANCE

Shortened URLs are numbered sequentially; the related long URLs are listed below for reference.

Introduction

00-01 https://www.httparchive.org/reports/page-weight?start=2017_04_01&end=latest

00-02 http://radar.oreilly.com/2014/01/web-performance-is-user-experience.html

00-03 http://www.pewinternet.org/fact-sheet/mobile/

00-04 http://www.pewinternet.org/2015/04/01/us-smartphone-use-in-2015/

00-05 https://www.ericsson.com/assets/local/mobility-report/documents/2016/ericsson-mobility-report-feb-2016-interim.pdf

Chapter 1

01-01 https://bugs.chromium.org/p/chromium/issues/detail?id=791658

01-02 https://en.wikipedia.org/wiki/Discrete_cosine_transform

01-03 https://www.toptal.com/developers/sorting-algorithms

01-04 https://github.com/kornelski/dssim

01-05 https://cloudinary.com/blog/progressive_jpegs_and_green_martians

Chapter 2

02-01 https://andydavies.me/blog/2013/10/22/how-the-browser-pre-loader-makes-pages-load-faster/

02-02 https://developer.mozilla.org/en-US/docs/Web/HTTP/Basics_of_HTTP/MIME_types

02-03 https://make.wordpress.org/core/2015/11/10/responsive-images-in-wordpress-4-4/

02-04 https://github.com/ausi/RespImageLint

Conclusion

03-01 https://www.httparchive.org/reports/page-weight?start=2018_01_01&end=latest#bytesImg

Resources

04-01 http://shop.oreilly.com/product/0636920039730.do

04-02 https://www.smashingmagazine.com/ebooks/the-webp-manual/

04-03 https://alistapart.com/article/responsive-images-in-practice

04-04 https://ericportis.com/posts/2014/srcset-sizes/

04-05 https://www.smashingmagazine.com/2014/05/responsive-images-done-right-guide-picture-srcset/

04-06 https://abookapart.com/products/responsible-responsive-design

04-07 https://abookapart.com/products/responsive-design-patterns-principles

INDEX: IMAGE PERFORMANCE

ABOUT THE AUTHOR

Mat "Wilto" Marquis is an amateur boxer, aspiring chef, halfway decent carpenter, and passable antique British motorcycle mechanic—when not making fast, accessible, responsive websites. He keeps busy.

As chair of the Responsive Issues Community Group, Mat spearheaded the effort to bring native responsive image solutions to the HTML5 specification, later going on to facilitate browser implementations and oversee the addition of native responsive image techniques to major CMSes. He has spoken at An Event Apart, edited for *A List Apart,* and published *JavaScript for Web Designers* with A Book Apart, completing what he describes as "like an EGOT, but for putting semicolons in the right places."

10

PRACTICAL PAIR PROGRAMMING

JASON GARBER

Publisher: Jeffrey Zeldman
Designer: Jason Santa Maria
Executive director: Katel LeDû
Managing editor: Lisa Maria Marquis
Editors: Sally Kerrigan, Danielle Small
Technical editor: David Khourshid
Book producer: Ron Bilodeau

ISBN: 978-1-937557-96-6

A Book Apart
New York, New York
http://abookapart.com

TABLE OF CONTENTS: PRACTICAL PAIR PROGRAMMING

Dedicated to the memory of Michael J. Sharp
(my college pair prankster),
and his pair UN investigator, Zaida Catalán.
May peace and justice prevail where they have blazed a trail.

FOREWORD

THERE'S A COMMON MISCONCEPTION that software engineering is an individual's job: one person at one computer writing code. While companies can successfully operate under this practice, they're missing out on all of the benefits pair programming has to offer.

Two heads are better than one. Collaboration leads to more creative solutions. Fewer mistakes are found in the code. If these are all benefits to pair programming, why don't we see more companies take advantage of it? Maybe because it's a new way of thinking about writing code—and it takes practice to get it right.

Let *Practical Pair Programming* be your guide to integrating this methodology into your everyday process. Jason clearly lays out the fundamentals: what is and isn't considered pair programming, the benefits the practice can bring to your work and team, and how to successfully configure a pair programming environment for both in-office and remote teams.

Jason also provides actionable advice on how to improve the pair programming experience for both yourself and your partner, from the perspective of someone who's spent hours at it himself. The guidance he offers here will provide you with the tools you need to make pair programming in your company both an effective and enjoyable experience. Whether you're a seasoned manager or new to your team, *Practical Pair Programming* will set you up for success.

— Kelly Vaughn

INTRODUCTION

IN THIS BOOK YOU'LL find practical advice on pair programming for the beginning programmer, experienced software engineer, team lead, or engineering manager. Everything I've written comes from my own pairing experience, having worked as a developer on teams that were resistant to Agile and Extreme Programming (XP) practices, up through becoming a manager of a successful software development firm.

Bigger and more mission-critical software projects require larger, more diverse teams. Counter-intuitively, the greater the number of contributors on any one project, the harder it is to coordinate and finish software on deadline. Pair programming perhaps strikes the ideal balance between solo work and software development processes that need a giant flowchart to be understood: not too rogue and not too rigid; nimble but without the risk of having just one pilot in the cockpit.

Can successful software be made by one super-smart solo programmer? Sure! But in my experience, pairing is safer and more enjoyable than working alone. In fact, as I think back to my big mistakes as a programmer or the times my company's projects went off the rails (and we had to write off hundreds of thousands of dollars), it's almost universally attributable to solo programming.

What pair programming isn't

Pairing doesn't mean doubling the cost to get the same output. I like to say it's the same cost for a product that's twice as good! So why do people say pair programming isn't efficient? Developer Sean Killeen posits that they're not thinking of the long-term velocity and overall team effectiveness:

> *I think it's because lots of people think short-term when they say "efficient." I program faster alone, and more effectively when not alone because I'm optimizing for the system and team rather than myself. (http://bkaprt.com/ppp/00-01/)*

Pair programming also isn't "backseat typing." An unfair balance of control at the terminal will be more annoying than a backseat driver in your car. In Chapter 2, we'll go over ways to ensure you and your pair get equal time driving and keep your commentary constructive.

Finally, pairing isn't about group code review. You may think it's more efficient to have people work individually, then revise with a buddy, but this isn't a creative writing class. Two people need to be involved in the creative process together, from inception through development, to capture all the benefits of pairing.

What pair programming is

Pair programming is two developers working on the same code using shared controls. In Chapter 1, we'll cover the many benefits pair programming offers, including higher-quality code, improved team communication and cohesion, and overall work satisfaction.

When two people are at the controls writing code, twice the empathy is employed for your users, teammates, and future selves. With two different sets of experience, you can train one another. If one of you needs to step away, the other can keep things moving briefly. And when something goes wrong, two brains are better able to solve the problem calmly and professionally.

How this book is structured

I'd recommend you skim the whole book to get the lay of the land. Then feel free to jump around and dig into whichever parts are most salient for you and your team.

Chapter 1 discusses why you should pair program: the benefits to yourself, your team, and your work product.

Chapter 2 lays down some fundamentals of getting started with pair programming—how you make the radical change from solitary, silent work to collaborating as an engaged, dynamic, and conversational duo, and avoiding pitfalls.

Chapter 3 helps you be the best pairing partner you can be and bring out the best in others so pairing is a sustainable source of productivity and joy. The approaches I present will help you become a better collaborator, even if you don't end up pairing much.

Chapter 4 deals with the nuts and bolts of getting set up for pairing to mitigate fatigue as best you can. A common complaint is that pair programming is exhausting, due in no small part to a physical or virtual workspace that's not set up with pairing in mind.

Chapter 5 looks at pairing in the context of a team and making it a part of your team culture without triggering a backlash. We then go on to explore ways that pairing on the team can get stagnant and how pairing feeds into a larger concept of the Community of Practice.

By the end of the book, I hope you'll be sold on the value of pair programming, and even more so, internalize the values that make pair programming so enjoyable. I want you to know what it feels like to work with colleagues who are eager to exchange knowledge, care more about quality work than their egos, are reflective and insightful, and want to see everyone's contributions valued. If these colleagues don't sound familiar, this book will help you be an example to your team, help move them in the right direction, or perhaps find a different team of well-adjusted humans that deserve your presence.

Pair programming changes you (in my opinion, for the better). Read on, and I'll show why that is.

WHY PAIR PROGRAM?

Together—one of the most inspiring words in the English language. Coming together is a beginning; keeping together is progress; working together is success.

—ATTRIBUTED TO EDWARD EVERETT HALE, NINETEENTH CENTURY AUTHOR, HISTORIAN, AND UNITARIAN MINISTER (http://bkaprt.com/ppp/01-01/)

COMPUTER PROGRAMMING HAS HISTORICALLY been seen as an individual effort. Time on the old mainframes was parceled out individually, and workers with more standing got higher priority. For decades, the stereotypical office has been made of cubicle walls and PCs—*personal* computers. Not sharing a computer has been an unwritten rule for nearly fifty years.

For some reason, the myth persists that computer people just aren't cut out for working together. Software architect and Agile transformation consultant Allen Holub remarked on Twitter:

> *It's interesting that, even though there is hard research showing that most people find pair programming...MORE enjoyable than working alone, a very vocal minority on twitter says that programmers can never work effectively with other people. (http://bkaprt.com/ppp/01-02/)*

The prevailing sentiment in the business world seems to be that technologists don't *want* to collaborate. Meetings waste time that could be spent pounding out lines of code. It's true that many programmers treat work like a maximization exercise: get as much compensation for as little risk and effort as possible. The problem I see with this approach is it reduces programmers to little more than machines themselves; even brilliant programmers are likely to plateau under these conditions.

Pair programming as a practice emerged from a subset of Agile methodology called Extreme Programming (XP), a set of human-centered software development practices that offers validation for bringing communication, simplicity, feedback, courage, and respect to your work. In my experience, it's been far more fulfilling than slogging through code on my own; I want to bring my whole self to work and learn from active collaboration with smart people. Beyond personal growth and fulfillment, the shift to pairing also brings forth improvements in team cohesion, clarity around business goals, and even produces better code. Here's how.

BETTER CODE, BETTER OUTCOMES

If more computing power or faster typing was all it took to ship software faster, you can bet we'd have a supercomputer on every desk and programmers would be hired by typing test, but in reality, a programmer who types 20 percent faster isn't going to be 20 percent more productive. Critical thinking, problem solving, and quick recall make up the majority of our effort. Producing lines of code isn't the objective—it's just the means for attaining the real objectives: correct business logic and intuitive user interfaces.

A second pair of eyes can catch a missing semicolon or find that single-character difference that is failing your test, but much more important than catching typos are the decisions that can't be caught by a linter or compiler. A second brain helps you give good names to classes, methods, and variables and write clearer documentation. It gives the pair enough headroom to think about architecture, apply helpful design patterns, and sometimes even come at a problem from an entirely new angle. It means you'll think through more edge cases in your business logic and have twice the empathy for users as you design how they'll interact with your software. Having twice the brain power is much more important than twice the fingers.

At Promptworks, we've observed that having a pair is not noticeably faster or slower than two individuals working independently over a short period of time (like an hour or four). In a 1999 controlled experiment in a classroom setting, Dr. Laurie Williams found pair programming took a team about 15 percent more developer hours than working as individuals. However, she found defects to be 15 percent lower, design quality higher, and the project completed in 45 percent less calendar time (http://bkaprt.com/ppp/01-03/, PDF).

Pairing helps a software team go faster in the long run because it avoids common hindrances:

- **Coordination costs.** Two programmers working on two copies of the same software have to plan what each will work on, resolve conflicts when they both touch the same part of the codebase, and read the changes that others have made so their future work takes it into account. With pairing, you're working on the same copy of the software, and you're both aware of how it's changing in real time. There are no merge conflicts between the two of you, nor catching up on what the other did.
- **Thinking through a problem twice.** A solo developer who needs her code reviewed will have to revisit the problem, explain her approach, and rationalize the solution to the other developers. Some of them may revisit the paths that she already eliminated. Unilateral decision-making is a genuine risk, but the need for code review strongly points to pair programming as a more efficient and less antagonistic alternative. Why have two sets of eyeballs looking at the code serially when they could be in parallel? By working together from the outset, you can avoid thinking it through twice and move on to the rest of your long list of features.
- **Throwing away work.** The better designed and built the software is, the longer its life and the more adaptable to changing business needs. Building the components of a sophisticated asset in silos and then expecting the resulting amalgamation to work optimally is a recipe for having to throw it away and build a new solution much too soon. Worse than the cost of replacement is the lost revenue when software can't change fast enough, holds back the workforce using it, or creates a costly security breach.

PERSONAL ACCOUNTABILITY

When pairing, you have a partner who holds you accountable and doesn't let you get away with lazy thinking, uncertainty, or failing to recognize the merit of your accomplishments. You hold yourself to your own professional expectations just by having someone hear your thoughts. It helps you live up to your potential, as software engineer Sarah Mei observed after pairing full-time for two months at Pivotal Labs:

> *Fundamentally, what I love about software development is writing code that people actually use. I love to finish things. So anything that makes me feel like I'm really [getting stuff done] makes me incredibly happy.*
>
> *When people talk about pairing, you hear a lot about how it "amplifies" their productivity. I am going to go on record with the truth, however. Pairing does not amplify my productivity. Instead, it erases all the bad habits I have that keep me from being a superstar on my own.*
>
> *When I'm pairing, I can really get shit done. (http://bkaprt.com/ppp/01-04/)*

Pairing is synchronous, so a person—not a deadline—is your reason to show up on time and not zone out as the mid-afternoon doldrums set in. You can help each other remember to take breaks, eat lunch, and time-box your code spikes. Even the most scrupulous developer is sometimes tempted to skip writing tests under pressure or move on before refactoring code.

"Pair pressure"—the best kind of peer pressure!—can help you avoid the bad habits that keep you from being a superstar programmer:

- **Acting on first impulses.** In your zeal to solve a problem, you are likely to try the first approach that comes to mind. By having to jointly negotiate how to approach the problem, you'll evaluate more alternatives within a pair than you would individually.
- **Rabbit holes.** Sometimes you spend too much time digging into a problem that doesn't really need to be solved right away. Your pair can help you see when you're getting in the weeds and excavating pointlessly.
- **Distractions.** Focus and a state of flow are critical to doing your best work. There's always a temptation to scroll through Instagram while the computer does the work, but pairing encourages sustained attention to the work at hand. While waiting for tests to run, you can talk about the prob-

lem, discuss what you're planning to do next, or look at the backlog together.

- **Cutting corners.** When your estimates are too optimistic or you feel guilty for having gone down a particularly deep rabbit hole, you may be tempted to make up for lost time by skipping the writing of tests, implementing only the happy path, or not giving attention to security. Your pair can be the angel on your shoulder, reminding you to do what's right.
- **Fear and shame.** Solo programmers lose time worrying whether they're right. They're afraid of looking foolish, making the wrong choice, or overlooking something that might seem obvious. A pair can piece together enough knowledge to feel confident that they're right—or admit when they can't figure it out! The rest of the team is more likely to trust the decisions a pair made because there was already some level of discussion, deliberation, and agreement.
- **Getting too clever.** Pairing can provide a shared commitment to pragmatism and levelheadedness that those who have to deal with your code, tests, and comments later will appreciate. Don't get me wrong—we use funny fake names all over our test code and documentation. But hopefully, your pair will stop you before you name a class `AbstractInterceptorDrivenBeanDefinitionDecorator` (classic Java Spring framework nonsense!) or write your own encryption function (utterly irresponsible foolishness!).

TEAM COHESION

Better code and more productivity should be an easy sell to any boss who needs at least two developers, particularly one who feels anxiety about the team's "bus factor"—a macabre but memorable metric for how concentrated the team's skills and project-specific knowledge are. What happens if the dev who hoarded all database work gets hit by a bus, or bitten by a badger? (My team is trying to make "badger factor" a thing.)

Pair programming reduces the team's reliance on one or two superstars, and even very similar developers who pair will discover strengths and knowledge they didn't know the other had. Other team-strengthening benefits accumulate with each project:

- **Learning new tools.** Over many years, we develop our own code manipulation habits and style. Good pairing can teach you better, more efficient ways to use your tools. If you've used the modal text editor Vim, for example, you can imagine how pairing with another Vim user could make you more efficient (or if you wanted to try Vim, how pairing would make it less daunting).
- **Providing hands-on training.** Like learning to speak a foreign language, you haven't really learned any new software language or pattern until you're able to produce it yourself. Seeing it done isn't enough, but working it out by yourself is often difficult and inefficient. Pairing is the perfect in-between.
- **Developing your own best practices.** You naturally converge on a set of conventions and good habits without needing to write a style guide or have a manager dictate best practices (a.k.a. "the way we did things when I was a developer").

With the expanded knowledge base that comes as a side effect of pair programming, every member of a team can become comfortable working in any part of the app, or at least be intentional about learning what is needed to become so.

PAIRING KEEPS YOU ENGAGED AND FULFILLED

It's great that pairing makes for better code, air-tight business logic, more intuitive user interfaces, less time being sidetracked while simultaneously building up your team—but even if none of that were true, I would still want to pair because it's fun!

Maybe it's just my work style, but I like having someone with whom I can process thoughts. I like piggybacking on my partner's ideas to come up with the best solution. The synergy gives me energy and pairing feels like an activity worthy of my time. I can stick with hard problems longer when I have a partner and accomplish big things with what feels like little effort.

Pairing deepens your appreciation for the work itself. Clients or superiors can appreciate the result but probably won't celebrate the little victories with you along the way. Your partner gives you an incentive to do the little things right and maybe even show off a little bit.

You have more courage when pairing. Software engineer Nadia Odunayo tweeted,

> *You need to play around with stuff and do silly things to learn. There's a whole class of actions you just don't take when pair programming either because you consciously or subconsciously censor them out...I think it should be the main way all production development takes place. (http://bkaprt.com/ppp/01-05/)*

Humans are meant to work together. Being given one task at a time to perform in a solitary bubble goes against how humans have been productive for millennia, so why should we accept this approach in software development—especially considering the high cost of mistakes?

Hopefully, at least a few of these reasons are compelling enough that you want to give pair programming a try. Now, let's see how it's done.

GETTING STARTED

YOU DON'T TAKE ON the 10-meter dive at your first visit to the pool, and neither do you need to plunge into spending all your working time as part of a pair. Pairing is a very different style of working; wade in gradually, timebox your pairing sessions around specific goals, and give yourself (and your teammates) time to adapt.

Nothing about pairing is particularly hard, but an open mind is crucial. In this chapter, we'll walk through some of the tips and tricks that I've seen from successful pairs. Be ready to bring your whole self to the task as you and your partner adjust.

WHEN TO PAIR

It makes the most sense to work as a pair when you're making decisions and dealing with complexity. That encompasses most of what we do as programmers, even when we're not writing actual code, so it might surprise you to hear that full-time pairing isn't the goal. As a practical matter, at my company we aim for 50 percent pairing. Everyone gets exhausted by pairing to some degree or another. Yes, the more experience you have pairing, the stronger those muscles become and the more endurance you'll have. The more of an extrovert you are, the more naturally it comes. But it doesn't always make sense to pair and even when it does, it might not be practical to get a pair's undivided attention.

Not-quite-pairing

The work quality is always better with a pair, but if you can't get a pair or you're looking to start with a few baby steps, these are some alternatives that are better than nothing.

- Having someone talk through a problem with you for fifteen minutes before diving into a solo task can be enormously helpful. Sometimes a brief conversation will save you days of building something the wrong way.
- "Rubber ducking," or talking something through to understand it better, is another thing we sometimes do in our

office. Even if the listener has little knowledge of the problem domain (or happens to be a yellow plastic bath toy), just articulating it can help solve the problem.

- You might try "passive pairing," where both people are working separately but look at the shared screens often enough to keep up with what's happening on the other side. You don't get nearly as much benefit as active pairing because you're not engaged in the same creative act, but at least you can't get as far down a bad path as you might on your own.

Passive pairing is a weak form of pairing and is best suited to programming tasks that aren't super critical. It runs dangerously close to what software engineering and process coach Alex Harms calls "side-by-side pairing," where the advanced developer works on something else and the person who is identified as "junior" does all the work and gets to ask questions once in a while. "We call things like this pair programming," says Alex, "and then people say, 'Pair programming sucks and I don't want to do it.' Duh! Pair programming takes work!" (http://bkaprt.com/ppp/02-01/, video)

These alternatives can be helpful when you can't pair. Just don't mistake any of them for the real deal—if it doesn't require two people's full attention, it's not pairing!

Splitting up: "It's not you, it's the task"

This brings us to tasks that are a poor fit for pairing: Research, reading, chores like manually converting templates between languages, and lots of copying-and-pasting. These kinds of tasks should be few and far between—we are programmers, after all, and automating mundane tasks is what we do—but when they do come up, it's usually obvious that overall throughput will be higher if the job is split up.

The cost of error should be low as well. If you make a mistake while soloing, it should be the sort of tactical defect that's caught by your test suite, compiler, or linter. If you're producing *strategic* defects (going down the wrong path), then you should get back to pairing.

When you transition from active pairing to another form of work, clearly communicate your intentions. It's easy to say, "How about we split up for five minutes to search for answers?" If you wordlessly start typing on your laptop, how is your pairing partner supposed to know whether you're abandoning them or doing something useful?

When we split up for a few minutes while pairing at Promptworks, we tend to mumble what we're seeing and reading, or at least make expressive noises. By this, you keep tabs on how close each of you feel to an answer and tacitly communicate when it's time to share what you've found. Keep a chat window open to paste links back to the shared screen.

SHARING TIME AND SPACE

When you're on top of your pairing game, you're both so focused on the code that you hardly notice who's typing. It's like you're sharing a brain among four hands, sometimes trading control back and forth several times in a handful of seconds, yet rarely typing over each other. It's powerful and magical in a way that begs for intense gesturing from Jony Ive (http://bkaprt.com/ppp/02-02/, video).

This level of "flow" might seem pretty far-fetched, but I can attest that I often feel it when I get an hour or two into a pairing session with a colleague. To get there, equality and fairness are key—and there are some basic starting points that will help any pair get off on the right foot.

Agreeing on your objectives

You should agree on the objective of your pairing session at the outset. If one of you thinks the goal is to fix bugs as fast as possible and the other thinks it's to learn Python, you might both be disappointed by the lack of progress you make in either direction.

In many pairing sessions, the goal is simply to complete stories quickly and elegantly, but there may be some secondary goals you want to talk about. Perhaps you want to also get better at test-driven development or to clean up some smelly code as you go. Once you have these objectives in mind, take a moment to mention them as you're starting and ask if your partner agrees.

Setting a schedule

Working together with shared controls to accomplish a task means you have to be working at the same time. This can be a challenge when pairing across time zones, when you have different obligations outside of work, or when you simply have different preferences for work time. Be intentional about your pairing sessions: coordinate starting and ending times with your pair so you can work effectively and negotiate schedules with family and extracurriculars in mind.

A *laissez-faire* attitude to scheduling can result in missed expectations and lots of soloing by default. When less-attached team members work whenever they want, the team members who are also parents and caregivers may feel marginalized if they miss out on the best collaboration moments.

Taking turns

Dynamic, effective pairs feel empowered to call out disparity: "You've been driving (typing) for a while. Mind if I have a turn?" When my partner says this, I don't hear, "Gosh, you're such a keyboard hog!" but more like, "I feel bad that you've been typing for so long. You must be ready for a break." Speaking for myself, I'm always relieved to pass the baton.

While you're still getting comfortable with pair programming, you might use a timer to take turns driving; this ensures equal time at the controls and helps break any habits of being a keyboard hog or a comfortable spectator.

You might also trade control by tying each turn to a cycle like that of test-driven development (TDD). Under TDD, you first write a test for the tiniest change in behavior, watch it fail, then write the minimum code that makes the test pass. You next take the opportunity to refactor the production code and the test code, and only then move on to the next small change in behavior. "Ping pong" pairing, as Ward Cunningham describes it, simply alternates who writes the test and who makes it pass. After perhaps many iterations, you will have satisfied all the acceptance criteria for the story and can consider the feature done (http://bkaprt.com/ppp/02-03/).

By working in this fashion, you ensure that both of you not only have equal time driving, but you get to challenge each other to only make small changes to the codebase, have the test suite passing after every change, ensure high test coverage, and collaborate on refactoring at each step.

Checking in and taking breaks

Spending multiple hours in a car with only one traveling companion tests anyone's patience; the same is true of pair programming. An important part of not getting fed up with a pairing partner is taking breaks, having a snack, getting some air, and generally giving each other space to be quirky, flawed human beings.

Take some of your breaks together to check in on how the work is going. If you're growing into the pairing relationship, reflecting on the pairing process is important. Do you type noticeably more (or less) than your partner, and do they mind the discrepancy? If you're pairing remotely, are you able to hear them clearly enough to communicate, or are they drowned out by background noises?

It's tricky to not get fixated on annoying noises and habits, and trickier still to bring them up in a helpful and sensitive way. Psychologists and counselors have made careers out of this stuff. Don't let it fester; speak to pairing partners about it with empathy and non-judgment. Be aware of subtle hints coming in your direction, too.

Taking a walk around the block is a great way to spend a five-minute break. I cannot overstate the value of looking away from a screen and into the distance. It's not just good self-care, it's pair care!

SHARING POWER

For those of us who recognize the value in working alongside colleagues as diverse as the users we're serving, pair programming can be a fantastic vector for leveling the playing field—if its participants are mindful of the power dynamics between them.

Software engineer Sarah Mei identified the problem with unexamined pair programming in heterogeneous groups:

> *Pairing has nothing to say about how to structure an interaction to avoid taking unfair advantage of power dynamics. One of its basic assumptions is that everyone feels empowered to contribute.*
>
> *When this is true, pairing is amazing. When it's not, it's a nightmare.* (http://bkaprt.com/ppp/02-04/)

Tech is a predominantly White cis male industry, and beyond the obstacles underrepresented groups face just getting a job, there are dozens of ways White men have privilege that they take for granted at work every day (http://bkaprt.com/ppp/02-05/).

When you feel comfortable in your pairing environment, check in with your partner rather than assume that your feelings are shared. If you're part of a dominant group, be it according to gender, race, or another characteristic, remember that people in underrepresented groups often find it risky to voice concerns that fall outside of the lived experience of their colleagues.

When you're the old pro

Aside from sociocultural factors, discrepancies in professional experience are a fundamental source of power imbalances. The experience and practical knowledge that comes from more years as a programmer or more time on the codebase can be valuable; drawing on a solution from ten years ago sometimes saves the day. But the less experienced person may also feel behind in skill, not valued, and at a disadvantage in every disagreement; they may not feel comfortable voicing a contradiction. As Malcolm Gladwell pointed out in *Outliers*:

> *In commercial airlines, captains and first officers split the flying duties equally. But historically, crashes have been far more likely to happen when the captain is in the "flying seat." At first this seems to make no sense, since the captain is almost always the pilot with the most experience. But...planes are safer when the least experienced pilot is flying, because it means the second pilot isn't going to be afraid to speak up.*

The privilege of having more experience can shut down valuable lines of inquiry and stifle innovation with old habits, so make sure you're deferring to a person with less power or status, even if you have to literally sit on your hands. Give them more time driving and make sure you're using interrogatives, not imperatives. Far better to allow yourselves to explore the wrong path together than to split up in frustration and head off through the wilderness in different directions.

When the "pro" leaves you in the dust

If you find yourself being undermined by your partner, an effective intervention is to paraphrase what's going on: "I feel like you think I'm wrong more often than I am," or "We always seem to try your way first." Describing the imbalance makes them aware without ascribing a motive.

Impact statements can help redirect their attention to how their actions made you feel: "I felt like you didn't think what I had to offer was worth considering." You can also take an inquiring approach to explore where they're coming from or use humor to defuse a tense situation. These are just a few techniques experts suggest to interrupt verbal microaggressions, and with a little adaptation, they can be used to correct pair power imbalances that diminish the contributions of one partner (http://bkaprt.com/ppp/02-06/, PDF).

BRING YOUR WHOLE SELF

I know pairing for the first time can be daunting. You have to decide when to pair, how to pair, agree on objectives, coordinate a schedule, share the keyboard, keep your sniffles in check, take healthy breaks, and make sure everyone feels empowered to contribute. With all this to juggle, wouldn't it be easier to keep working alone and not risk disappointment?

Don't worry; you've got this! It all just boils down to bringing your whole self to the programming task and expanding your definition of success to more than lines of code produced. Remember, it's also about team resiliency, better code choices, and ultimately better business outcomes.

With a few dozen pairing experiences under your belt, it becomes routine enough that you start to see ways it could be even better with a few tweaks. You'll want to get more out of the experience and give more to your partners. You might be facing your first pair that really tries your patience or having difficulties and wondering if you're the problem. That's perfectly normal! Our next chapter looks at ways you can be an even better pairing partner.

BEING A BETTER PARTNER

My grandfather once told me, "Marriage is not about finding the right person but rather about *becoming* the right person." In other words, a lot of a partnership's success is within your control.

Pair programming may not have the permanency and legal implications that marriage does, but it's a pretty intimate thing to let someone else see exactly how you work. Complicating the arrangement is the fact that you might have little choice in who you're partnered with. If you don't trust and respect them, it can be a real struggle. "I only like pairing when my partner is a pleasure to work with," software engineer Ryan Kulla tweeted. "So I try to be too" (http://bkaprt.com/ppp/03-01/).

Working with difficult people is a fact of life, and the earlier you develop the skills to receive their energy and turn it into something positive, the quicker you'll succeed in your objectives and advance in your career. Don't write someone off just because you're having difficulty with them in the moment—people and circumstances can change!

Let's dive into some good pairing habits you can develop that add value to the pairing relationship and leave everyone feeling better for having engaged in it.

THINK OUT LOUD

If you were to listen in on a pair, you'd often hear such things as:

- "What do you think? Is this right?"
- "Do you mind if I drive?"
- "Let's see if that worked."
- "I'm going to grab the mouse."
- "Can I look at something?"
- "I'm thinking the problem is... What do you think?"
- "Go ahead."
- "Sounds like we have different opinions. Let's try yours first."

This level of chatter is in fact a fundamental habit of pairing: There should be a dialogue running almost continuously. The driver (the one controlling the keyboard at the moment) is constantly thinking out loud in a practice called "reflective articulation," which helps the navigator (the one not typing) understand what they're doing and keep up with what's going on (http://bkaprt.com/ppp/03-02/, PDF). The navigator should be acknowledging the driver's narrative, filling in the gaps, questioning their choices, noting potential problems, helping remember what that thing over there was called, and helping direct where to go next.

It's hard to remember to think aloud when we've spent so much of our lives in school and solitary work environments keeping our thoughts inside our heads, but with practice, it can become second nature. Remember: Silence is selfish. Go ahead and share what you're thinking, whether you're the driver or the navigator. If your partner goes silent while continuing to work, "Hey, catch me up with what you're thinking" is a friendly prompt to come back to the pair and contribute to the shared experience.

It won't take long to realize that you and your partner may have completely different styles of thinking through a problem. Because reflective articulation is so important, asking the right questions when you're not following (or agreeing with) your partner is critical.

I've learned from business leaders and psychotherapists how powerful curious, genuine inquisitiveness can be. Often the best solution isn't one either I or my partner thought of initially, but rather a hybrid we developed by piggybacking off each other's ideas and gently guiding each other along with a series of thoughtful questions.

Good questions are open-ended, asked with genuine curiosity, and non-judgmental.

- **Inquire about their reasoning.** If you ask, "Why did you make that choice?" you acknowledge that there were multiple approaches and they selected one, whether they realize it or not. You get to hear what they rejected and why. If they didn't consider anything else, hopefully they'll ask you what other ways *you* see.
- **Consider alternatives.** "How else might we accomplish the same thing?" invites you to come up with alternate solu-

tions. "Is there another name that would be more semantic?" gently questions whether their choice conveys the right meaning (and we know naming things is hard!). "Is there something we could abstract from this?" invites reflection on function/class size and the single responsibility principle.

- **Be open to experiments.** Maybe the alternative your partner just suggested sounds outlandish to you. Don't waste too much time debating hypothetical principles. Save your work and try the alternative on for size. Maybe you'll like it once you see it, and there's little in the computer world that can't be undone or reverted.
- **Ask whether the juice is worth the squeeze.** An important job when you're the navigator is to provide a "subliminal process check" and speak up when you think you're working too long, trying too hard, or going too far on a task. Try questions like, "Is this something we should spend more energy on, or is it good enough? Is there something else could we be doing that's more valuable?" Weighing the value of what you're working on versus the effort required should always be in the back of your mind.

It's important to employ non-confrontational questions to keep yourselves in a critical-thinking space without putting each other in a defensive mode. Always keep in mind the overarching objective and make it explicit when necessary: you're working together to discover the best solution.

CHECK YOUR EGO

When developers fear losing their identity, their personal style, and their sense of control, it presents a real challenge to effective pairing. I've heard many stories of developers intentionally obfuscating their code or adopting an extreme personal style to make themselves more indispensable, perhaps reasoning that if they don't rule their corner of the codebase and defend it from all intruders, they can be replaced easily. Others might go to the other extreme and have a crisis of confidence, thinking they don't have anything to contribute. These are both examples of unmanaged ego, and it's probably the number one threat to successful pair programming.

Pair programming is a practice that helps moderate ego, because we're all simultaneously teachers and students. Learning from a colleague means finding the balance between questioning their assumptions while remaining open to having your own assumptions questioned in turn.

Looking at a language, framework, problem domain, or codebase through the eyes of a newbie can be a real gift; you drop your expectations and preconceived ideas and see things with an open mind, curiosity, and fascination—a state of mind called "beginner's mind" in Buddhist practice. You notice what's going on, try to see the details, and don't take anything for granted. A beginner exposes where the code doesn't adhere to the Principle of Least Astonishment (POLA), which is when a piece of code does exactly what you'd expect it to do from reading over it.

If you suffer from too little confidence, pairing can be an opportunity to see inside someone else's work and realize that they really aren't any smarter, faster, or better than you. "I find that pairing regularly is great for my confidence, getting to see everyone else typo and Google stuff too," programmer Danielle Sucher tweeted (http://bkaprt.com/ppp/03-03/).

Wherever you are on the software engineering growth curve, you're probably the best person to teach the knowledge you recently acquired to the folks just behind you. It's a gift for you as well, because by articulating the thinking, circumstances, or history behind why things are done a certain way, you'll get an even better grasp yourself on the principles you've already learned.

Growing as a person who can pair confidently with anyone requires introspection, acceptance, and commitment to the practice when it would be easier to quit. In the words of IBM CEO Ginni Rometty: "Growth and comfort don't coexist" (http://bkaprt.com/ppp/03-04/).

Of course, the only person over whom you truly have control is yourself; no matter how much humility and non-defensiveness you model, you may still find yourself paired with someone whose ego becomes a real problem. This brings us to another important practice in pairing: getting comfortable with giving and receiving feedback.

GIVE AND RECEIVE FEEDBACK

Each member of the team needs to be open to giving and receiving critical feedback. Being a good pairing partner means staying engaged, wrestling with interpersonal challenges, and not checking out and walking away when you experience adversity. Yes, it would be easier to hide behind your own screen and ice out a difficult collaborator, but you're just putting off a larger conflict.

In my opinion, honesty and kind-but-fair micro-confrontations are better than repressing resentment. I believe (or at least operate as if) everyone is trying their best and would want to improve if given the right information. I've found success with a few different approaches:

- **Soften the criticism by asking permission first.** "Can I offer some feedback?" you might ask. "Can I bring up something I noticed?"
- **Frame it as an observation.** "So I noticed we've been leaving a lot of comments about what the code does. I wonder, is that something we should be doing?" (Even if you're sure it isn't, make sure you ask sincerely.)
- **Emphasize what you would improve, not what went wrong.** "Next time, I would like to spend more time driving, because I need to get a better feel for where things are in the codebase." Or perhaps, "Next time we should try ping pong pairing, so we each have equal time driving. Would you be open to that?"
- **After a pairing session, conduct a nano-retro** to quickly evaluate it and make improvements. On the count of three, each person scores the session on their fingers from zero to five. Take turns sharing what improvements would have made you give it a five and record the improvement ideas for the next time you pair together.

When you're on the receiving end of critical feedback, it can be hard to take! You may feel misunderstood or even attacked. But try to see it as a gift, because new information is the only way to grow and we all have things we can learn about ourselves and our work. Don't explain or defend; just offer a simple "Thanks for the feedback" so the person offering it feels heard. Review the feedback later and decide what action you want to take.

When you implement a suggestion and find it successful, it's good to share it with the team (if not too personal) so others can benefit from your learnings. As a group, talk about what's going well with pairing, what's not working, and what you'd like to change. Perhaps you need a better hardware setup, a subscription to a better remote pairing tool, an environment with fewer distractions, a less library-like atmosphere, longer or shorter sessions, or different parameters around rotation.

Becoming a better pairing partner is all about curiosity, experimentation, and reflection—thinking about how things could be better and giving it a shot. Not every idea is a good one, but it costs very little to give something a try. Clear, direct communication will establish trust, which is ultimately what makes our pairing highly efficient and our work product the best it can be.

4

THE PAIRING ENVIRONMENT

THE KEY FEATURE OF pair programming is shared control, which usually means shared hardware, but might be virtual in the case of remote pairing. With shared control, you can't turn the plane in two different directions at once. If you can both work on different code at the same time, you're not pairing!

Whether you and your pair are a few feet or a few hundred miles from each other, it's important to take the time to get set up properly so you have parity with your partner and prevent computer-related injury or fatigue. The setup matters a great deal for the long-term sustainability of your pairing practice. Be aware of and advocate for your needs and you can enjoy pairing for a long, long time.

IN-PERSON PAIRING: THE IMPORTANCE OF HARDWARE PARITY

At Promptworks, we prefer having the same desk, chairs, monitors, and power supplies at each station for uniformity and interchangeability. We have unassigned, standardized desks at our company so a team can trade partners as necessary and no one has to worry about shuffling hardware around. As Forrest Gump said, "That's good! One less thing."

We determined early on that we didn't want to maintain dedicated pairing computers separate from our individual machines. Some people say that's pairing heresy—that the pair computer should be neutral ground—but we don't think it's worth the IT hassle. Instead, we bring our own laptops and take turns hosting. It lets us share new tools or configurations we're trying out and get to experience another person's setup. That way, we all gradually converge toward the same configuration.

It's important to have the same equipment on both sides of the pairing workstation, particularly the same monitor, because operating at different resolutions will make it difficult to mirror the screen. We've seen some weird monitor behavior at Promptworks, even with two monitors that the operating system ought to see as the same. Using two completely identical monitors, bought at the same time, seems to work best.

We provide cubbies for storing personal items and peripherals near the pairing area. We discourage people from leaving behind chargers, plants, mugs, fans, photos, or anything else that marks your territory; "nesting" discourages flexibility and makes it less likely that you'll change up pairing partners or have someone drop in to pair for a minute.

Arranging the furniture

For ideal pairing, a normal desk with sides or drawers won't do. What you want is a table—or better yet—two small, identical tables that let you sit on opposite sides. Ideally, the environment is quiet enough that you can hear each other easily at a normal conversation volume, but not library-like silence where you'll feel self-conscious for thinking out loud non-stop.

If you share the same monitor, as you might when first dabbling in pairing, you'll want to sit side-by-side and pass the keyboard and mouse back and forth (Fig 4.1). This works well enough to start and many people do it frequently for short stretches. You'll want to get a second keyboard and mouse as soon as possible, though (FIG 4.2). Sliding the keyboard or shuffling your bodies back and forth gets old in a hurry and makes it easier for bad pairing habits (such as keyboard-hogging) to form.

Two keyboards mean you don't have to pass or shuffle, but you're still looking at the monitor from the side when they are designed to be viewed head-on. If you can, get two monitors so each person can look at their own screen (FIG 4.3). Your back and neck will thank you!

Once you're each looking at your own screen, you may as well sit on opposite sides of the table and offset yourselves, so you can see each other diagonally (FIG 4.4). If you use two separate desks, you can slide the right side forward about eight inches, so you're even closer (FIG 4.5). The empty desktop space between you is useful for papers and pens, food, and other shared artifacts.

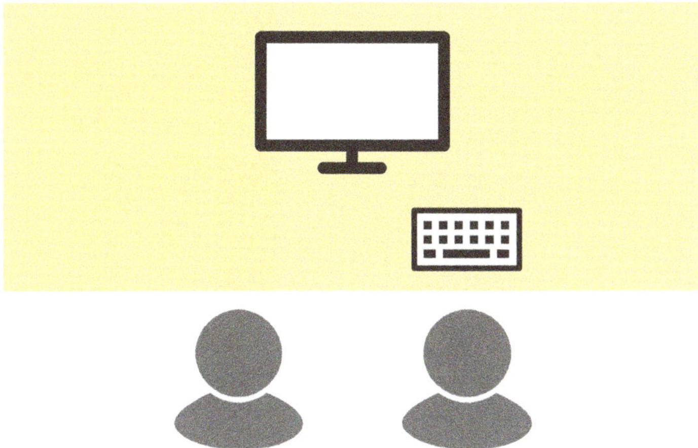

FIG 4.1: The "Please Pass the Butter!" configuration makes it unambiguous who is driving, but passing the controls gets tiring.

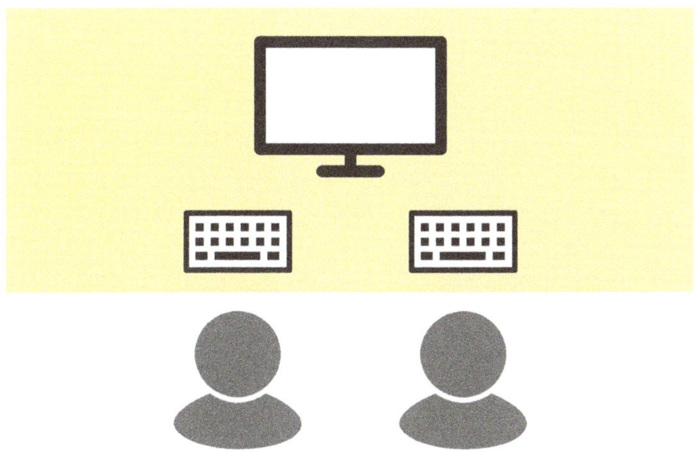

FIG 4.2: The "Tennis Doubles" configuration allows trading control more often, but viewing the screen at an angle can become uncomfortable.

FIG 4.3: The Mission Control setup gives each partner all the peripherals to which they are accustomed.

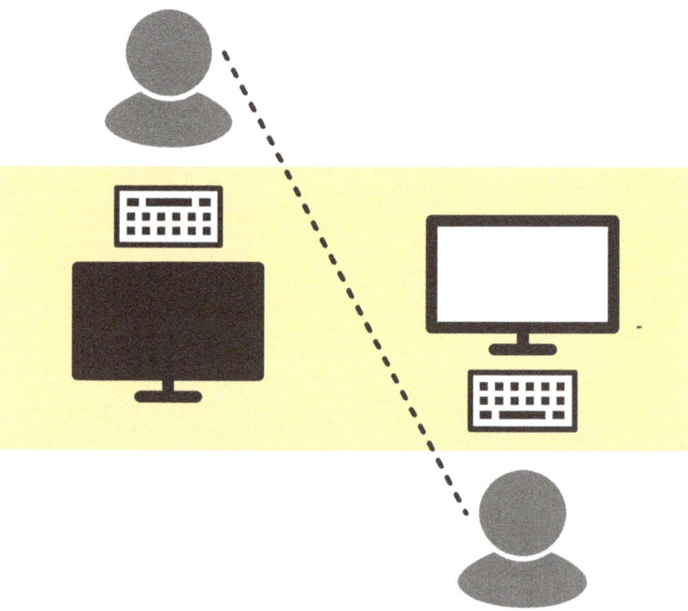

FIG 4.4: The "Mr. Darcy" improves upon Mission Control by allowing eye contact...albeit at a distance.

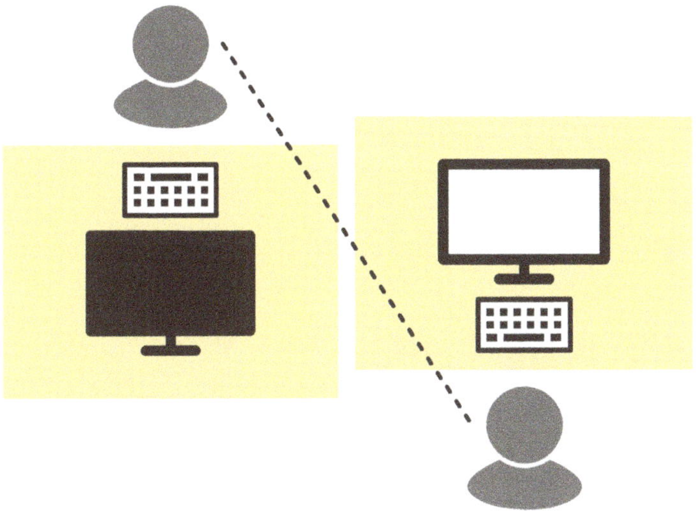

FIG 4.5: The "Tête-à-tête" maximizes human-computer and human-human ergonomics. It also works great in an open office environment with a row of offset pairing workstations.

This is a great arrangement—you don't have to speak loudly, your partner is just off the left side of your monitor, easily in your peripheral vision, and it takes up less space since your partner's desk is partially to the left of your chair. If you mount the monitor on an arm, make sure there's room to position it perfectly at eye height directly in front of your body.

REMOTE PAIRING

Remote pairing can be very effective and an absolute necessity—a few of my friends have done it every day for many years! But in full disclosure, I've found it to be orders of magnitude more difficult than in-person pairing because of the technological hiccups. All sorts of things can get in your way, from connection troubles to software shortcomings. Technical issues can easily result in burnout.

Mid-pairing session is not the ideal time to figure out why your audio drops out or why your mouse is lagging on a shared screen. Here are some things to check out before you decide to conduct your first remote pair programming session:

Network connection

Pair programming requires a high degree of synchronous communication and instantaneous feedback, which demands a good internet connection. Most household internet service is designed for downloading a lot of content, but when pairing, your upstream connection gets a workout as you share video, audio, and your computer screen or control signals. Latency and dropped packets can also be a problem, even if you're paying for a lot of bandwidth. See the Resources section for useful troubleshooting tools.

Get familiar with your router's admin interface and see if you're maxing out your bandwidth in either direction. If upstream bandwidth seems to be the barrier you can't overcome, a shared server or co-editing integrated development environment (IDE) might be better options, eliminating screen sharing from the upstream channel.

- **Enable QoS or WMM,** so your video and audio streams aren't hampered by a software update in the background or a backup on another computer.
- **For the fastest Wi-Fi, set your WLAN to WPA2 and AES encryption only** (the latest standards; try to avoid WPA and TKIP, which are older and less secure). Put your laptop on a 5 GHz channel, and scan for a channel with the least interference.
- **Clear a path to your Wi-Fi.** Avoid Wi-Fi repeaters and radio-frequency-opaque obstacles. When placing access points, experts recommend finding a central location for the Wi-Fi access point placed above head height with no more than two rooms and two walls between the access point and devices (http://bkaprt.com/ppp/04-01/).

- **Radio waves will always lag behind wires, no matter how advanced the technology gets.** If Wi-Fi is your source of latency and lost packets, try connecting via wired ethernet, even if that means running some Cat 6 cable through the attic or under a baseboard. A voice and data installer (not an electrician) can get it done right for a few hundred bucks and can certify their work by using a fancy network tester.
- **If you have the option, switch to a fiber internet connection** for the very best performance and symmetric connectivity—i.e. as much upstream bandwidth as downstream (http://bkaprt.com/ppp/04-02/). These providers offer aggressive introductory pricing to gain subscribers and recoup their last-mile infrastructure investment, but don't be fooled into buying "High Speed internet" (a.k.a. DSL) when fiber isn't available. They're tricky like that.

Video

Your first thought when considering remote pairing is probably how to share the computer, but don't forget how much of pairing is about human interaction! You need to see and hear your partner almost as well as you do in person for effective interpersonal communication and to catch subtle visual cues like a furrowed brow or a faraway look. Switching windows to look at your pair's face gets old in a hurry; the most ideal way is to have a dedicated screen for the video chat, usually placed slightly to the side of your monitor. An iPad works well.

In Joe Kutner's *Remote Pairing: Collaborative Tools for Distributed Development*, Joe Moore, a developer with Pivotal who has been remotely pairing full-time since 2010, pointed out that being self-aware and disciplined is even more important when you're remote pairing—and video can help widen that channel:

> *I find that [video] is invaluable. I want to be able to see people's faces. I want to know if they're confused, if they're laughing, or if they're looking down at their phone.*

If you can, opt for one of the premium video conferencing platforms, not a free service like Google Hangouts or Skype.

Our company tested many in 2016 and preferred the reliability and quality of Zoom—and still do, as of this writing.

Audio

MacBook Pro speakers have gotten quite good in recent years, but the more isolation your microphone has from your speakers, the less noise cancellation work software like Zoom has to do. Headsets with a boom microphone are most remote workers' preference, though some people prefer a high-quality directional microphone like the Blue Snowball rather than wearing a headset.

Screen sharing

Your video conferencing software might have screen sharing built-in, so it's easy to request or give control over the software you're already used to. In our case, that's Zoom. If screen control is your primary consideration, you can try software like Screen.so, which is optimized for responsive pair programming. Screen gives each person their own mouse pointer, lets you sketch on the screen, and has impressively low latency.

Sharing your screen with your pairing partner is super easy... until it's not. It can completely consume bandwidth and the lag can increase as the hours go by. If you don't already use a text-mode editor and the shell, this might be an excellent time to consider them because the more graphical your tools are, the more difficult remote pairing can be. Sharing a terminal and programs running from the command line is more reliable and takes just a fraction of the bandwidth.

What you need in order to share computing resources somewhat depends on the kind of development environment you have. When we're remote pairing at Promptworks, we generally use SSH, tmux, and MacVim in text mode for editing code, but we still need screen sharing for the browser and sometimes a graphical git client. This way, both partners can see everything that goes on—copying and editing files, running code, and seeing test output—without having to share an entire screen. Vim stays nice and responsive for both of us, and if the browser lags a bit through screen sharing, it's not a very big deal.

When we're developing mobile apps, we generally use command-line runners to build the apps, but have to use screen sharing for the mobile device simulator and the occasional visit to XCode or Android Studio.

Collaborative editors

Your code editor or IDE can facilitate collaborative editing by connecting to your pair's editor over the internet. Once linked, they work together to share the same editing environment—either partner can edit and run code as if they had a physical pairing setup or screen sharing, except that each person can have their own editor configuration, color scheme, shortcut keys, and keyboard layout.

The most prevalent editor is VS Live Share, available for Visual Studio and VS Code. It comes with a shared terminal, co-debugging, and localhost tunnels out of the box. You'll need to install additional extensions for sharing a browser, git, audio chat, and so forth, but it's a lot more responsive that screen sharing and could replace most of it. We've sometimes experienced some weirdness when it gets out of sync, so your mileage may vary.

If you prefer editing code in Atom, Sublime Text, IntelliJ, Emacs, or Neovim, check out Floobits or one of the other options in the Resources section.

Shared servers

Some teams like to have a server that pairs log into to pair program remotely. The environment is neutral, already set up with the team's agreed-upon tools. It can be cloned or regenerated at a moment's notice and treating it like a disposable server means you can use DevOps tools to set it up quickly and repeatedly. This helps the team converge on a uniform environment with room for one-off customization that a pair finds necessary for a given project.

With a remote server, you don't have to worry about firewalls, NAT, or that you're working on your partner's computer while they stepped away. Both partners have equal access to the webserver if your app requires one, though you'll still have to figure out how you both interact with it remotely.

Most pairs that use a shared server are using text-based editors like Vim or Emacs and multiplexing their terminals with tmux. This setup uses very little bandwidth, and theoretically, you can still pair from a coffee shop or airplane. More likely, you're jumping on when your partner isn't available (we don't pair 100 percent of the time!) and want to pick up right where the two of you left off from wherever you happen to be.

If you're using a graphical editor, you might need remote desktop capabilities from your server. The industry term is virtual desktop infrastructure (VDI), and since you'll be screen sharing with remote desktop protocol (RDP) or virtual network computing (VNC), the location and reliability of the provider matters a lot. See more specific hints in the Resources section.

ABOVE ALL: PARITY

However your setup looks, the important thing is that you're ready to focus on getting stuff done when you sit down. Creating the right environment enables successful pair programming, but it doesn't assure success on its own. Alex Harms surveyed seventy-six people to figure out the best hardware setup for pairing and was surprised to find that whether the respondents loved or hated pairing had nothing to do with the furniture or the equipment (http://bkaprt.com/ppp/04-03/, video). It was all about both people being focused on the code.

Above all, make sure your pairing environment puts you on an equal footing so you can focus on the advantages it enables: being confident you're making the right decisions, avoiding distractions, and being encouraged to engage hard problems longer and do the right thing more often.

PAIRING IN THE ORGANIZATION

SO FAR, WE'VE TALKED ABOUT pairing as if it's just you and a partner with total agency in how you do your programming work. In reality, you're probably part of an organization or at least a team that has an opinion on how, when, and with whom you program. You might think you won't be able to pair program in your situation, or that your boss would never get on board with it (though there's a good chance they would love the results). In this chapter, we'll navigate how to incrementally add pair programming to your organization at the right pace and level of subtlety to give it a fair shot.

SITUATING PAIRING IN YOUR TEAM

Before you eagerly dive into pairing, you need to be circumspect: What is the team's attitude toward pairing, and how will it affect your ability to find a partner and successfully work together, even for short stretches? Will it attract resentment from your peers or a skeptical look from anyone in management?

Talking to management

I'll be honest: I'm a manager myself, and I'm most inspired by employees who come to one-on-ones and team retrospectives prepared with questions, ideas, or topics they've been thinking about. It shows that the employee values my leadership and cares about my managerial agenda.

If no one on your team has paired before and you want buy-in from the top before you begin, consider: what are your manager's objectives and priorities when it comes to pairing? Are there larger company values (knowledge-sharing or cross-training) or objectives (reducing churn, defects, help-desk calls, or missed deadlines) that would support a pairing initiative?

As you identify opportunities around big-picture goals, team improvement, and career development, you can open a conversation about pairing to test the waters.

- **Start from shared values.** You can lay some groundwork just by being a good listener and staying curious about the problems management deals with on a regular basis. Learn their thoughts on coordination costs, time wasted on red herrings, reducing training costs, or the consequences of a programmer's over- or under-confidence. What are their ideas to reduce wasted effort and improve output quality? Don't get too evangelical or push any agenda—but do pay attention to opportunities where pairing might offer advantages.
- **Tap into their experiences.** Your manager has probably been building software for a long time. What have been their experiences with doing code reviews, talking through problems with a coworker, or sharing creative control? How have they seen cross-training or mentorship work best?
- **Take interest in sharing knowledge.** A manager who is responsible for personnel development should be looking for ways to spread the knowledge and experience that more senior team members have. You can suggest pairing part-time—either with someone more junior than you or with someone you'd like to learn from—as a career development opportunity. You'll either look generous with your knowledge and time or hungry to learn, both of which are attitudes most managers want to encourage if they're even remotely serious about developing a robust and effective team.
- **Emphasize the value of risk mitigation.** Single points of failure are dangerous, as we discussed with the bus factor. Surely your manager has been left in the lurch when someone quit or took a sudden leave of absence. If you demonstrate attention to the business risks that pair programming mitigates, not only will you support a case for pairing, you'll also build affinity with your manager and show them support. You might also point to research showing improvements in the code as a result of pairing; what are the consequences if your team allows a big mistake to slip through?
- Annual reviews, check-ins, and even one-on-ones are great times to discuss pair programming. With a little prior reflection, you can align it with personal and team goals. Don't let these opportunities to talk to your manager sneak up on you!

Building ground-level support

It's great to work with your manager's blessing if you can get it, but even if you can't (or, more likely, your manager is too busy to think about implementing a top-down, team-wide pairing effort), you might find just as much success by adopting some of the practices of pairing with your colleagues gradually and non-disruptively. The goal is to approach it like an experiment, testing the hypothesis that pair programming produces better software faster than two people would individually.

1. **Find your co-conspirator(s).** Who is most tuned-in to XP and continuous improvement? For teammates who seem open, propose that you experiment together with pair programming. If they're more reluctant, ask if they would be open to helping each other with stories from time to time.
2. **Try a few short sessions with a lightweight setup** (screen sharing or collaborative editor; act like you're remote even if you're close by) to see if you work well together.
3. **Keep the momentum going.** If you're not explicitly pairing, you can start by simply saying, "Wow, I really like working together on stories. Can we do this more often? How about for a half-hour every Friday?" A month later: "This is great! Can we increase our time to an hour?"
4. **Identify some KPIs** (key performance indicators, in manager-speak) that pairing is helping. Productivity is highly subjective, so think about what matters to your boss and your team. Tracking the number of story points completed or defects produced can be meaningful. What matters might be subjective, like familiarity with the codebase or the amount of confidence you feel, but you can still assign it points or a rating scale to measure it.
5. **Start pairing slowly at first**—short, occasional sessions without a lot of pressure. You want it to work, and jumping in too quickly might jeopardize the experiment. Don't overestimate how adaptable you are. It takes time to get used to a new way of working.

Take some notes after each pairing session so you can look back over your progress later. Whatever metrics you're tracking, the more diligently you measure them and track how these KPIs improve as you pair, the better you can defend your choice and get buy-in to make it an official practice on your team. What did you work on? What did you learn? What domain knowledge, tools, or parts of the system did you become acquainted with because of your partner? You might be enjoying pairing, but if it's not leading to quality and productivity gains, you'll have difficulty getting the rest of the team or your manager on board.

GROWTH AND ADVANCEMENT

If pairing does take hold on your team, you might have some new problems to manage: getting stuck in a rut or having overly prescriptive pairing.

Pair rotation

We've talked about how pairing eliminates silos, but if two members of the team get in a rut of always pairing with each other, they can create a silo of their own. No matter how well-intentioned the rationale may be, any imbalance in pairing frequency is leaving some knowledge on the table.

To combat this, many pairing teams draw a pairing matrix on a whiteboard or keep a spreadsheet that tallies how many times any two people have paired. This way, you can correct for imbalances without having to explicitly make a pairing schedule. You can see who pairs together a lot and steer toward the less common pairings when you have the freedom to do so.

Pair rotation sounds simple enough in theory, but in practice, it's a lot harder than you'd think. Do you break up a pair in the middle of a long-running story? There are pros and cons. Do you have an anchor that sees the story through to the end, or does that create a power imbalance because the anchor becomes the de-facto owner and will probably end up driving a lot? These are things to work out in your retrospectives. Remember, the team should be willing to try anything once, as long as it's a small change that doesn't kill your productivity. Once you've tried something, be honest about how it compares and whether it's worth continuing.

Avoiding institutionalization and calcification

You may have fought a long hard battle to get pairing accepted among your team, but now you have a new challenge: resisting central planning and rigid institution of pair programming. Among managers, a common reaction to a new way of working is to mandate, manage, and control it. It's pairing by fiat: Somebody in charge makes a plan that assigns who is pairing with whom and on what story. They define exactly how pair programming works, so everyone will do it right. A pairing schedule goes on the wall, and procurement gets a purchase order for ten chess clocks.

In some organizations, this is the best you can hope for, but the ideal is to self-organize based on what needs to be done. It's a bit like the difference between project planning by Gantt chart versus an Agile or Scrum board. The former doesn't take in all the information and can't keep up with changes on the ground as they happen. It gives a false sense of security that all the uncertainty is being managed when really, it's better to define the objectives clearly and let smart people figure out how best to get there.

If your boss is pushing rigid pairing practices, the best way to deal with these mandates is to approach them with an inquisitive mindset. Ask what they're hoping to get out of the pairing schedule. A few weeks later, ask them how it's working. A few weeks after that, ask if they considered a pairing matrix to accomplish the same goal.

If you are the manager who wants your team to pair, be intentional about where you want to see your team headed and the steps to get there, don't push it too fast, and remember that these practices serve the outcomes; we don't serve the practices for their own sake. If there's another way to get there, so be it!

Wherever you fall on the org chart, remember to keep an open mindset of experimentation and "trying anything once." That's how organizations keep up with changing best practices and create a community of continuous learning and self-reinforcement.

BUILDING A COMMUNITY OF PRACTICE

There's an old story of a newly married couple that bakes their first brisket together. The meat turns out delicious, but the husband asks the wife, "Why did you cut off the ends? That's the best part!" She answers, "I don't know; that's the way my mother always made it." They ask the mother why, and she gives the same response. Finally, they ask the grandmother, and she says, "Because my pan wasn't big enough!"

In programming, we also tend to do things just because we've always done them that way, or we followed someone else without really examining if they need to be done or if there's a better way. Pairing gives us the opportunity to see how someone else works, the mental space to ask "why?", the courage to try completely new things with a partner, and the opportunity to share what you learned with the broader team.

Pair programming doesn't only transfer technical knowledge—like how to use a framework, how a codebase was architected, or tools and techniques to make your programming more efficient. It also transfers implicit knowledge—the experiences, routines, strategies, and intuition that members of a team accumulate over the arc of their careers. When this knowledge is shared among a team, an informal Community of Practice (CoP) can form, where individuals lean on each other to share insights, gain knowledge, and advance their practice.

At its core, a CoP is about a self-motivated commitment to making software the best way possible through a set of shared practices and values. It's a critical mass of continuous learners who naturally share their knowledge and humbly open themselves to the wide world of things they don't know.

Pair programming is an important tactic (but not the only one by any means) to develop a strategic CoP among software engineers. Pairing helps develop implicitly shared practices that transcend two perspectives through pair rotation, cross-pollination by proximity, and collective reflection on the pairing process.

CONCLUSION

UNTIL YOU'VE HAD SOME really great pair programming experiences, you may not believe just how enjoyable and empowering it can feel. You feel like you're on fire—a dynamic duo that is more than the sum of its parts. When you have to go back to programming alone, you feel like you're missing half of yourself.

Like any powerful tool, it matters who wields it and how it's used. Pairing can join people together and make new technologists feel like they have a place in the programming world, and it can also exaggerate power differences and make a person feel like even more of an outsider. Be mindful of the power you have and of those who come to the pairing table with a history of having their contributions ignored and devalued. Be sure to keep a running dialogue, give up control easily, be open to feedback, and reflect honestly on what's working well and what's not.

Even great pairing experiences can still leave you feeling like you just did double the work—perhaps because you did! The intense focus and lack of distractions are tiring, so an ergonomic pairing setup and good pair-care are key to make the practice sustainable. Make sure you have parity in a dozen ways between you and your partner, so it's not too easy for one to dominate—and if possible, get comfortable pairing IRL before you try it remotely.

I hope you find pairing as fulfilling as I have and that you develop your own insights into what makes pair programming work well on your team. My wish is that every team is able to lower their stress and produce better software through broader adoption of these collaborative coding techniques.

In the end, we're all looking to improve ourselves, get more done, and work more happily with others. When you're deeply immersed in the joy of pair programming, you'll start looking for opportunities to pair on non-programming tasks, from unloading the dishwasher to reconciling the checkbook. There's little work that isn't better when shared with a partner!

ACKNOWLEDGMENTS

I'D LIKE TO THANK Mat Schaffer for turning me on to pair programming and for devising our original tête-à-tête desk setup. Thanks to Dan Shipper for the idea to collect our learnings into a book and to Jon Long for spotting the manuscript's potential and connecting me to the perfect publisher.

The torchbearers of pair programming who were defining and refining the practice long before me, deserve special thanks: Laurie Williams, Ward Cunningham, Kent Beck, Alastair Cockburn, Martin Fowler, Ron Jeffries, Bil Kleb, Bill Wood, Robert Kessler, and Joe Moore—to name a few. I'm grateful that they not only had the vision to practice pairing but also took the time to refine it with their peers and write down what they learned. I owe much of my career happiness to them.

To my editors, Lisa Maria Marquis, Sally Kerrigan, and Danielle Small: thank you for cutting many a silly joke and pointless peregrination to find the few good words that made me sound passably smart. Every first-time author should have such an amazing team. ABA CEO Katel LeDû, thank you for believing I had something important to say and knowing how to turn it into a viable book.

Finally, to my wife Karena: thank you for putting up with this project for the last year. I know how astonishing it must be that I started something without appreciating how much work it would take or the tradeoffs I'd need to make. Your steadfast encouragement and insistence that I close the computer and look at a tree every once in a while, brought me through.

RESOURCES

Agile and XP

In this book, I've assumed you're at least a little familiar with Agile and XP. If you're not or you want to dig in deeper, I recommend the following resources:

- In Rachel Davies's XP talk at NewCrafts 2017, "What Ever Happened to Being eXtreme?", she discussed what modern Extreme Programming includes, where it came from, and its most important aspects. She also revisited old-school XP and what it has to offer even though it's been forgotten by the mainstream (http://bkaprt.com/ppp/06-01/, video).
- Though things like continuous integration (CI), small feature branches, and test-driven development (TDD) are the modern norm of effective engineering teams, Extreme Programming Explained: Embrace Change by Kent Beck and Cynthia Andres remains a great reference and an important read if you're coming from a background where XP principles aren't practiced.
- ExtremeProgramming.org has an interactive map that puts pair programming in the context of an Extreme Programming project. You can zoom out to see its relationship to testing, refactoring, standups, and Agile processes (http://bkaprt.com/ppp/06-02/).
- Build confidence in your test-driven development (TDD) skills and practice ping pong pairing with some TDD katas (http://bkaprt.com/ppp/06-03/).

Pair programming under a microscope

- The book Pair Programming Illuminated by Laurie Williams and Robert Kessler devotes a whole section to various combinations of expertise, introversion, gender, culture, ego, and so on. If you're struggling to make a particular pairing relationship work and the basic habits of humility, confidence, receptivity, communication, and compromise aren't working for you, perhaps consult Chapters 12–23 for advice!

- If you really want to get into the economics of pair programming, the same book has an Appendix B that presents a detailed economic analysis. For a broader look at academic pair programming studies, see this meta-analysis (http://bkaprt.com/ppp/06-04/, PDF).

Managing resistance and anti-patterns

- "Does Pair Programming Have to Suck?", Alex Harms' talk at Ruby Midwest 2011, is an accessible and frank look at how pairing can either go really well or really badly, depending on how it's practiced. (http://bkaprt.com/ppp/06-05/, video).
- "10 Reasons Pair Programming Is Not For The Masses" by Obie Fernandez looks at why pair programming, though highly effective at Hashrocket, isn't more widely practiced (http://bkaprt.com/ppp/06-06/).
- Framed as "etiquette," this article by training site Techtown lists sixteen behaviors that help pair programming go well (http://bkaprt.com/ppp/06-07/).
- The Recurse Center's social rules (not to be confused with their Code of Conduct) help create a "friendly, intellectual environment where you can spend as much of your energy as possible on programming" (http://bkaprt.com/ppp/06-08/).

Code quality

These books will help you be a better navigator as you continuously review the code you're writing.

- Practical Object-Oriented Design by Sandi Metz (http://bkaprt.com/ppp/06-09/).
- Clean Code by Robert C. Martin (http://bkaprt.com/ppp/06-10/).
- Agile Technical Practices Distilled: A Journey Toward Mastering Software Design by Pedro Moreira Santos, Marco Consolaro, and Alessandro Di Gioia (http://bkaprt.com/ppp/06-11/).

Pair rotation

- This pair programming matrix Google Sheet created by Pivotal Labs can be used to highlight hot spots if two people pair disproportionately often. Copy the sheet and replace the cartoon characters with your faces or names (http://bkaprt.com/ppp/06-12/).
- Git Pair Trix is one example of an automated matrix that reads the git authors from commit messages in your repository (assuming you're using the pivotal git-pair script) and produces text output showing the matrix (http://bkaprt.com/ppp/06-13/).

Pair code authorship

Git version control is designed for collaboration but assumes that a single person is making the commits. Since that isn't the case when pairing, we might want to give the credit—or blame—to the right people. Here are a couple tools that will let you temporarily make commits as a pair.

- **git-duet:** Both your names will go on the commit messages—one as author and one as committer. You can set it up to alternate who is who if you wish. You can use git duet-install-hook pre-commit to set a hook that reminds you if you haven't specified who is pairing for a while. Note that you have to use git duet-commit, git duet-revert, and git duet-merge to get both names on the commit unless you set `GIT_DUET_SET_GIT_USER_CONFIG` to `1` (http://bkaprt.com/ppp/06-14/).
- **pairwith:** This simple utility just adds a Co-Authored-By line to the body of your commit messages (http://bkaprt.com/ppp/06-15/).

Collaborative editors

- Microsoft Live Share for Visual Studio, VS Code, and Visual Studio Codespaces (which can be used directly in GitHub) provides the most advanced collaborative editing experience, including collaborative debugging and terminal sharing (http://bkaprt.com/ppp/06-16/).

- Floobits enables collaborative editing for Atom, Sublime Text, IntelliJ, Emacs, and Neovim (http://bkaprt.com/ppp/06-17/).
- CodePen (http://bkaprt.com/ppp/06-18/) or CodeSandbox (http://bkaprt.com/ppp/06-19/) allow you to collaboratively edit front-end code in a browser.

Terminal sharing

- tmux is a terminal multiplexer that lets you have multiple windows and panes in one terminal session. If this interests you beyond checking out a primer online, pick up the Pragmatic Programmers book tmux: Productive Mouse-Free Development by Brian P. Hogan, because tmux and the customization thereof is a deep, deep subject (http://bkaprt.com/ppp/06-20/).
- Many people prefer iTerm over the Apple-provided Terminal app. It has more configuration options and integrates nicely with tmux. With this integration in place, you can almost forget tmux is running because you don't have to use tmux commands to manage your windows. Just click, scroll, highlight text, split, and resize windows like you're used to and your partner's will, too (http://bkaprt.com/ppp/06-21/9)!
- tmate is a fork of tmux that makes sharing a breeze. When you start the session, it gives you an SSH connection string you can share with your pair. They just paste it in their terminal and they're connected to your session without any VPNs, SSH tunnels, or fixed IPs (http://bkaprt.com/ppp/06-22/).

Screen sharing

- Zoom is a market leader in video meetings for good reason. Zoom's video and audio compression is fantastic, their echo cancellation is second-to-none, and you can actually see your partner and their screen at the same time if you have multiple monitors. We've done side-by-side comparisons with

Google Meet and vastly prefer Zoom. It's free for one-to-one meetings of unlimited length. We have Zoom integrated with Slack, so the `/zoom` command pops open a new Zoom meeting in an instant. From there, you can share your screen and give your partner control. Either person can type or run the mouse, but there's just one mouse cursor. The shared whiteboard is easiest to use when you have a tablet with a stylus (http://bkaprt.com/ppp/06-23/).

- We used to use Screenhero all the time for remote pairing. It was low lag, included audio, and allowed each person to have their own mouse pointer, which was handy for trading control back and forth quickly. Then Slack bought it in 2015 and turned it into their video chat feature, killing off some of the best functions before removing screen sharing entirely in 2019. Fortunately, the original authors have written new software to fill the Screenhero void. It takes some cues from Zoom (like scheduling meetings, using meeting codes, and showing a live thumbnail of your partner's face) but puts collaborative screen sharing at the center of its feature set. Screen is available for Mac, Windows, Linux, iOS and Android (http://bkaprt.com/ppp/06-24/).
- When Screenhero was dissolved, three French devs built USE Together. It's reasonably priced (free for students!) and is available in an on-premises solution if your organization is cloud-averse. The chat is voice-only, though, so you won't be able to see your partner (http://bkaprt.com/ppp/06-25/).
- If you're in a Mac-only environment, check out Tuple, screen sharing software made explicitly for pairing. It tucks away in the menu bar, automatically enables Mac's do-not-disturb mode, and gives you loads of insight into and control over your stream quality (going up to 5k resolution with very low latency). As of this writing, it's a little more expensive than the others, but highly endorsed by respected engineering teams. The developers say Windows and Linux support is coming (http://bkaprt.com/ppp/06-26/).

Pairing servers

- You can use Amazon WorkSpaces (http://bkaprt.com/ppp/06-27/) to spin up Windows or Linux desktops in a nearby datacenter. There are similar offerings on Microsoft Azure (http://bkaprt.com/ppp/06-28/) and Google Cloud (http://bkaprt.com/ppp/06-29/).
- macOS and iOS developers have fewer virtual desktop options, but a few include MacinCloud.com (worldwide datacenters), MacCloud.me in Cleveland, and xcloud.me in Zurich. MacStadium (US and Europe) is doing some cool stuff with Kubernetes to manage macOS VMs (http://bkaprt.com/ppp/06-30/). If you're doing iOS development, it's not a bad way to go.

Keyboard tools

- Karabiner-Elements is useful for keyboard remapping, needed if one of the pair uses a different keyboard layout (e.g. Dvorak) or is used to just a few keys being remapped—such as swapped Control and Caps Lock or the backtick as escape. I'm grateful that Takayama Fumihiko implemented my feature request to allow mappings to only apply to specific keyboards. It's saved many in-person pairs from fighting or struggling with different keyboard preferences (http://bkaprt.com/ppp/06-31/)!

Network tuning

- PacketLossTest.com will test your upload and download speeds, lost or late packets, and jitter (the variation in packet delay) to help you figure which part of your network connection might be to blame for poor performance (http://bkaprt.com/ppp/06-32/).
- iPerf is a sophisticated command-line app. If you're remote pairing, run it in server mode on one end and client mode on the other. Test with UDP packets to measure jitter. You can use a public server, but they're often busy. `iperf3 -u`

`-i 1 -c bouygues.iperf.fr` is an easy way to start (http://bkaprt.com/ppp/06-33/).

- The Zoom desktop client provides network statistics, which are described in this article. The article lists acceptable ranges for latency, jitter, packet loss, and video resolution and framerate that make good guidelines for any remote pairing with audio, video, and screen sharing (http://bkaprt.com/ppp/06-34/).
- If you're toying with different Wi-Fi routers, repeaters, or mesh networking, the tools and techniques Jim Salter has developed at Ars Technica can be useful, especially if your Wi-Fi has other simultaneous users that put pressure on your pairing bandwidth. Access point placement is way more important than the top speed numbers on the product box or your internet plan for minimizing glitches when remote pairing. He has ten rules for getting the most out of your Wi-Fi (http://bkaprt.com/ppp/06-35/). If you really want to optimize, his testing tools and techniques can help you figure out the best equipment and layout in your own home or office (http://bkaprt.com/ppp/06-36/).
- At a network level, remote pair programming looks a lot like online multiplayer gaming. League of Legends ranks hundreds of internet providers by latency, packet loss, and jitter and provides many suggestions for troubleshooting your connection and reducing lag (http://bkaprt.com/ppp/06-37/, http://bkaprt.com/ppp/06-38/).

REFERENCES: PRACTICAL PAIR PROGRAMMING

Shortened URLs are numbered sequentially; the related long URLs are listed below for reference.

Introduction

00-01 https://twitter.com/sjkilleen/status/1144684073119571969?s=21

Chapter 1

01-01 https://books.google.com/books?id=Wg5MAQAAIAAJ&lpg=PA80&ots=jfzNfMhikz&dq=Addresses%20of%20the%20President%20of%20the%20U.S.%20and%20the%20Director%20of%20the%20Bureau%20of%20the%20Budget%20edward%20hale&pg=RA10-PA14&ci=109%2C445%2C785%2C93&source=bookclip

01-02 https://twitter.com/allenholub/status/1144631354044272641?s=21

01-03 https://collaboration.csc.ncsu.edu/laurie/Papers/ieeeSoftware.PDF

01-04 http://www.sarahmei.com/blog/2010/04/14/thoughts-on-two-months-of-pairing/

01-05 https://twitter.com/nodunayo/status/686295215532015616

Chapter 2

02-01 https://youtu.be/OQXEzwXtzJ8?t=424

02-02 https://www.youtube.com/watch?v=_ynXKHC9Wo4

02-03 http://wiki.c2.com/?PairProgrammingPingPongPattern

02-04 https://twitter.com/sarahmei/status/991028340571103232

02-05 https://geekfeminism.wikia.org/wiki/Male_Programmer_Privilege_Checklist

02-06 https://academicaffairs.ucsc.edu/events/documents/Microaggressions_InterruptHO_2014_11_182v5.pdf

Chapter 3

03-01 https://twitter.com/rkulla/status/440165393823305728

03-02 https://c2.com/doc/episodes.pdf

03-03 https://twitter.com/DanielleSucher/status/440178048403390465

03-04 https://fortune.com/2014/10/07/ibms-rometty-growth-and-comfort-dont-coexist/

Chapter 4

04-01 https://arstechnica.com/gadgets/2020/02/the-ars-technica-semi-scientific-guide-to-wi-fi-access-point-placement/

04-02 https://broadbandnow.com/guides/dsl-vs-cable-vs-fiber

04-03 https://youtu.be/OQXEzwXtzJ8?t=326

Resources

06-01 https://vimeo.com/221024846

06-02 http://www.extremeprogramming.org/map/code.html

06-03 https://kata-log.rocks/tdd

06-04 https://www.idi.ntnu.no/grupper/su/publ/ebse/R11-pairprog-hannay-ist09.pdf

06-05 https://www.youtube.com/watch?v=OQXEzwXtzJ8

06-06 https://blog.obiefernandez.com/content/2009/09/10-reasons-pair-programming-is-not-for-the-masses.html

06-07 http://techtowntraining.com/resources/blog/etiquette-for-pair-programming

06-08 https://www.recurse.com/social-rules

06-09 https://www.poodr.com/

06-10 https://www.oreilly.com/library/view/clean-code/9780136083238/

06-11 https://leanpub.com/agiletechnicalpracticesdistilled

06-12 https://docs.google.com/spreadsheets/d/17qgykS1zviaHDQQ5-dJ49c1X-0sRf3Lss0q9_R9UASN8/edit?usp=sharing

06-13 https://github.com/thiagoghisi/gitpairtrix

06-14 https://github.com/git-duet/git-duet

06-15 https://github.com/patricksmith/pairwith

06-16 https://visualstudio.microsoft.com/services/live-share/

06-17 https://floobits.com/

06-18 https://codepen.io/

06-19 https://codesandbox.io/

06-20 https://pragprog.com/titles/bhtmux2/

06-21 https://www.iterm2.com/

06-22 https://tmate.io/

06-23 https://zoom.us/

06-24 https://screen.so/

06-25 https://www.use-together.com/pair-programming/

06-26 https://tuple.app/

06-27 https://aws.amazon.com/workspaces/

06-28 https://azure.microsoft.com/en-us/services/virtual-desktop/

06-29 https://cloud.google.com/solutions/chrome-desktop-remote-on-compute-engine

06-30 https://www.macstadium.com/

06-31 https://pqrs.org/osx/karabiner/

06-32 https://packetlosstest.com/

06-33 https://iperf.fr/

06-34 https://support.zoom.us/hc/en-us/articles/202920719-Meeting-and-phone-statistics#h_82592927-e937-43cd-a442-7a913b3d4d4d

06-35 https://arstechnica.com/gadgets/2020/02/the-ars-technica-semi-scientific-guide-to-wi-fi-access-point-placement/

06-36 https://arstechnica.com/gadgets/2020/01/how-ars-tests-wi-fi-gear-and-you-can-too/

06-37 https://lagreport.na.leagueoflegends.com/

06-38 https://lagreport.na.leagueoflegends.com/en/steps

INDEX: PRACTICAL PAIR PROGRAMMING

ABOUT THE AUTHOR

Jason Garber is COO and cofounder of the software firm Promptworks, where he leads internal operations and guides client work. He carries the same entrepreneurial mindset and attention to detail that launched his first company back in 1997, when he was a 14-year-old web developer. He is a passionate advocate for Ruby on Rails, clean code, and automated testing. He lives in Philadelphia.

CPSIA information can be obtained
at www.ICGtesting.com
Printed in the USA
JSHW052039031122
31748JS00003BA/1